The Street Is My Home

Youth and Violence in Caracas

The Street Is My Home

Youth and Violence in Caracas

Patricia C. Márquez

Stanford University Press • Stanford, California

Stanford University Press
Stanford, California
© 1999 by the Board of Trustees of the
Leland Stanford Junior University

Printed in the United States of America

CIP data appear at the end of the book

For my three mothers
Luisa, Irina, and Elvira

Acknowledgments

I wish to thank Professor Laura Nader for her time and knowledge and for supporting and encouraging my love of asking questions. I wish to thank my dearest friend and colleague, David Eaton, for our endless discussions and his careful reading of my work; I thank him for encouraging me to maintain confidence in this project.

I am grateful to Professors Nancy Scheper-Hughes, Margarita Melville, and Ruben Oliven for their support and attention to my work. I wish to thank María Massolo and Paco Ferrándiz for their patience with my writing hysteria and their helpful comments.

In Caracas, I am indebted to the Association for Street Children for their initial support in helping me to meet the youngsters on the Sabana Grande boulevard. In particular, I wish to thank my friend and association member Gustavo Estanga for helping me shed some of my *gringuismos* and learn how to do things "Venezuelan style." I also want to thank the National Institute for the Welfare of the Minor (INAM) for allowing me to conduct research at one of their centers. I am grateful to Franz Huiguen for sharing his notes on the Sabana Grande *chupapegas*.

Although many youngsters helped me with the research, I

want to thank those whose contribution to this study has been invaluable and who also wanted to see their names printed in what they called "Patricia's book." I thank H. Jiménez for being so good-natured and willing to open up; A. Machado, who, although always distrustful of my questions, allowed me to enter his world and meet his family; Armando for showing me the city with a big smile; and Joseíto Arciniegas for letting me read his poetry and for remaining a constant friend through his weekly phone calls.

At the Carolina Center I am grateful to the staff. I am most indebted to some of the youngsters. I thank O. B. Montes for writing so much information about himself and his friends, even copying into a notebook all the graffiti scribbled on the yellow walls; and Félix, Oswaldo, Jerlin, Heilson, and all the others for making our afternoon meetings so enjoyable. Special thanks go to Maikel, who by the end felt my project was also his and insisted in suggesting an appropriate title for it, "Los problemas críticos y tristes y sus virtudes del país llevan a los menores a su peor fracaso en Venezuela" (The critical and sad problems of the country as well as its virtues lead youngsters to their worst failure). By worst failure he meant "el expediente de la vida, no el expediente de los tribunales. Una mancha negra en su corazón, mancha negra que lleva uno en la agenda de la vida" (the file on one's life, not the court file. It is a black spot on the heart, a black spot in one's life history).

I am grateful to FUNDAYACUCHO and LASPAU for financing four years of my graduate studies. I also thank the Humanities Research Center and the Center for Latin American Studies at the University of California at Berkeley, and the Lowie Fund of the Department of Anthropology for partially financing my fieldwork. I am indebted to the Instituto de Estudios Superiores de Administración (IESA) for providing me with the time and support for transforming my thesis into a book.

Special thanks go to my editor, Shirley Taylor, who endured my Spanglish with patience, and to Linda-Anne Rebhun. And last, I want to thank Isabel Martínez and my husband, Juan Cristóbal Palacios, who were always helpful and very understanding of my mood swings and my frustrations.

A note on the text: All translations from the Spanish are my own.

P. C. M.

Contents

4 pages of photos follow p. 80

The Street Is My Home

Youth and Violence in Caracas

Introduction

There are approximately 40 million street children in Latin America (Tacon 1981, 1983). Why, if Latin America has only 10 percent of the world's population of children, does it have about half of the world's street children (Aptekar 1991)? Although no current statistics exist on the number of street children in Venezuela, over the last decade the number of children begging, working, hanging out, and sleeping on the streets of the capital city, Caracas, appears to have been rapidly increasing (Barrios, Cárquez, and Frigo 1989). What does it mean to grow up—to be a child or an adolescent—in a context of everyday violence and in the midst of an economic, social, and political crisis?[1]

In this study I apply a "vertical-slice" approach (Nader 1972, 1980) in discussing the socioeconomic and political conditions that have led to the sudden increase, over ten years (1983–93), in the number of young people on the streets of Caracas.[2] At the same time, I examine, through their everyday experiences in work, relationships, and networks and their choices and expectations for the future, the meaning of being young for people living on the streets. I discuss the relationships among these young people, their families, and the adults with whom they come in contact, such as street merchants, policemen, and social workers. Additionally, by studying public discourse on street children and the children's interactions with adults, I outline the relationship between street children and the larger social setting within which they live.

Moreover, I examine how the identities of displaced youth in Caracas are formed within a context of scarcity and violence, describing the ways in which young people manage to gain material wealth and create meaning in their lives as well as the risks they are willing to take in such pursuits. Above all, I want to show how these young people define, live, and experience life on the streets, with all its violence, in the larger context of national and global events, such as hyperinflation, generalized corruption, the deterioration of public services, and decreasing oil prices.

Approaches to the Study

There have been only a few anthropological studies of young people living on the streets. Many studies on the problems faced by street children have been strongly influenced by psychological and sociohistorical models of childhood and adolescence (Aries 1961; Blos 1979; Coles 1986a, 1986b; Erikson 1950; Freud 1958; Gillis 1974; Minge-Kalman 1978; Muñoz and Pachón 1991; Walvin 1982). These models are not completely adequate in explaining what constitutes youth for people between the ages of nine and eighteen who, for a variety of reasons, have little or no family support and who spend most of their time on the streets.[3] For instance, studies examining the mental development and psychological processes of street children (Coles 1986a, 1986b; Barrios, Cárquez, and Frigo 1989) often fail to describe these children's daily experiences or their participation in a larger system.

In this study, I move away from psychological models by examining how young people in Caracas develop selfhood and values, not just as mental categories but through experiences and relationships that generate choices and decisions at specific times. Their daily lives do not necessarily reflect the conflicts and conditions attributed to the stages outlined in Western psychological models. Rather, the conflict that exists in these young people's lives stems from tangible conditions such as hunger, fear of abuse, and the lack of safe places to sleep (cf. Scheper-Hughes 1992).

Young people on the streets of Caracas are compelled to develop a complex body of knowledge very different from that of privileged young people in the city. They have to learn how to get food, where to find shelter, how to avoid falling into the hands of the authorities, and how to decide with whom to share their profits. Although extensive journalistic and descriptive accounts capture aspects of the daily lives of street children in different cultures (Muñoz and Palacios 1980; Maturi 1987; Allsebrook and Swift 1989), they only briefly explain how these children exist as part of a larger society riddled with unequal class, gender, and race relations.

Psychological anthropologist Lewis Aptekar's research of street children in Colombia (1988, 1989, 1991), in contrast, represents pioneering work in the study of children living on the streets. Aptekar's analysis of the relationship between the lives of street children and the economically and politically dominant classes, which view the street children as a threat to the patriarchal family and to the social order, places these children in the context of the larger society. I expand on Aptekar's approach by examining Venezuelan national attitudes toward young people on the streets in the context of their everyday lives. National media, municipal institutions, and legal policy have all drawn attention to street children as a problematic social group. In this study, I describe modes of actual interactions among these children and between them and others in downtown areas where these children are most visible to the nation and I consider the challenge not only to the traditional patriarchal family of the dominant classes but also to the systems of labor, education, and criminal justice that influence the daily lives of children on the streets, their alleged delinquent behavior, and rumors about them.

Until recently, most research in anthropology, with exceptions such as Mead's work in Samoa (1928) and Whyte's work on gangs (1943), has focused on adults as the normative group (Whiting and Whiting 1987). Anthropology has either dealt with young people as secondary or it has focused on rites of passage in developing psychological and symbolic interpretations based on biosocial definitions of life stages (cf. Whiting, Kluckhohn, and Anthony 1958; Young 1965; Schlegel and Barry 1979; Ottenberg 1989). Rites of passage, at least as they have been classically defined, may not even exist for street children. If such rituals do exist, then they may mark passage to prison or to death. Anthropological studies have also focused on the social organization of young people in the context of institutions such as "male houses" or dormitories (Elwin 1968). For young people living in the streets, established social institutions are not the norm; instead, social organization involves groups based on friendships and economic factors (Aptekar 1988; Allsebrook and Swift 1989).

In their studies of Latin America, journalists, psychologists, and other social scientists have considered the "increasing poverty," resulting from political and economic crises, and foreign debt to be the main causes of the growing numbers of street children (Castro and Samenzato 1978; Barrios, Cárquez, and Frigo 1989). But poverty alone neither explains how the dominant classes justify or perpetuate this situation nor accounts for society's ambivalence toward these children (Aptekar 1991). Relying upon poverty as a reified category does not allow us to explore the relationships of young people on city streets and the community, the rehabilitative social agency system, the media, and legal and social policies. Deciding simply that "children are on the streets because of poverty" leaves little room for understanding the actual lives of these people. For example, it does not acknowledge the complex process of moving from marginalized *barrios*—which in Caracas are squatter settlements—to the streets. Poverty alone does not explain why a street glue sniffer sometimes prefers playing video games to eating a good meal. And it does not explain why economically deprived young people are driven to kill to obtain a pair of expensive Nike shoes instead of food or shelter.

Defining "Street Children"

To examine the variety of socioeconomic and political conditions behind the increase in street children, it is first necessary to know who the street children are and how they came to live on the streets. Putting all these children into the category of "street children" glosses over the heterogeneity of their lives. This term—which I often use, with trepidation, for lack of a better one—by definition separates young people on the streets from their families and their communities of origin. The origins of most street children in the downtown areas of Caracas are far from clear: Who knows what their family situations are and how much time these youngsters actually spend on the streets? These young people actually play an important role in the economic survival of their families, and we need to learn more about their childhood and adolescence in order to understand their kinship ties and the type of labor they perform.

Aptekar (1989, 1991) argues that in Colombia the majority of street children maintain some sort of contact with the family and are not always the victims of sudden family abandonment. In large poor families, parents or stepparents often push the highest-functioning children to survive on their own or to produce an income on the streets. Parents and siblings deliberately teach young children early independence and self-assurance. Similarly, my research in Caracas indicates that many youths on the streets are not abandoned but have left the barrios to find goods, money, and a different sort of life (see also Pedrazzini and Sánchez 1992). Contrary to popular belief, many of these youngsters are not vagrants but, as in Colombia, working children who may be playing a vital role in the survival of the family, with the streets as the locus of their economic activity.

Street children earn money through legal activities such as shoe shining, rag collecting, and food selling (cf. Muñoz and Palacios 1980), but they also engage in illegal activities such as thievery, drug selling, and prostitution. Just what constitutes subsistence and what constitutes delinquency depends on one's point of view; however, what society views as delinquency may not be seen in the same light by street children. One of my main concerns in this study is to present the youngsters' own perspectives on what activities they consider delinquent and their reasons for engaging in them.

Certainly, child-rearing practices within families may influence delinquency among young people; but in Venezuela, the primary forces driving young people on the streets to sell drugs or to steal have more to do with socioeconomic and political factors, such as the extremely unequal distribution of wealth. In the majority of cases, whatever the structure of these children's families, people from the barrios lack access to basic social, political, economic, and legal institutions and to survive are often forced into a parallel informal economy. Therefore, these young people's crimes are sometimes their only means of survival. Thus, their delinquent acts represent, among other things, economic strategies.

Part of the difficulty in understanding this new urban phenomenon of rapidly growing numbers of young people on city streets is the failure to take into account the kinship ties of these young people and the expectations of their communities. Indeed, the childhood and adolescence of young people on the streets must be redefined as a new social form and situated in particular family structures in a contemporary context of complex urban dynamics.

Society's Perceptions of Street Children

Contradictory sentiments about street children, as well as the perceptions and reactions of the dominant classes, permeate and shape state policies. Yet there is no doubt that their delinquency and victimization are interrelated, and that the point of their intersection is actively shaped by the children themselves and by the dominant classes and the state. My analysis concentrates on three main domains that shape the recent discourse on street children: personal relationships between youngsters and adults in downtown areas, media coverage, and state and legal policies.

State welfare and disciplinary systems and the dominant classes have attempted in various ways to deal with young people who do not attend schools, who work in the informal sector, and who are not under rigid family surveillance. Often those in power, that is, professionals who head state welfare institutions and other NGOs, express passionate mixed feelings about those considered street children, who, sometimes in violent ways, threaten and challenge the existing social and moral order. Increasingly, authorities use schooling, laws, and parental guardianship to place young people in urban environments under the control of the family and the state (Meyer 1977). But young people who live on the streets, who fend for themselves, and who are forced to make decisions about their own survival are very different from most other children in many aspects. Their very independence and self-assurance mark them as deviant and contest the traditional meaning of childhood.

Criminalizing street children is one way to bring them under state control. Trotman (1986) has shown that both behavior reflected in patterns of violence and labeling, such as definitions of criminality, show intimate links with the dominant classes' struggle for political and economic hegemony. In much of Latin America, the crimes of young people on the streets sometimes involve theft and murder. It has been increasingly the case, however, that the mere presence of children on crowded city streets is considered criminal, resulting in harassment and institutionalization by local authorities (Violante 1985; Dimenstein 1991). In the national culture, the presence of children on the streets constitutes a living accusation, pointing out the widening gap between the upper and lower classes and the failure of existing child-welfare projects.

The population of Venezuela is very young; its median age is approximately 21 (OCEI 1992). How is this younger half of the Venezuelan population surviving in a time of inflation, political uncertainty, and increasing levels of poverty? Some of the questions this study attempts to answer concern the larger socioeconomic aspects of street children's lives. What is the relationship between the rising criminalization of street children in Venezuela and the growing social inequalities and political unrest? To what extent is recent discourse on young people on the streets a reflection of the dominant classes' fear of family disintegration and moral and social disorder?

Connections: Youth on the Streets and Geographical Boundaries

The Sabana Grande boulevard is the area, geographical and imaginary, where many young people live out their youths. It is the place where those called street children do not merely survive but constitute complex forms of social organization, develop emotions, acquire knowledge, and formulate strategies for survival and for recreation. People's daily practices on the boulevard take many forms: telling anecdotes, complaining, protesting, being questioned, suffering beatings, begging, slashing, or stealing. In this study I hope to provide a space for new discussions of what it means to grow older in the context of the streets as I reveal the creativity and complexities of the lives of young people on Sabana Grande.

The city of Caracas, huge and diverse, with approximately four million inhabitants, including children living on the streets all over the city, is an overwhelming site for a study of street children. I therefore had to limit my area of concentration and I chose the thirteen-block area of the Sabana Grande boulevard.

I chose this boulevard because I wanted to understand the ways in which young poor people inhabit and experience spaces such as streets, parks, *ranchos* (shantyhouses), and state institutions. I wanted to focus on those places in the city where different groups of young people connected by what Willis (1990) terms a "common culture" of life on the streets spend their time. To do so I established relationships with various young people who became my subjects and analyzed emerging socializing processes for barrio youth, who are continually moving out of the barrio, to the streets, and to state institutions.

When I began my fieldwork, which went on for a year, in January 1993, I focused primarily on approximately fifteen youngsters between the ages of nine and eighteen whom I had met on the boulevard. I soon realized that I needed to move beyond the boundaries of the boulevard, for these young people were constantly traveling all over the city. Several of the younger ones, who were known as *chupapegas* (glue sniffers), spent time with their families in the barrios, bathed in the Bellas Artes area (on the west side), looked for glue and money in places such as Catia boulevard in the industrial western section, were invited twice a week to the house of a wealthy philanthropist, and were arrested and taken to police headquarters or to the facilities of the National Institute for the Welfare of the Minor (INAM). The older ones moved about even more as they tried to get off the streets, got involved in "hard" drug consumption and distribution in particular areas, or found new ways to survive.[4]

As I got to know the city with the young people themselves, I realized that far more of them lived on the streets than just those who were most visible because they occupied certain "unnatural" spaces (places where in theory poor-looking people shouldn't be) or because they disturbed the social order with their ragged clothes and cans of glue. Many street people were connected not only by the geographical locations they shared, such as INAM, police headquarters, or the boulevard, but by local perceptions about them and their everyday practices.

It was at two of INAM's centers that I first realized how huge a proportion of young people were on the streets away from school and the constant tutelage of their families. The two centers I studied were Los Chorros, for youngsters between the ages of seven and thirteen, and the Carolina, for boys between fourteen and eighteen.

In this study I distinguish among groups of young people, sometimes arbitrarily and always in an attempt to avoid reification, in order to understand the process of growing older on the streets. I discuss the chupapegas, the *monos* (youngsters from the barrios), who are also called *jordans*, and the *malandros* (thugs) of the boulevard, and the children of Los Chorros and the Carolina Center.[5] The groups are not mutually exclusive: the chupapegas, for example, often spend time at Los Chorros. Youngsters living on the streets near the Sabana Grande boulevard and in the barrios share a culture of often violent practices and expectations. They also share the identity of the marginalized youngster growing older on the eve of the collapse of the oil boom of the 1970's and early 1980's, the Venezuela Saudita. For these young people, individual status is often equated with the acquisition of particular consumer goods, such as shoes, video games, motorcycles, and Walkmen. These youngsters share a contradictory dream of fast and easy consumption at a time when, for the poor, morally acceptable ways of getting these goods no longer exist.

In the course of my fieldwork I met several people older than eighteen who had been "street children" and now were either off the streets (sometimes in jail) or still living on the boulevard. Through them, I was able to establish some connections with some "street adults." Although my focus was on younger people, I did get a sense from these adults of what growing older meant for street people who had been children at a time when, as my friend Aquiles (who is in his mid-thirties) says, "taking someone's life meant something serious."

The monos and malandros on the boulevard were a prime target for the police because of their particular style of dressing, walking, and talking. They were constantly harassed. But the *woperós* (middle-class youth), though equally visible, were hardly ever bothered by the police or perceived as undesirable by the community. The woperós were not seen as a threat but more or less as buffoons, because of their long hair and their eccentric style of dress. On the boulevard, the monos and malandros, who were considered potentially dangerous, lived alongside the "eccentric" woperós.

All my informants were males. Some young females live on the streets, but there are fewer females than males, and they are also less visible and harder to contact. Although I met four street girls on the Sabana Grande boulevard, I felt that to work with them would have required a different approach from the one I was using with the males in my study. Their daily lives, though similar in many ways to those of the males, involved activities that would have been impossible to examine in one year. For example, many of them are involved in prostitution, and exploring this survival strategy and its risks would have required establishing a whole different set of connections. And because the INAM institutions for females are separate from those for males, I would have had to divide my time even more.[6]

A *Caraqueña*'s Fieldwork in Caracas

In many ways my fieldwork was structured by my own fear and by what risks I was willing to take. As a native caraqueña educated in the United States, I brought to my fieldwork a cultural and emotional baggage that limited my options in some ways but that expanded my understandings in others. At the same time, my subjects' perceptions and stereotypes of Venezuelan upper classes and North Americans very much influenced their reactions and the ways in which they chose to present themselves to me.

I grew up in an upper-middle-class neighborhood on the east side of Caracas. Up until I started my research, I had many prejudices and fears about what I was studying, that is, a group of people—"marginals," "delinquents," "monos"—of whom I had been taught all my life to be at least a little afraid. For the first time I was visiting places such as the Carolina that I had only heard about through sensationalized media programs and through rumors about "bad" things having happened there. I had to learn to see my native city through a different lens from the one I grew up with, and I had to explain my behavior to my grandmothers, sisters, cousins, and friends, who could not understand my interest in these places.

Before beginning my fieldwork, I used to walk around the boulevard, shopping or meeting friends for coffee. At the time, I regarded the begging young glue sniffers as simply annoying, while some of the older street people seemed more threatening. I was, and in some ways still am, one of those *sifrinas*, or uptown girls, who are terrified of Caracas, and especially of being out on the streets. I had grown up sharing the experience of family members who had had their cars stolen, been shot at for refusing to let go of a wallet, or had been threatened with a razor blade while inside their car in a traffic jam.

When I returned to Caracas after many years of studying in the United States, it appeared even more chaotic and violent than I had remembered. During my first months there, the noise, the heat, the traffic, and the pungent smell of certain areas made me retreat to the comfort of my grandmother's apartment and beat myself over the head for having chosen this field site and research topic. Moving between the spheres of the two Caracas, the poor and the wealthy—the distinction between the two is that obvious—was not easy. On the streets I would wear jeans, T-shirts, and ordinary tennis shoes, hoping that none of my relatives would spot me, especially when I was surrounded by the youngsters; for if they did, I would have to put up with their endless comments about the type of work I was doing. Until I got used to the grime covering the city—and many of my subjects—I would come home desperate to jump into a hot shower, feeling that I was itching all over or that the smell of the chupapegas would always stay with me. One of my relatives once suggested that I shower daily with *quitapiojos* shampoo (for lice) and wash my clothes with strong lye soap.

All these differences between my work on the streets and my daily life within my own social circle influenced the way I constructed my research. For example, this discrepancy limited the hours I visited the boulevard. Even though I knew that many young people were there at night, I almost never stayed out later than nine P.M. It also limited the areas I was willing to visit with the youngsters; although I was dying of curiosity, I never entered what street people called the Bellas Artes caves—abandoned concrete cylinders at an old construction site. It also took me a while to adjust to the bureaucracy that sometimes kept me from getting into state institutions. My friend Gustavo Estanga from the Association for Street Children patiently insisted that I stop being so *gringa* and start doing things Caracas style.

I was usually not afraid of the young people with whom I worked, but I was afraid of the older people who often manipulated them to sell drugs or to steal. I was also afraid of some of the staff at the several institutions I visited who could be oppressive and, for lack of a better word, cruel toward the children. I was afraid of the data I was uncovering to which I was not supposed to be privy, such as the way the INAM constructs the case files of delinquent individuals. I was afraid of the police, who thanks to the suspension of constitutional guarantees in 1993, could haul people off to headquarters and leave them there for no apparent reason, search homes without a warrant, and worse. Most of all, I was afraid of the violence the youngsters suffered from and were capable of perpetrating.

A last consideration concerns the construction of my ethnography. Even though I have finished my research, I continue to live in Caracas. I have maintained contact with many of the chupapegas, monos, and malandros I met; I also keep in touch with many street community members and people working with them. Many of these people expect an outcome from the research in which they participated. Because I am still here in my field site, I cannot escape what I have said or written about them and their communities. And even if Edison, Prince, Wilson, or any of the other youngsters I worked with never get to read my work, they, and their anxiety over what I might say about them, linger in my heart as I write.

In this study, translating has been problematic. By this I do not just mean the confusing enterprise of translating passages from my native Spanish into English. What I have found extremely difficult has been to convey most accurately the richness and creativity of the youngsters' language and stories. I am still struggling to communicate meanings and histories of certain places, political figures, television programs, events, and even smells, which, for those from Caracas, are quite significant but for others are perhaps meaningless.

I have tried to answer, I hope successfully, the question of how to first notice and to then articulate that which appears obvious to me. If I hear Wilmer's tale about being thrown into the Guaire River by a man who wanted to seduce him, his horror and humorous recounting of it make sense to me. How do I convey that sense to others in North America, who cannot imagine what the Guaire represents to most caraqueños? Wilmer recounted to me his journey down the river, during which he regretted having lost his Converse sneakers in his attempt to scale the concrete walls that channel the dirty waters. I can so easily picture where he struggled in vain to get out of the water. He told me of his agony when an old man yelled to a group of training firefighters, "Look, there's a fish in the water!" As Wilmer swallowed the dirty water, he abandoned his worries that the river was leading him either to the Orinoco River or to the Carolina Center—here I should pause to add that the Orinoco River is far away in southern Venezuela and that the Guaire goes nowhere near the Carolina—and yelled, "I am not a fish! Get me out of here!"

Wilmer's story struck me as very funny and very tragic. When I tell others this story, the question that I ask myself, when they look at me with either pity for choosing such a "depressing" topic or with admiration for being so "brave" for working with these people is: How can I convey that for all its depressing aspects, the humor and the creativity with which the youngsters presented their lives to me, and the very humanness of their stories, made my fieldwork at once enjoyable, disturbing, challenging, and thought provoking.

1 · The Streets of Caracas

There are no sounds on the streets of Caracas.
Everybody walks quietly, melancholic, grave.

—FRANCISCO DEPONS, early-nineteenth-century traveler

On February 27, 1989, popular violence broke out in Venezuela's major cities. Journalists in Caracas called it "el día que bajaron los cerros" (the day the shantytowns came down from the hills). For five days large crowds of people took over the streets, entering shops, looting, breaking windows, burning tires, and stealing cars. In Caracas, approximately one million people broke the rules regulating public movement and expressed their growing anger and frustration. The February events in the capital city were popularly titled "el Caracazo." Both the poor and marginal living in the shantytowns of the surrounding hills and many considered middle class were no longer passively accepting price inflation, food shortages, and the collapse of social services. The collective but unorganized and spontaneous realization of rampant inequality translated into practices of overt, desperate, and surreal violence epitomized in media images of people from different strata of society running wildly out of shopping malls, pushing supermarket carts full of cartons of milk, television sets, and Coca-Cola bottles amid smoke and ruins.

This popular uprising speaks of new dimensions of order and space. The "red zones," the dangerous areas of the urban imaginary, were no longer confined to the barrios. February 27, 1989 marks in public consciousness the transformation of the urban topography into a single "bad area" where nothing and nobody appears safe. The masses entered in direct confrontation with the state, which until that point had felt it had control of the streets. At every class level, people were afraid, since nobody knew what would happen outside their homes. For those who did not participate in the uprising, rumors, sights witnessed, and the constant sound of gunshots were enough to convey the chaos and the general discontent of the population.

The uprising, which turned into a brutal massacre when the police and the military intervened, was a turning point in the contest over urban boundaries, some assumed, some quite evident, and it changed the sociocultural and political dimensions of the control of spaces.[1] There have been other demonstrations of civil and military unrest on the streets of the capital city since. In this landscape of disorder, seemingly powerless people have opened a dialogue with a deaf state by crossing these urban boundaries. Since the Caracazo, the streets of Caracas have more openly become a site of struggle among the different forces of the state, such as the police, dominant groups, and marginalized groups. In the mid-1990's, demonstrations on the streets encompassed a wide range of frustrated citizens: the old, who do not receive their pension increases, teachers asking for better working conditions, and the *motorizados* (motorcycle messengers) protesting police harassment.[2] The mere presence of these people in places that were formerly out of bounds for them becomes increasingly more menacing to the dominant social order.

The presence of relatively large numbers of marginal young people on the streets, no longer contained in the barrios, threatens the hegemonic control of major parts of the city. After February 27, 1989, young people seemed to embody the perennial threat of the poor taking control of the boulevards, the bus terminals, the shopping malls—any public space. For many, their presence is similar to the kind of affront that middle-class housewives feel when their maids dare to sit down with them in their living rooms. For the elite, the children and adolescents on the streets (monos, malandros, and chupapegas alike) are disturbing because they seem to represent the ugliness and uncivilized ways of the barbaric "other" (De Freitas 1993). However, the actual increasing presence of young marginals in city spaces means much more than simply an expansion of "barbarism." Young people's lives on the streets, considered in a national economic and cultural context, constitute a powerful statement about the creation and perpetuation of different kinds of violence.

The Oil Boom and the Illusion of Wealth

Venezuela in the twentieth century has been drenched in the flow of oil wealth, a wealth that made possible the construction of a nation with a representative state of centralized power visually embodied in a figurehead, the president-caudillo. Over the years, Venezuela developed what Roberto Briceño-León (1990) calls a society with a "rentier mentality," in which people competed for oil wealth using whatever means possible.[3] Venezuela has seen its own brand of massive "fast capitalism" (Watts 1992).[4] As a consequence, until recently, oil revenues gave the country the opportunity to expand and improve, which in turn provided the political and economic possibility of eventually accommodating divergent interests (Karl 1987; Coronil 1988).

The transformation of the social spheres of Caracas was a clear result of the effect of oil on the geographical, social, cultural, political, and economic landscapes. But these landscapes underwent further changes when the dream of "The Great Venezuela" was shattered in the 1990's.[5] Since the early twentieth century, Venezuela has been directly dependent on oil revenues. The nation's petroleum export industry began under the long dictatorship of Juan Vicente Gómez (1908–35). In the 1950's, under another autocratic regime, that of dictator Pérez Jiménez (1948–58), oil wealth further benefited a growing commercial bourgeoisie (Coronil and Skursky 1992; Coronil 1988). In 1960, Venezuela, along with Iran, Iraq, Kuwait, and Saudi Arabia, formed the Organization of Petroleum Exporting Countries (OPEC), collectively restricting the world's supply of oil and setting market prices. It was not until the global price increase of oil in 1973–74, however, that the majority of the Venezuelan population, living under a democratic regime, found a variety of opportunities to obtain a share of the wealth.

Especially during the first term of Carlos Andrés Pérez (1974–79), increasing oil revenues (oil prices quadrupled) allowed relatively high living standards for the entire population. A collective dream of unlimited wealth and modernization emerged; for many Venezuelans in all strata of society, the notion of progress involved the chance to travel at least as far as Miami, which became a mecca of consumerism. The nation associated progress with the rapid flow of imported high technology and goods. Venezuela began to project an international image of development.

The dream began to shatter during the government of President Luis Herrera Campíns (1979–84). On February 18, 1983, a day now popularly known as "Black Friday," the first devaluation of the bolivar since the early sixties occurred. Until then the existence of petrodollars had prevented serious social conflict by allowing the nation an at least superficial resolution of its many structural problems. As in the rest of Latin America, in Venezuela the unequal distribution of income became acute throughout the 1980's: in 1989 the poorest 20 percent of households in Venezuela had 4.8 of the income, while the wealthiest 20 percent had 49.5 (World Bank 1994, 221). In the late 1980's, the erosion of the oil economy became more evident to the general population: it was harder to obtain credit, to earn higher salaries, or to fund the universities properly. Venezuela was in a crisis.[6]

Pérez was elected to a new term in December 1988, succeeding Jaime Lusinchi (1984–89). During this term, Pérez took on a huge foreign debt (approximately 43 billion dollars), the taint of moral scandals left by former president Lusinchi, and a population that expected and looked forward to the same wealth and distribution it had enjoyed during Pérez's first term. In spite of the enormous corruption of the previous government, which had left the country with a devalued currency and rising inflation, Pérez dared to celebrate his coming to power with a lavish inaugural ball with guests from all over the world, a display no doubt meant to show the public that he was optimistic about turning the country around.[7]

Pérez and his ministers approached this second term with a proposal of a neoliberal free market adjustment program from the International Monetary Fund, called El Paquete, similar to what in Mexico was called the Ajuste. El Paquete claimed to be more realistic about the increasing debt crisis and promised to deal with four areas: commercial reform, fiscal deficit, financial reform with open bank competition, and labor reform. The government avoided the question of who would shoulder the cost of social reforms, and it soon became evident that commercial reform was mainly being promoted, thanks to diverse political and private interests. The improvement of collapsing social services was for the most part placed aside.

The February riots of 1989 were not unusual in Latin America. Similar conditions of oppression existed in other nations, and since the mid-1970's more than half the major countries of Latin America and the Caribbean had experienced social upheavals in direct response to austerity measures (Walton 1989, 308). In most cases, the protests had been precipitated by economic policies urged by the International Monetary Fund, operating in collaboration with other lending agencies such as the World Bank, the United States government, and a consortium of private banks. The protests were often directed at other institutions, taking the form of food riots, general strikes, and political demonstrations. The protesting masses were frequently the urban poor from shantytowns.

Since the collapse of the illusion of wealth in Venezuela, the everyday violence and misery of the shantytowns have become public knowledge. The wealthy more or less ignored the continuing deterioration of living standards for El Pueblo—the masses—as long as it remained in the hills, where ranchos seemed to spring up in the most precarious places.[8] As long as poverty and violence stayed confined to the barrios, along with the people living there, those in power remained at ease. The ranchos could be thought of as invisible, even pretty: one could gaze up at the hills at night and imagine that the lights made the city sparkle like a Christmas tree.

Collective Anxiety and Everyday Protests

In the Venezuelan consciousness the only event that matches the Caracazo is the collective celebration in January 23, 1958, of the fall of dictator Jiménez's government, which plunged the country into acute political and economic crisis. Crowds filled the streets calling for jobs, condemning the oil companies for their support of the military government, and looting the homes of members of the Jiménez clique (Karl 1987, 80; Coronil 1988, 53; Coronil and Skurski 1992, 292).

Ever since "el día que bajaron los cerros," the major streets of the capital city have become an arena for expressing social discontent. As sociologist David Harvey notes, objective improvements in quality of life are often effected through social struggle (1989, 227), and in Caracas, the masses have realized that the only way their voices will be heard is if they take control of their own spaces, the streets. Current protest practices have been shaped by the recent collective memory of the masses taking control of the streets: two other major rebellions followed the Caracazo in 1992, on February 4 and on November 27. Both were conducted by military groups, who themselves were protesting the government of Carlos Andrés Pérez instead of suppressing the masses.

Today, a general aura of uncertainty and despair hangs over the streets of Caracas, and every time a *golpe* (coup) is rumored—which now happens more and more frequently—people run to stock their homes with food or to buy dollars while they still can. But the collective memory of the February rebellion lingers on a more subtle level in that it induces a fear of everyday manifestations of public discontent, while creating opportunities for its existence.

The anxiety created by unpredictability—"Will there be food?" "Will the military rule if there is a coup d'état?" "What will happen to my family?"—involves, and to some degree shapes, the dynamics of each new protest. And each new protest arouses fears about the disruption of the social order. More and more, news articles carry headlines such as "La ansiedad colectiva será el síndrome de hoy" (Collective anxiety is today's syndrome) that reflect the experience of the general population:

> February 27 will be remembered as the day when the Venezuelan's tranquillity was shattered, even though the causes of that explosion had been festering for decades. Since that day it has been the custom to board up the supermarkets, grocery stores, and small

shops every time an alarm goes off or there is a rumor of an important political event. (Marielba Núñez, "La ansiedad colectiva será el síndrome de hoy," *El Nacional*, May 23, 1993)

This anxicty is exacerbated by the deterioration of the city's infrastructure—an annoyance that seriously tests the patience and endurance of the caraqueños. Everywhere, the urban landscape shows shocking contrasts: streets strewn with holes, old buildings alongside slick new ones covered in brown and green mirrors, falling-apart cars parked next to imported BMW's, and the presence of more marginal people working and living on the streets. This contrast of old and new, rich and poor, also reveals an increasing gap in the distribution of wealth.

Protests are now an everyday occurrence. Old people who have not received their pension checks rally in front of Congress, a historic site and tourist spot. Teachers who can no longer live on their meager salaries strike, taking over major streets. University students demonstrate every Thursday afternoon and shut down the Central University.[9] And this collective voice transforms the social landscape.

Yet the collective voice of each protest is most often muted through repression. For instance, in May 1993, there was a march called by the fifteen national public universities to demand a fair budget. Ten thousand people all over the country, including deans, professors, staff, and students gathered at Central University to ask the government for 35 million bolivares (approximately 3.5 million dollars) so that the schools could stay open for the remainder of the year. Although the event started peacefully, it ended up in what is popularly call a *disturbio* (outbreak).[10]

The march moved from the Central University of Venezuela to downtown Caracas, where the leaders decided to continue on to the Congress. However, national guards blocked the way, and the crowd was forced to stay at Plaza Bolívar, where it proceeded to denounce the government and the current economy. At this point, the protest was augmented by assorted groups of people banging pots and pans.[11] Police forces then showed up firing tear-gas bombs. When the university deans finally gained access to Congress, they openly accused the police of provoking violence.

Violence and the fear of conflict in Caracas have changed everyday life. They have transformed personal and business schedules, social relations among neighbors, and the use of public spaces. When there are uprisings the government imposes curfews on minors, and several constitutional rights such as the freedom of public assembly are suspended. People are frustrated that they cannot stroll through the city for fear of arrest or violence: adults have self-imposed curfews, because they fear armed robberies and assaults. Even whole neighborhoods close themselves off to unidentified people. Those who can afford it place armed guards outside their homes or on their streets, thinking they can keep protesters or delinquents at bay by putting up gates with hired gatekeepers who grant permission to enter only to desirable visitors.

In effect, Caracas is now in a state of siege. The walls that surround the properties of the well-to-do grow higher and higher, and even among the less well off and the poor, there is anxiety, uncertainty, and hopelessness. But while some seek to protect themselves in their fortresses, others cannot escape the bullets flying inside their thin rancho walls.

Por Estas Calles: **Mass Media and Social Consciousness**

"Por estas calles . . . "

Por estas calles la compasión ya no aparece
Y la piedad hace rato, que se fue de viaje
Cuando se iba la perseguía la policía

Oye conciencia, mejor te escondes con la paciencia
Por ningún lado se encuentran rastros de valentía
Quienes la vieron dicen que estaba pálida y fría
Se daba cuenta que estaba sola y sin compañia
Y cada vez que asomaba el rostro se le veía
Por eso cuidate de las esquinas
No te distraigas cuando caminas
Que pa' cuidarte yo solo tengo esta vida mía
Por estas calles hay tantos pillos y malechores
Y en eso si que no importan credo, raza o colores
Te las juegas si andas diciendo lo que tu piensas
Al hombre bueno le ponen precio a la cabeza
Y los que andan de cuello blanco son los peores
Porque ademas de quemarte se hace llamar señores
Tienen amigos en altos cargos muy influyentes
Y hay algunos que hasta se lanzan pa' presidente
Por eso cuidate de las esquinas
No te distraigas cuando caminas
Que pa'cuidarte yo solo tengo esta vida mía

"On These Streets . . . "

On these streets compassion no longer exists
And mercy has long left us
As she was leaving police persecuted her,
Listen, conscience, you'd better patiently hide,
You can't find traces of courage anywhere
Those who saw her said she was pale and cold
She realized she was alone, without company,
And every time it showed on her face.
Therefore, beware of corners.
Don't get distracted when you walk
Because I only have this life to take care of you
On these streets there are so many rascals and thugs
And in these beliefs, race or colors don't matter.
You take a risk if you say what you think
The head of the good man has a price
And those with white collars are worse

Because besides screwing you they make you call them Mr.
They have very influential friends
And some even run for president.
Therefore, beware of corners
Don't get distracted when you walk
Because I only have this life to take care of you.

For people in Caracas, the emerging violence is partly understood and experienced through popular culture. Technology has made this easy, since even the poorest ranchos have television sets, and popular culture, with its songs, soap operas, and jokes, provides caraqueños with a common language that enables them to discuss and understand the different types of violence—structural, political, symbolic, and individual—experienced at different levels of society. In the "common culture" (Willis 1990) of the mass media, caraqueños find idioms for social commentary that help them make sense of the current crisis in Venezuela.[12]

Soap operas in Venezuela, as in the rest of Latin America, are prime-time programs consisting of a series of sequential one-hour episodes, which are shown every day except Sunday.[13] Unlike serials in the United States, soap operas last for approximately six to eight months. They are often combined with music and have become increasingly a venue for social and political commentary. For instance, the soap opera *Por estas calles . . .* and its opening song of the same name are one example of the symbolic creativity through which caraqueños humanize and give meaning to their lives in the midst of a national crisis (see Willis 1990, 2). *Por estas calles . . .* created idioms and characters that allowed the establishment of a dialectic between society and people in the media—a dialectic in which the real and the fictional often merge.

Por estas calles . . . began in June 1992 as an alternative soap opera. It did not have as its title the name of its heroine (such as Abigail, Topacio, Cristal, Kassandra, and so on) and it did not focus solely on a romantic story line.[14] Though it was written to have only 250 episodes, to be shown from Monday to Saturday from nine to ten P.M., it was so successful—it captured about 70 percent of television viewers—that it was extended for over two years. As the series continued, new episodes combined fictional events with real ones, such as water shortages, the *carros bombas* (exploding cars), and the 1993 national election campaign.[15]

During its two-year run, the series introduced a cast of characters who used a vocabulary that helped to illuminate what was happening on the streets. I will discuss here five male characters whose roles touch on three themes of the complex social fabric of violence and life on the streets: Don Chepe Orellana and Dr. Valerio, Eudomar Santos and Rodilla, and the "hombre de la etiqueta" (Tagman). In the course of my fieldwork, I met people on the streets who constantly used these characters as personal frames of reference.

Don Chepe Orellana and Dr. Valerio embodied powerful political and structural violence (that is, violence associated with their formal position in institutions, class, and so forth). Although Don Chepe, the governor, along with those who surrounded him, personified all the major scandals surrounding various politicians of the last decade, his character appeared to be primarily based on former president Lusinchi, who was manipulated by his private secretary (now wife), Blanca Ibañez ("Lucha" in the soap opera). For people on the streets, a dialogue was taking place between the television characters and the Lusinchi-Ibañez duo, especially during times of increased media coverage, such as when Lusinchi was on trial and his soon-to-be-wife was hiding in Costa Rica. Together the characters Don Chepe and Lucha went through an election—which happened at the same time as the Venzuelan national election in December 1993—developed all sorts of illegal schemes to gain more power, and eliminated their political enemies using brutal force. From Monday to Saturday, Don Chepe and his companions were the tragicomic parody of real-life current politics, portraying the inefficiency, bureaucracy, and corruption that have plagued the Venezuelan governments of the last decades.

Another character, Dr. Valerio, was a caricature of the upper-middle-class scoundrel. He ran a private clinic and spent his time coming up with schemes to obtain more power and more money. He had connections with certain groups that stole equipment from public hospitals and sold it to private clinics for less than market price. Dr. Valerio, like many well-known white-collar crooks, boasted about his cleverness in cheating the system.

Dr. Valerio was juxtaposed with Eudomar Santos in the soap opera and in the viewers' imagination as two different versions of Venezuelans' famed *facilismo* (smoothness). They shared two women and the desire for fast money. Eudomar Santos was a barrio man in his late twenties who, although he had more scruples than Dr. Valerio, also wanted to get rich the easy way. Dr. Valerio was light skinned, well-educated, and a respectable member of society. Eudomar Santos was dark skinned, and he was looked down upon by those in power as a petty crook and a mono. Santos was always looking for a *chamba*, an odd job often to be found in the informal economy. Like Dr. Valerio, he was always in search of an opportunity.

In the course of the series, Eudomar tried all the odd jobs he could, including working as an employee of Don Chepe and Lucha. His proverbs and expressions, such as "¿Qué es lo que está pa'sopa?" (What's going on?) were the everyday talk of the "easygoing mono." Eudomar represented a mono who, although not contributing to the official economy, reproduces the broader system of corruption in microcosm. The majority of the youngsters at the Carolina Center with whom I spoke, however, respected and liked Eudomar but considered Dr. Valerio "funny, but a typical *yupi* [yuppie] from the east [side of Caracas]."

The most unexpected surprise of the series was the character

Rodilla (which literally means knee), a fourteen-year-old boy who was a sort of a barrio malandro. Rodilla appeared in the second year of the soap opera and brought the ratings back up. He was of the generation after Eudomar Santos, representing the new gangs of malandros who terrorize the barrio with their guns. Rodilla opened a debate about how he was simultaneously an agent of individual violence and a victim of structural and symbolic violence. It was not a coincidence that this character, interpreted by a young actor of humble means, was such a success. Rodilla represented, and at the same time was, the young mono. The actor spoke the malandro language in the soap opera, but his own manner of speech outside the program was not that different. The boy became the most important actor in the soap opera, because he epitomized the tastes, styles, problems, and dreams of the majority of the young audience. To some in the audience, Rodilla was also the marginal young person fighting to survive poverty in spite of the odds. Not everything about him was violent; on the contrary, with time the boy showed that he was willing to change, only to find that the conditions of life made it difficult for him to do so.

Rodilla definitely rubbed salt in one of society's open wounds. He personalized the current degrees of violence in the city. In fact, at the height of the character's popularity, Rodilla, or "los Rodillas," became an identifying term; newspaper articles about crime used the name Rodilla to refer to minors. Rodilla represented a new kind of hero or the young generation of criminals who are plagued by all kinds of ambiguities. Rodilla in *Por estas calles* . . . was indeed responsible for a great degree of individual violence (assaults and robberies), but every time he tried to change, he found he was not able to. Like many young people I met on the streets and at the Carolina Center, Rodilla felt that no matter what he did he was always treated harshly and with distrust. For example, when Rodilla was arrested for committing a crime of which he was innocent and sent to an INAM center, he was treated roughly and sent home to his mother, who was a drug addict and made him work for her distributing drugs.

Just when Rodilla had become most popular, a judge ruled that the character should be banned from the program because "Rodilla did not portray a good example for society"; she added that it was to the detriment of the actor's mental health to depict such a delinquent character. (María Yolanda García, "Tribunal de menores ordenó suspensión del personaje Rodilla" [A minor's court ordered the suspension of the television character Rodilla], *El Nacional*, April 28, 1994.) A protest ensued, in which viewers argued that Rodilla was in fact a "positive" role model among all the "negative" role models in life because he stood for those who were trying to get away from a life of crime. For example, he was trying to find a suitable home by fighting for his adoption by a hard-working woman. After a few weeks of pressure, the judge allowed Rodilla to appear on the program again, thereby losing the battle to shield the public eye from Rodilla and the controversies surrounding him.

The most ambivalent character in *Por estas calles . . .* was Tagman, who embodied the anonymous violence happening at different levels of society. He started out in the series as an unknown person who took justice into his own hands. He would kill someone whom he considered delinquent and leave his trademark, which was a tag on one of his victim's toes. As the soap opera developed, it was revealed that the Tagman was a police officer whose son had been killed at the beginning of the story by an unknown person. In his pain and rage, he became a vigilante. He argued that there was no social justice anymore, and because he found the law that he was supposed to uphold corrupt and inefficient, he took the law into his own hands.

Tagman became a popular metaphor for the faceless violence in Caracas, a symbol of those who share the feeling that real justice has to be done from behind a mask.[16] For the state, the anonymous violence of the Tagman represents that of those protesting on the streets with T-shirts wrapped around their faces, or that of the young hooded students who protest at the university every Thursday, or that of the even younger students who protest outside the high schools over issues such as transportation fare increases. But from the state's point of view it appears that this violence is embodied in more sinister symbols than the Tagman, such as the *mano peluda* (hairy hand) or *mano negra* (black hand). Newspapers often report on the dark force of the mano peluda, which they suggest has an important, but unexplained, role in disturbing the social order.

According to those I met on the streets, the mano negra was made up of a body of hooded police agents who kill youngsters at their whim. These policemen go into the barrios in groups, sometimes on motorcycles, and take their victims.[17] The Tagman was also a policeman, and the chupapegas of Sabana Grande likened him and the police forces to the death squads who kill street children in Brazil. Following this view, the Venezuelan state in its desperation at the slowness of the judicial system, and in order to solve the "delinquency problem," used the rationality of Tagman, that is, anonymous violence. Some of the youngsters I met also thought that Tagman symbolized the subtle violence of the bureaucratic system because of the tag he always left on his victim's toe. In other words, he represented the humiliations ordinary people suffer daily to gain access to basic services, the long lines they have to endure to conduct the most simple procedures, and the confusing number of papers they have to produce to carry out any transaction. Tagman embodied tags, papers, stamps, lines—an inefficient system in which for those without economic resources everyday life is becoming increasingly hellish.

Tagman, in his anonymity, also represents the phenomenon

of ordinary citizens taking justice into their own hands. Vigilante violence has in fact become more common in Venezuelan cities. In several communities, residents look upon vigilante action as the only alternative to solve intracommunity violence. At the Carolina Center, I met two youngsters, Jerson and Felipe, from the barrio 23 de Enero, who were both caught stealing and had previous records for stealing from several restaurants. They belonged to an enigmatic vigilante group called the Tupas, who in order to fight violence in the barrios stole money from the wealthy.[18] With this money they bought weapons and goods such as food, clothes, and medicines that they then distributed among people in order to gain support for their cause. They said that the group had started to fight off the malandros, who were terrorizing the barrios, but in the end, they themselves became just another group of malandros. The great majority of the Tupas, like the malandros, became corrupted by money and drugs. Secrecy was important, and members of the group refused to elaborate on how the Tupas were organized or what they did. Today in Caracas there are several groups such as the Tupas and many others that are more public.

The song "Por estas calles . . . " was an instant hit for the singer Yordano as soon as it premiered with the soap opera. The lyrics of the song, like the experience of violence itself, do not make complete sense. The words tell of the surrealist fear of everyday life on the streets, in which one has to beware of corners; on the streets of the city everybody is vulnerable, especially women who are alone. Who is truly in danger and who are the perpetrators of violence? the song asks. The streets are full of thugs, but the white-collar crooks, the ones you have to call "señores," are worse. And some of them even run for president, so be careful where you walk.

Anthropologists Carolyn Nordstrom and JoAnn Martin describe patterns of violence as embodied and elaborated cultural processes, and "not as fragmented phenomena which occur outside the arena of everyday life for those affected" (1992, 5). *Por estas calles . . .* allowed people in Caracas, regardless of their socioeconomic backgrounds, to share a "common culture" that touched on experiences and understandings of violence much like their own. It gave people on the streets—malandros, policemen, politicians, booksellers, and *buhoneros* (street merchants)—a common language of characters and situations through which to make sense of everyday life in the capital city.

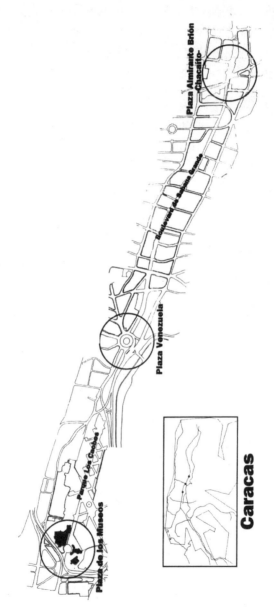

Caracas

The Sabana Grande boulevard

2 • Young People on the Streets of Caracas

The Sabana Grande Boulevard

I remember my weekly trips to Sabana Grande with my grandmother when I was growing up. While she drove her green Oldsmobile along Abraham Lincoln Avenue, popularly known as la Calle Real de Sabana Grande, my sisters and I, sitting in the back seat, looked out at the plethora of jewelry, clothes, and shoe shops. When I was in high school in the early 1980's, Sabana Grande was transformed into a boulevard. The Calle Real was closed to traffic, and there were three new metro stations built along it: Chacaíto, Sabana Grande, and Plaza Venezuela. At one end of the boulevard closer to the Plaza Venezuela were several outdoor cafés, the most famous of which was the Gran Café. There students, tourists, and chess players gathered to share some moments of intimacy in the crowded city.

This boulevard was different from the Sabana Grande of my childhood. It was much more a meeting place for people from all parts of the city, a place of reference. There were more stores and more people walking along the streets. There were also more buhoneros selling clothes, crafts, and books outside the shops and taking up walking space with their stands.

My grandmother often laughed at my concern over the fast transformation of the boulevard. When she was young, Sabana Grande consisted of an open field with a streetcar station, and people used to go there for vacations. In 1920, at the age of seven, my grandmother got dysentery and the doctor sent her and the family to rest in Sabana Grande. The family spent three months in a rented house in the Callejón Negrín, which is today very close to the large traffic-jammed Avenida Libertador, right above the boulevard.

In the 1930's, Caracas was made up of approximately 200,000 people, only 6 percent of the total population. In 1935, the dictator, Juan Vicente Gómez, died after twenty-seven years in power, and with his death a different type of government emerged. The new democratic process brought with it the use of government funds to rebuild the city. Big plans for a new modern city appeared, such as the Frenchman Maurice Rotival's Plan Monumental para Caracas (monumental plan for Caracas). The plan was never fully carried out, but from that moment on the city started to grow and people began to move from the *centro* (downtown) to the east side of Caracas. Today the capital contains approximately four million people out of a total national population of 21 million (OCEI 1992).

According to the chronicler Caremis, this expansion of Caracas started with the military dictatorship of General Perez Jiménez in the 1950's. Perez Jiménez built a very important infrastructure, including the Caracas–La Guaira highway and the Central University. At this point the movement from west to east began to take force within the city (Troconis de Veracoechea 1993). This movement, along with increasing population density and immigration, accelerated urban growth, transforming Caracas from a small central city to a rapidly expanding larger city, growing toward all the cardinal points, but especially east.

Caremis believes, however, that it was not until the 1960's, when democracy was again emerging, that Sabana Grande became a commercial center for wealthier groups. At that time it was still partly residential, but European immigrants were opening their shops along the Calle Real, selling clothes, shoes, cosmetics, and jewelry, among other signs of newfound wealth. In the late 1970's and early 1980's, the state started the construction of the metro to alleviate the heavy traffic going west to east to west.

At present, approximately 15,000 people walk daily down the Calle Real, with its five hundred stores (Carolina Ledezma, "Sabana Grande: un rincón para los olvidados" [Sabana Grande: a corner for the forgotten ones], *El Nacional*, April 5, 1994). With the new transportation system, people living in the shantytowns on the hills can easily come to this commercial center designed for tourists and the middle class. For Caracas's four million people, the boulevard is one of the few places left to gather and to socialize.

But unfortunately, the boulevard is now overcrowded and dirty, and visitors, merchants, and police call it "out of control." Certainly it has become a visible representation of the daily violence lived in the city. Fear and repression are now everyday experiences for consumers and locals. At Christmas in 1993, a newspaper article told of the shop owners' daily tragedies. The headline read, "El hampa se muda a Sabana Grande" (The *hampa* moves to Sabana Grande), and the article went on to explain that crime has moved to all the commercial establishments in the area. Not one business has been able to escape that group of undesirables called hampa.[1] In the first week of December 1993, shops lost fifteen million bolivares (approximately 150,000 dollars) to robberies. According to the article, the shop owners feel unprotected, since many consider the police to be accomplices of the situation and say that when the police come around it is "only to rip us off" (es para matraquear) ("El hampa se muda a Sabana Grande: roban 15 millones en los ultimos días" [The *hampa* moves to Sabana Grande: 15 million *bolivares* have been stolen in the last few days], *El Nacional*, December 15, 1993).

The street merchants, artisans, and booksellers also live in continual fear that they will be sent somewhere else and lose their income. The municipal government (*alcaldía*) and the police try to control the increasing population of street merchants and the areas where they work, but these efforts only increase the corruption and bribe taking. Street merchants are never sure which policeman will take a bribe to let them have a larger stand or to overlook expired or nonexistent permits. Recently a television talk show called its program of the day "Sabana Grande: tierra de nadie" (Sabana Grande: no-man's-land). An artisan who was interviewed insisted that the title was wrong: Sabana Grande was "tierra de policía" (the land of police).

It is the young hanging out on the boulevard, maybe snatching a bag, who should be most in fear of the increasing police repression. It seems a war on the young people of the street, especially the dark-skinned ones, has been declared. It has become increasingly common to see a group of policemen walking or riding motorcycles along the boulevard, carrying Uzis and other weapons. Often they stop groups of young people because they look suspicious, like "vagos y maleantes" (vagabonds and thugs).[2] Policemen ask them for their identification papers, and more often than not these young people will be harassed for the way they look, chupapegas, malandros, and monos alike.

The media portray Sabana Grande as filled with garbage, criminals, prostitutes, street children, and any number of other offensive things, like a modern-day Latin American version of Hieronymus Bosch's *Garden of Earthly Delights*: "The lack of adequate police attention has favored the invasion of beggars, street children, and groups of vandals who do not hesitate to destroy the lights of this boulevard" (Ledezma, "Sabana Grande"). These "invaders" have taken the boulevard from the middle class and the tourists. The poor and so-called marginals no longer stay in the cerros but come down to share spaces that were never designed for their use or their presence. The boulevard has become a "red zone," the media say, and the wealthy cannot tolerate the transformation of their urban landscape, in this case a recreational and commercial zone, by the "shantytownies." This transformation of Sabana Grande is often associated by the authorities with stereotyped marginal practices: promiscuity, delinquency, prostitution, and drug dealing. In this manner police forces structure and justify various forms of social control such as repressive police *operativos* (operations).[3]

I now turn to a consideration of the different categories of street youth in Caracas. The terms I discuss are not mine; rather, they are categories that the young people, policemen, street merchants, and frequent visitors used when they spoke of life on the boulevard.

The Chupapegas

Whatever the time of day, anyone who happens to be in the Gran Café can see boys, walking in groups of two or more, all carrying soda cans or plastic bags. To the uninformed, it appears that those ragged-looking youths are drinking soda from the cans, but frequent visitors and locals know they are actually breathing shoe glue. They are also conspicuous for their dirty clothes, which are often too big for them. On the boulevard they are known as the chupapegas (they are sometimes called *huelepegas*, which also means glue sniffer). Even others who sniff glue and live on the streets refer to them that way. A chupapega may refer to his *pana* (buddy) as a chupapega, along with much cruder epithets, such as *mamahuevo* (cocksucker).

During 1993–94, I met about twenty chupapegas along the boulevard, mainly in the Gran Café area, but I know from other people working with them that there are more, perhaps forty or fifty. The number of boys varies, of course, as boys go home or are sent to institutions for a period of time or simply vanish, going to another part of the city or even to "el mundo de los acostados" (the realm of the dead). Although the chupapegas spend most of their time on the boulevard, they do not always stay there. They move around the city to hide from the police, to avoid *culebras* (enemies, literally snakes), or to follow friends or other people for companionship or the desire to find a "better" place to sleep. Sometimes they visit shoe factories on the outskirts of the city, looking for leftover glue. Other times they even leave Caracas to go to the beach for some fun.

The chupapegas are the youngest people living on the boulevard. Most of the ones I met were between the ages of ten and fifteen, but there are even younger ones. The chupapegas are the youth who embody the most contradictory sentiments and who provoke them in others. On the one hand, they are looked upon as very young marginals and delinquents—too young to be so terrible, to have so much freedom to "do as they please." They have been described by some people on the boulevard as "la peste" (the plague). On the other hand, in some ways the youngest street people on the boulevard embody innocence, vulnerability, and dependency, traditional Western ideals of childhood.

I was rarely able to find out from a chupapega just how long he had been on the streets. When I met most of them in February 1993, several had been on the streets for at least a year. Yet when I asked one young chupapega, Alexander, how long the Gómez brothers, who were from the same barrio as he, had been on the streets, he answered "all their lives." Even in the barrio the Gómez brothers had lived on the streets; until they were seven or eight years old everyone saw them running around naked.

The Gómez brothers were among the best-known chupapegas in Sabana Grande and had stayed on the boulevard for the longest time. Their lives present an instructive example of how life on the street can harden these young people, especially as they go from sniffing glue to trying harder drugs, such as *bazuko* and crack. The older brother, Gómez, who was thirteen when I first met him in 1993, had a very warm attitude. Though he was a frequent glue sniffer, he always greeted me and other people. But by February of the following year Gómez had become increasingly aggressive.

At first Gómez was even liked by police agents. The Unidad de Protección Vecinal (UNIPROVE), officers of a special unit designed to work with minors, said they preferred him to the other chupapegas. When I was at Los Chorros once, I saw Gómez hug the officers there, who told me that Gómez was a "nice" one. Then one of the officers distinguished between "nice" and "behaving well," for Gómez was still considered "a demon." He explained that on several occasions he had had to tie Gómez and his group to a tree and shower them with a hose to calm them down.

Yet the last time I saw Gómez, in May 1994, he was considered by those in the community to be one of the most bellicose of the boys. He now smokes the highly addictive bazuko and picks fights with others.[4] The change is perceived by other friends. Pechundío, an older chupapega, told me with concern that a man named Tíochino (short for Chino's uncle) was transforming Gómez: Tíochino was exchanging sexual favors for bazuko. Glue is a child's drug, whereas adolescents move on to harder drugs and consequently harsher drug effects, as well as more problems related to drug distribution and violence.

Gomita, the younger brother, was one of the leading chupapegas. When I met him during the summer of 1992, he was ten
years old, always dirty and high on glue. Gomita experienced
sudden mood swings: one moment he was talkative and smiling
and the next he was quiet or aggressive. I met him in different situations, such as on the streets, at Los Chorros, and in the hospital, and he usually remained aloof. What I know of his background I learned from Gómez, who with Gomita, was a leader of
their group. Gómez was a natural leader; he could communicate
better than the others with older people and he was sweet and
talkative. He could organize games, robberies, and trouble, and he
could deal with the consequences better than the others. Gomita
was also a natural leader, but for a different reason: he was able to
manipulate other street people into doing things while not as-
suming any responsibility himself. He was also very clever at
playing the "poor child" when confronted by an adult.

The majority of the chupapegas I met belonged to the group
led by the Gómez brothers. The others who stayed together during the year were Caracortada, el Feto, Rafaelito, Parra, Chino,
Gerald, and Mascota.[5] They were always hanging out together,
playing video games and sniffing glue. The boys' addiction to
glue was very strong. I never saw a chupapega so upset as when
someone took his cans of glue from him. Even in difficult times,
it seemed their most urgent need. One time Mascota had cut his
hand and it became infected. I watched la Gata give him a shot
of penicillin. Afterward he kept looking at the Previsora (a large
building next to Plaza Venezuela) clock. Mascota said he was
waiting until it was 6:00 P.M. He felt that the shot would take effect by then and he could once again sniff glue.

Glue sniffing is the most striking feature of the chupapegas'
daily lives.[6] Shoe glue is very easy to obtain, for it is sold cheaply
in hardware stores or by shoe repairmen on the streets. Although
I asked most of the chupapegas why they sniffed it so often, I

never got an answer more elaborate than "I like it," "It makes me forget that I am hungry," or simply, "It makes me forget." Some of them told me about how much fun it was to be high on glue because it gave them hallucinations in which they saw fantastic monsters and "satanic creatures." There may not be a more elaborate reason. Pleasure is wonderful and escape desirable: How much pleasure or escape do these boys have?

One boy, Edison, who used to be a glue sniffer when he was at the Bellas Artes area, gave me a piece he wrote about glue sniffing.[7] He poetically expanded on the chupapegas' version of sniffing "to forget for a while" by describing the harsh and violent reality the boys try to escape.

> What answer can a can of beer in the middle of the Pacific give? The answer is solitude, an ailment which upsets and sickens us. You should all think a little, place yourselves in the spot where that can in the middle of the ocean is, and you will know how a street child feels. That child, an innocent being who for hunger, for coldness, or for lack of love sniffs glue. He consumes it to forget the hunger or the pain. That creature seeks a way to forget that every night he sleeps on the cold floor with an empty stomach. He sleeps wondering whether there will be anything to eat the next day. That is how that child's routine goes, waiting for someone to show him pity, someone who will understand the misery in his heart and provide him with something. The rain: some like it and others love it, because they have a safe place to sleep. But for street children it is annoying, because if they don't run fast to a shelter they know what awaits them. You may think there are good places to escape the rain. How safe can they be? Even when we find a place where we don't get wet, we still have to keep from getting cold. We look for cartons to cover ourselves. Combine the cold with the hunger that you feel, and then you will understand why we say, "Good thing that glue exists, otherwise how could I stand this."[8]

As Edison so poetically describes, sleeping is often difficult on the boulevard. The chupapegas have to fear both the police and

criminals of various sorts, and so they go to places such as parking lots, abandoned houses, or sewage drains and they sleep together, not only for protection but also for warmth. The closeness of their bodies also expresses a different kind a warmth, the
warmth they experience as part of a group, which is not visible
to the uninformed middle-class observer.

Chupapegas experience a normal, congenial erotic attach-
ment that they do not view as homosexuality. Both physical intimacy and sexual exploration are common among them. There
are many rumors among the children about the sexual encounters they have while sleeping close to one another. I heard one
say to another "toma tu tetero" (come for your baby bottle)
while pointing to his genitals, but as soon as I showed interest in
understanding what was happening, he grew quiet. I did learn
that the chupapegas regarded their closeness as homosexual (*de
marico*) only when it was imposed and not a natural part of their
sexual self-discovery.[9] They made several comments about who
was a "homosexual" or "sort-of-homosexual"; for example, they
called el Gordo ("Fatso") a marico because he was always jumping on top of them. His behavior did not have a place in their intimate practices. During the day, el Gordo tended not to hang
out with the rest of the group. The fact that he was much bigger
and a bit older, and therefore more capable of imposing his sexuality on the younger, smaller boys, most likely contributed to his
status as a "marico" and an outsider.

The places where chupapegas sleep are called *caletas*, or, as
one of my acquaintances, Prince, described them, "un hueco
donde duermen" (the hole where they sleep). Caletas are often
more enclosed than a bench or the open streets—a corner in an
empty lot or parking lot, an abandoned house, or some odd area
in a metro station that offers a bit of privacy. There is one such
sleeping place in the metro station in Bellas Artes, not far from
the Plaza Venezuela. Though the station is in the middle of a

crowded street, the young boys run up a steep inclined wall to a ledge that offers some refuge from the city. I went there despite my embarrassment at running up the wall in the middle of the day while all the people entering the metro station stared in disbelief at the sight of a woman in her twenties running to the top of the entrance with a bunch of street children. The boys had made the caleta comfortable with a couple of old mattresses that someone had given them and a few old clothes for blankets. One young chupapega I met described one of these places:

> There is one behind the funeral house San Martín, one block from the Orfeón Hotel. It is a hole like most of the caletas. It is a more or less a long surface underneath the sewer where there are some cables. You enter through the drain. (Haven't you seen the Ninja Turtles?) You open the drain and enter like a mole, and once you have arrived you find your mattress and your blanket. That one is for four people.[10]

When the chupapegas find a suitable caleta, they watch it for some days and then move in, in what they call an "invasion operation"; this process is like the start of a shantytown in miniature. Chupapegas frequently share the caletas with adults, especially good spaces such as condemned houses and abandoned construction sites in the area just off the boulevard. These caletas are not permanent, of course. To the best of my knowledge, the chupapegas do not stay in a caleta for more than a couple of months—until the police, the owner, or someone's enemy finds them.

The youngsters often fight among themselves—they can fight ferociously over a pair of shoes or a sleeping space, for example— but they also share food and in other ways take care of one another. In emergencies they almost always take care of their group. For instance, on one occasion el Feto almost lost his finger when he cut it on broken glass while breaking into a store. The entire group searched for a place to go and finally entered a private clinic, where they made a racket until the doctors took care of their friend.

The chupapegas' favorite activity, other than sniffing glue, is playing video games. Their street culture is highly transnational, and so the chupapegas often identify with the characters portrayed in the video games. Through the games the chupapegas also become familiar with the sensuality and efficiency of modern technology. Nestor García Canclini's description of the effect of video games on young people is appropriate: In the "mirrored screen where power is portrayed, there is the fascination of fighting against the large forces of the world using the latest techniques without the risk of direct confrontations. They dematerialize and disembody danger, providing us with the sole pleasure of winning against others, or the possibility, when losing, of just losing a few coins" (García Canclini 1993, 286). The chupapegas sometimes spend their money on games instead of food; and they ask passersby either for food or for video-game chips. Store supervisors do not like them because their mere presence annoys the other customers, but they tolerate the boys if they have come with money to buy chips. If they are only hanging out and waiting for someone to give them a game, bothering the clientele, they are shooed away, sometimes with force.

Whenever they can, chupapegas swim in the fountains, sometimes in the fountain at Plaza Venezuela, but most often in the more secluded fountain of Parque Los Caobos, which adjoins Bellas Artes. The chance to bathe in these public fountains depends mostly on the police, who can decide on the spur of the moment to allow it or to kick them out. Most chupapegas and other young people in Bellas Artes like to wash about once or twice a week, though others do it less often because they say they do not have clean clothes to change into. Moreover, it is not good strategy to be too clean: the chupapegas think people give

them more money or food when they look dirty. They also believe that being dirty can save them from being taken to police
headquarters, because when they smell horrible the police do
not want them in their patrol cars.

Most of the chupapegas are quite obviously undernourished,
yet they seem to have an amazing physical resilience. Gomita,
for example, was run down by a car and got an ulcerated wound
on his leg. The doctor could not do a skin graft because the
tissues were too weak from malnutrition and because the wound
would also take a long time to heal. However, in a short time
Gomita was walking again as if nothing had happened. Sadly,
the chupapegas leave most of their wounds untreated, because
they know that in most medical places they will not be well received.[11] Since most public hospitals are on the verge of collapse,
a ragged-looking boy is generally not welcomed with open arms,
and indeed is sometimes told to go somewhere else.

Even though they go hungry at times, the chupapegas can get
plenty to eat on the boulevard. It all depends on what strategies
they use. On more than one occasion I saw several of them ask
for food in front of a pizzeria. They would go in groups and first
ask for soup. If they did not get it, they would start jumping
around and screaming. The waiters would grow tired of this and
finally give them food. If the waiters didn't relent, there was a
good chance that they would lose customers. Parra, who was
thirteen, had been on the streets for more than two years. He explained one of his strategies to me: "I go to the Gran Café and begin to spit, making a lot of noise, and then people stop eating
and leave. They leave their food on the plate and then I eat it."
This trick does not work everywhere, of course. In Bellas Artes,
Gerovi, who was fourteen, explained to me that he was more
successful at getting food than his two friends, the brothers Jorge
(age fourteen) and Hector (age thirteen). They would always enter the same place and ask insistently for food, making a lot of

noise. Waiters disliked them and kicked them out. Gerovi said he was very quiet and well mannered when he asked for food and was therefore more successful. He had been in the area for eight months, and people knew him and left him alone. Once, the three boys and I encountered two police officers, who wanted to know what the boys were up to. Although one of the officers said that the boys should go somewhere else, the other one told Gerovi that he was not like the other boys and could therefore stay, since he never bothered people or businesses.

The main Sabana Grande group (Gómez and Gomita's group) sometimes harassed other chupapegas with whom they did not get along. Jorge and Hector, for example, moved from Sabana Grande to Bellas Artes because they were being attacked by the group. Hector said that he got tired of having his shoes stolen, and he did not like sniffing glue all the time. Once when he was bathing with his brother, Jorge, at the fountain in Los Caobos, the other chupapegas took his clothes, leaving him only his wet undershorts. Jorge was a heavy glue sniffer, but his friend Darwin was a culebra of Gomita, and this drew Hector into his problems.

Some chupapegas avoid these types of conflicts by remaining more independent, such as Plandefuga (literally, escape plan), who gained his independence through his mastery at fleeing from the Los Chorros youth center. He had been on the streets for more than three years and usually walked by himself in the *calle de los hoteles* (hotel row). Plandefuga was a half brother of the Gómez boys (they have the same father), but they did not acknowledge the relationship, which perhaps explains why he traveled alone.

What happens as the Sabana Grande chupapegas grow older? How do their lives change as they become taller and stronger, when they begin to grow facial hair, and when their hormones begin to stir? What kinds of survival skills do they develop once they are no longer perceived as children, chupapegas, or *malandritos* (little malandros)?

I only have partial answers to these questions. I knew the chupapegas during the period of one year, during which the changes they underwent did not at first seem that radical. At the end of the year, most of the chupapegas were taller and stronger, but they still looked like boys. Only one of them, el Gordo, whom I described earlier, had grown to such proportions that he looked more physically threatening than the others and more like a teenager than a boy.

Not all the glue sniffers are younger than fourteen. There are older chupapegas, such as Wilmer (eighteen), Pechundío (nineteen), and Jonny (nineteen), who started sniffing glue at around age thirteen when they arrived on the streets, and have not stopped. The bodily deterioration of these older boys is very noticeable. They are thinner, and their hair is very dry; their gaze is distracted, and they have a more pungent body smell, which is probably related to the toxic effects of the glue.[12] Also, in contrast to the younger chupapegas, they generally like to keep out of trouble. The younger ones in the Gómez-Gomita group seemed to enjoy creating havoc on the boulevard, and certainly they had more energy for such behavior. The stakes for the older ones are higher too: the police are less tolerant of them, and if they are caught committing a transgression, they could go to La Planta or another adult jail.[13]

One older boy with this attitude was Wilmer, who was eighteen at the time of my fieldwork, though he looked fourteen because of his small size and his thinness. At the beginning of the year he could always be found hanging out with the chupapegas. But then he got caught in a robbery with other people, some of whom were minors. The minors were kept for a few days in Los Chorros, but he had to stay for three months in La Planta. The last time I saw him in December 1994, he simply wanted to stay

out of trouble; he wanted to be more responsible and was looking for a job. Wilmer already had a baby daughter in the barrio,
and though he still sniffed glue, he tried to take care of her. Unlike the younger ones, who used whatever money they got to
play video games, Wilmer took any extra money he got to the
mother. The other boys, who were a few years younger than
Wilmer, constantly made fun of him for always worrying about
buying diapers, because at their age, the idea of having children
seemed far-fetched.

The other two older glue sniffers I met, Pechundío and Jonny,
hung out with the younger ones. The community reacted to
them differently from how it reacted to the younger children.
Pechundío, who was nineteen, had been on the streets for six
years. Although he was no saint, he kept a lower profile than the
younger ones and tried to stay out of trouble. He could usually
be found walking on the boulevard holding a can of glue. Jonny,
who was also nineteen, did not get along with the Gómez-
Gomita group and hung out with other younger people. Usually
he was with a group of four: the brothers Jorge and Hector, Darwin, and el Mudo ("the mute"). The brothers were harassed
mostly by Gomita and Parra and finally left the boulevard to go
to Bellas Artes. Darwin was referred to as the "earthquake," because he was always breaking into stores or harassing passersby.
El Mudo, too, had to move to Bellas Artes, because he had some
culebras on the boulevard. He was twenty-five years old, and according to another street person, was deaf because of a beating
his father gave him when he was little. Jonny liked to play the
leader with this group, telling them what to do. At some point he
wanted to help them and got involved with an evangelical group
interested in placing the younger ones in a private rehabilitation
center. But the police and the community were tired of Jonny.
He was often caught and sent for a few days to the police headquarters, until one day he finally got sent to La Planta for three

months. Later on he went to Nuevo Circo (another hangout place with many street children), where he had a large group of followers.

As time passes, tolerance of both older and younger chupape-gas wears thin. The community of merchants and buhoneros grows tired of them as crime rates on the boulevard continue to increase. Visitors and locals also grow impatient with their beg-ging, stealing, or just hanging out. Under pressure from the re-cent state declaration, "guerra contra el hampa" (war against the hampa), the police are becoming more brutal and have decided to create a public spectacle out of punishing the chupapegas. For example, one time they handcuffed several chupapegas and force marched them to police headquarters in public view. Jo-seíto, a twenty-one-year-old living on the streets, looked in shock from his corner. He wanted to protest the police's brutality, but he had already received "un calienta culo" for making a loud comment.[14] The youngsters were dragged to the police station, where an officer came out and asked the others about the event. Then he told the officers to let the boys go. The purpose of this public punishment was threefold: to humiliate the boys, to warn other youngsters, and to reassure merchants and visitors that protective measures were being taken.

Growing Older: Malandros and Monos

Although, as discussed earlier, some glue sniffers grow older and continue to sniff glue until they die or get killed, most glue sniffers on the streets of Caracas appear to experience radical changes as they grow older. Suddenly it is not enough to goof off with the others in their group. I met many older street boys on the boule-vard with this attitude. Some boys who continue to live on the boulevard drop the dirty chupapega look and participate in more organized crime such as drug selling. Others like Edison, Wilson, and Benjamín, who stopped living on the streets and sniffing glue, begin to work and study but retain some ties to the boulevard.

With the passing years, young people on the streets have new needs. They become interested, among other things, in women, larger amounts of money, other types of drugs, or a safer life. As they grow older, boys suffer different consequences for the same behavior. Boys who are fifteen to eighteen years old seem more threatening to the public, especially if they have dark skin. Their knife fights, bazuko addiction, and motorcycle theft bring greater repercussions than the purse snatching and glue sniffing of the younger chupapegas. The older a boy, the more likely that he will be labeled a malandro, mono, or jordan.

Whether a young person on the boulevard is considered a malandro or a mono, or both, depends on his style, attitude, and skin color. The terms malandro and mono, in the popular imagination, represent hordes of young people hanging out on the streets of Caracas. They are old categories, but they have acquired new meanings with increasing crime rates, inflation, and desperation. Rough classification helps one to make sense of the large numbers of young people on the boulevard, the streets, and the barrios.

Yves Pedrazzini and Magaly Sánchez define a malandro as "a person representative of a way of living, thinking, and talking of the young people in the popular barrios" (1992, 98). Prince defined a mono as "un pelabola del barrio que se viste de marca y se corta el pelo de una manera para disfrazar su pelabolismo" (a loser from the barrio who dresses in brand-name clothes and cuts his hair to disguise his poverty). Depending on who defines them, these two categories are not necessarily mutually exclusive. For most upper-class people, any young person who has dark skin and lives in the barrio is a malandro or a mono.

For the barrio dweller, a malandro can be more a hero than a villain:

> At the shantytown the malandro is the son of Mrs. . . . The malandro is the best-known person in the shantytown. He is the point of reference for adolescents and children. He is admired at least as much as television characters because they are similar but real. The malandro is the successful man, because he has the opportunity to conduct and have what mass media and the environment consider the ideal lifestyle. (Sosa 1993, 308)

On the boulevard when the young person is known to be involved with drugs, to be a troublemaker, or to interact aggressively with others, he is considered a malandro. Monos are more concerned with wearing *ropa de marca* (brand-name clothes) and picking up girls than they are with drug dealing or car stealing. However, both malandros and monos on the boulevard work hard to develop a particular kind of self-image. They are usually clean and try hard to wear brand-name clothes, such as fancy Nike sneakers, Chicago Bulls shirts, and Pepe blue jeans.[15] They become indistinguishable from other malandros and monos who come from all over the city. Wanting to look good or "tener plata para levantar jevas" (to have money for women) are powerful motivations for stealing.

If malandros or monos get into trouble, they are not treated as lightly as the chupapegas are. Police are rougher on them and do not let them go as easily. If they are over eighteen, they may be sent to jail. If Wilson, Edison, or Benjamín were caught doing something illegal, they would not be seen as "street children" causing mischief, but as malandros committing serious transgressions. They have outgrown their cute rascal image.

Roy has been on the streets of Sabana Grande since he was eight years old. At the age of fifteen he was considered a malandro. I met Roy two years before beginning my fieldwork, when he was thirteen. He was in Los Chorros, standing with a small group of boys underneath a mango tree. When I asked him why he standing around instead of playing basketball with the rest of the boys, he told me that the teacher was making him stand there for the entire day because of his disobedience. He soon escaped from Los Chorros and went back to the boulevard, but he was sleeping at the house of El Abuelo (grandfather), a teacher in Bello Monte rumored to let street children sleep at his house in exchange for sexual favors.

In 1994, Roy spent most of his days and nights hanging outside a video-game store near Chacaíto, waiting for people to come by to sell drugs to them. He looked like a malandro, with his fancy clothes and haircut, short on the top with curls on the back. During the past year he had been caught by the police many times. He was tired of being caught by the police in Maripérez (a neighborhood near Plaza Venezuela), because they always handcuffed and beat him, and most humiliating, made him clean up police headquarters. On one occasion when he got into trouble he was shot in the leg. Soon after, the authorities caught him and sent him to the Carolina reeducation center. After a week and a half he escaped. The other residents there told me that "José Gregorio [as he called himself there] liked to pretend he was a malandro, but he was only a *chalero* [charlatan]."

Three Members of the Association for Street Children

I met three of my young acquaintances, Edison, Wilson, and Benjamín, through my work with the Asociación Muchachos de la Calle (Association for Street Children), a small NGO that provides friendship and some basic services to children living on the streets of Caracas. Sometimes the association pays for meals or snacks for them. If a child is sick or injured, often a member will take him to the hospital and even pay for the needed medicine. The association also tries to keep track of when and where the children from Sabana Grande boulevard were institutionalized and to find out about their family situations. In addition, the association always tries to find private institutions (orphanages) for these children. These three boys had been members of the association for a long time but had only recently left their street home in the Bellas Artes area, partly because of increasing police harassment and too many enemies and partly because, since many boys had moved to other parts of the city or had gone home, their group of glue sniffers had broken up. They often compared themselves to the chupapegas on Sabana Grande, saying they used to be just like them, looking dirty and sniffing glue the whole day.

At the beginning of the year, the three of them were moving around the city and converging at Plaza Venezuela, at the eastern end of Los Caobos Park. Only Edison was sleeping there. Even though they were still living on the streets, one of their main concerns was their appearance. They tried to stay clean and were always interested in nice clothes. Benjamín was at that point picking up cans for recycling, and he got very dirty from searching through trash cans. But he always had his black plastic comb in his back pocket and used it all the time. Whenever the association had an event, the three of them often showed up with jeans still wet from having been washed the night before: looking good was worth the discomfort of wearing wet clothes.

I met Edison during the summer of 1992 when he came to one of the association meetings at Plaza Venezuela. He was sixteen years old. The first time we met he was wearing jeans, a sleeveless shirt, and boots, an outfit that earned him the nickname el Comisario (commisary) along the boulevard. To do my research, he said, I had to understand that he and Wilson had become *guerreros* (warriors). They both showed me their strong bi-

ceps and body scars to prove it. To me they didn't seem like warriors at all, but simply a pair of vulnerable young malandros.

When I met Edison again in January 1993, he was back on the
streets. He felt guilty about letting the association down and not
trying to get off the streets, but he nonetheless started hanging
out with other minors who were stealing and taking drugs. Edison was enjoying a life of easy money and had many girlfriends.
After he got caught a few times, he asked the association to help
him get a job and moved back to the barrio where he had most
recently lived. He began to work part-time as an office boy, and
the association offered him the chance, through talking at conferences and on radio shows and with children on the streets, to
be a role model to other young people. With this work his attitude changed. He decided to study, and he aspired to an intellectual image with a stolen pair of round glasses.

It would be too simple to say he had changed from a bad glue
sniffer to a good hard-working little intellectual. Edison thought
his identity was undergoing a transformation from street warrior
to intellectual; individual changes were prompted by his own expectations for the future, pressure from the association, and his
desire to regain his family's respect. But the process of change
was difficult, because Edison could not easily adjust to other people's expectations about his job performance and a different routine. For various reasons, he had quit jobs several times. He quit
a job at a bakery after only a few days, because he had to work
ten hours a day to make the equivalent of 25 dollars a week,
when he could make that or more in one day on the streets.
Touchingly, he gave free pastries to any person who came in asking for food, arguing that others had done the same for him in
the past. He also worked with an NGO for a brief time but found
the routine of picking up paper for recycling very boring and
skipped work whenever he felt like it. Finally, he left this job and
started another one, and he enrolled in a film school.

Philippe Bourgois argues that many of the men in East Harlem he studied enter the legal labor market at a young age, but before reaching 21 years of age, almost none of them fulfill their childhood dreams of finding stable, well-paid legal work (1995, 144). The jobs most inner-city youths get as mail room clerks, photocopiers, and messengers propel many of them into wrenching cultural confrontations with the upper-middle-class white world (1995, 145). In those jobs they encounter the racism and subtle badges of symbolic power expressed through wardrobes and body language, all of which leads them to abandon their jobs and enter the informal economy of the barrio. In the case of the youths on the streets I met in Caracas, the reason for abandoning their jobs in the formal economy is related less to racism and dress differences—"the search for respect"—and more to their inability to cope with tedious routines, rules, and schedules. For instance, on one occasion Edison asked Wilmer about his job at an auto parts store near the boulevard. Wilmer said he had not shown up for about two weeks and now he could not return because he was too embarrassed to see the owner, who had been very nice to him. Wilmer went on to explain that it was difficult to go to work when you did not have a stable place to sleep. It was hard to wake up at six in the morning when you had to worry about being attacked at night and, worst of all, to do so when you did not have an alarm clock nearby. Edison then admitted that he had left the job at the Ministry of the Environment Recycling Program after two months because he could never show up on Mondays and he was also too embarrassed to confront Jose Alberto, who had offered him the job. Furthermore, even though these youngsters would agree with moral arguments in favor of an honest job, from an economic point of view it does not make much sense to them—as it does not for many youngsters in Spanish Harlem—to work hard and regularly for the same amount of money they could make in a few hours stealing.

Strolling down the boulevard, Edison is generally considered by the middle and upper classes as a mono, as a young person who is dressed in a particular way, always clean and neat. Because of his gentle manners and his awareness of making a good impression, Edison does not look threatening to locals and visitors in the way Roy or Wilson might. He is just someone from the barrio who likes to hang around the boulevard. In 1995, he voluntarily joined military service. Perhaps fittingly, after six months the "street warrior" was awarded the "cadet of the month" mention for his great skills in battlefield training.

Wilson's family comes from the predominantly Afro-Venezuelan Barlovento area (the mid-north coastal part of Venezuela). Wilson was about sixteen when I met him, but he was much taller and stronger than most boys his age, and partly on that account and partly because of his dark skin, he looked more threatening than Edison. Many of the locals called Wilson a malandro, even though they recognized that he had changed since he began working at an ice cream parlor. In popular consciousness he could be considered either a malandro or a mono.[16]

Wilson was eight years old when his father died, and soon after he left for the streets of Caracas. He became part of the Bellas Artes group, which is where the association started its work. In 1992, he moved to Plaza Venezuela when the Bellas Artes group was dissolved. In February 1993, Wilson was living on the streets and in the Pinto Salinas barrio, which is a major drug-distribution center. He looked very dirty and was getting into trouble with drugs. At some point he got shot in the leg. Fortunately, the bullet went through and out, lessening the chance of infection. In March 1993, the police caught him for stealing a motorcycle and took him to police headquarters at the División de Coche. When I visited him, the police were pushing him around like a criminal—even though according to the law minors cannot be treated as such—making him sit on the floor while I stood there for a few minutes and talked to him. The social worker referred to him as *indocumentado* (without identification papers). Even though Deanna, the president of the Association for Street Children, and I told her that I had his identification papers at home—he had given them to me for safekeeping—she still thought that Wilson was undocumented and a liar. As proof of Wilson's lies, the social worker showed us his case file and pointed to his real name: Florentino. We told her that Wilson was his street name, but we did not succeed in changing her opinion of him.[17]

The last time I saw Wilson, in March 1994, he was again off the streets, living with his maternal grandmother in a dangerous barrio. During the year he had been in and out of the house, depending on family dynamics (there was a lot of yelling in the house, and Wilson's mother often came over high on bazuko and joined with Wilson's grandmother in berating him), and he was still preoccupied with his appearance: he was eternally worried about looking strong and virile. Wilson had attended school until the third grade, but unlike Edison, he was not interested in further schooling. He seemed mainly interested in a *pinta* (outfit), with nice sneakers, Chicago Bulls insignias, and so on. He always criticized my clothes, mainly jeans and T-shirts, saying that I looked like one of those devious woperós.

Benjamín was the third person in the Bellas Artes group whom I came to know. He showed up at a meeting of the Association for Street Children in February 1993. At that point he was a ragged and dirty *recogelata* (can collector), always walking around the city with a bag of cans on his shoulders; he often exchanged the cans for bazuko in Pinto Salinas. In spite of his appearance, Benjamín was the most peaceful of the three. During the time I knew him, he never got into serious trouble with the police.

Benjamín had been on the streets since he was twelve. When his mother died he had no choice but to leave his neighborhood, since his father had other women and had deserted the family, and his older sister could not take care of him. He had been a heavy glue sniffer, but in April 1993, a friend of his who shared living space with him in an abandoned house in Chacaíto invited him to his evangelical church. Benjamín started to attend and entered a detoxification program there. Soon after, he became an evangelical, changing from the recogelata of the boulevard to a clean-cut religious young man. He did not want to ever get into trouble again. Once, when Benjamín was fourteen years old, he was caught for stealing. It was his first time at police headquarters, and he was very scared. Since he had no documents with him, he decided to exchange his identity with a sixteen-year-old malandro named Giancarlo, but unfortunately, the latter had a record of several transgressions. When Benjamín realized what he had done, he tried to explain his mistake to the police, but the police had decided that he looked like a street malandro, and whether he was Benjamín or Giancarlo was of no consequence to them. As a result, Benjamín was sent to La Planta, and it took four months after association members brought his identification papers to go through all the bureaucratic procedures to secure his release.

Throughout 1993, Benjamín not only stopped taking drugs but he also went back to his old neighborhood on the outskirts of Caracas and regularly visited his twelve-year-old brother, who had been adopted by a family after spending several months on nearby streets. Benjamín also made amends with his sister. In the past he had been very angry with her for not being able to take of him, but now he realized that she could not have taken care of him properly because she was only a few years older than he and had been going out with a man who did not want him to live with them. He also went to visit his sick father, who was living in a barrio with one of his women and who had never taken care of him. In December 1993, with support from the association, Benjamín borrowed a wheelchair for his father. The last time I heard about Benjamín from my association friend Gustavo, he was selling pencils (by jumping inside buses) in downtown Caracas and was about to join Edison in the military service.

As we have seen from the stories of these boys, some chupapegas, as they grow older, try to leave their lives on the streets to become students, painters, or evangelicals, and some just drift into the lifestyle of the malandros, participating in illegal acts. Yet in the popular imagination, all chupapegas just become more dangerous, or at least more threatening. The process of change for young people on the streets of Caracas does not just consist of a biological transformation of the body: it is a process involving the three bodies—the individual, the social, and the political (see Scheper-Hughes and Lock 1987). Street children's life-cycle progression from child to man interacts with the political and social progression of perceptions: from vulnerable to dangerous, from soft to hard drugs, from needing care to needing punishment, and so forth.

The social differences between boyhood and manhood have serious implications for people defined as poor and black. In Venezuela we pretend that we live in a racial democracy and think of ourselves as *café con leche* (literally, coffee with milk)—a racial amalgam of African, European, and Indian elements. We do not experience the same type of virulent, hate-filled discrimination and segregation found in the United States (Wright 1993, 126). However, as I have tried to make clear in this chapter, the social forces shaping the lives of street children speak of the much more subtle forms of racism that are pervasive in Venezuelan society.[18] The color of the boys' skins negatively affects their ability to get money and food from the general public at the boulevard. Lighter-skinned chupapegas, such as Gómez, are often favored—or at least tolerated—by police officers and staff members at INAM state centers. As they grow up, dark-skinned children become more threatening to shop owners, visitors, and buhoneros on the boulevard. For instance, even though Edison and Wilson spent a lot of time together, people referred to Wilson as more of a malandro and as worse behaved than Edison because of his Afro-Venezuelan ancestry and his muscular body. I confess that I, too, felt less intimidated by Edison when I first met both of them.

The physical and social transformations of these boys have clear political implications. Minors' laws no longer protect young people once they turn eighteen. However, as pressure from the upper classes to control them increases, people like Benjamín, who are under the legal age, can be sent to adult jail even if it is illegal. Also, as they grow older, their undocumented status, whether actual or imputed, has dire consequences for their future, because it can limit their access to basic services such as health and education. The lack of identification papers is one way in which these young people on the streets are denied citizenship, with all its rights and privileges. These young people are being failed by a state that cannot provide housing, employment, custody, and schooling, as laid out in the United Nations' Rights of the Child Declaration (Convención Internacional de los Derechos del Niño)—of which Venezuela has been a signatory since 1991.

Woperós

In this era of electronic music and a revival of 1960's clothes, particular groups of mostly middle-class youths are emerging. These groups of youngsters sit outside their buildings in the east side of the city or in public spaces such as the boulevard. Some are referred to as woperós because of the rock music they listen to.[19]

Woperós, like malandros and monos, have a particular style of speaking, dressing, dancing, and interacting. Large numbers of woperós hang out in front of the Recordland store on the boulevard. They usually have long hair, baggy pants, thick belts, and boots—a style much like that of northern European youth groups. The woperós are never mistaken as malandros and monos, who fancy the African-American basketball culture, with short haircuts, designer jeans, and huge sneakers.

Music preferences also set the groups apart. The differences in taste perhaps can be traced to an old divide, which associated the Caribbean salsa with the popular classes (Rondón 1980) and the Americanized *changa* with the rich youngster (*pavito*). Woperós listen to electronic and reggae music and what one of my mono informants calls "merengue de ricos" (merengue for the rich). In contrast, malandros and monos listen to salsa music, and some of them are highly knowledgeable about it.

Preferences are not necessarily mutually exclusive, and by this I do not mean to imply simplistic class splits. But it is fair to say that woperós are generally thought of as higher class than are malandros or monos; even when a woperó is from a low-income home in the same barrio as a mono, he will indicate his superiority to that mono. It is part of the woperó style to assume a more middle-class identity. (I will discuss the interactions between woperós and monos in further detail in Chapter 6.)

At Home on the Boulevard: Into Their Twenties

To some young people, the boulevard becomes a way of life. Even when they are in their twenties, some still beg in the area or occasionally work as booksellers or street merchants. Others are enticed into selling drugs, organizing robberies, or snatching bags, working from the boulevard. After years of being in Sabana Grande, they have strong networks there (which can include the police, with whom they are sometimes in cahoots). I have met several older people (twenty to forty years old) who, though they do not live on the boulevard anymore, still go there to organize illegal activities. Many of these older people play the role of a teacher. They interact with the younger boys on the boulevard or in a shared caleta, and they teach the chupapegas the tricks of the streets: how to get more money while begging, how to break into cars, how to make master keys. Pechundío remembers an older boy on the streets who taught him how to get more money begging simply by tying one arm to his back so he would look maimed. Often men who are too old to be protected by juvenile laws recruit youngsters to do their dirty work for them. Although as I've said, I have not worked with many of the older people, I did manage to get close to two of them, Prince and Cheo.

Prince of Dreams: A Life on the Streets

Prince—short for his pseudonym, Prince of Dreams—was twenty-one years old when I met him. He had been on the boulevard since he was fourteen. Even though he slept at the house of an adopted aunt in a nearby barrio, he continued to spend most of his days and nights on the boulevard. He put it well when he told me the boulevard "is an addiction. You can't ever leave it."

Prince came to the boulevard one day by chance and ended up staying. Life there appeared more promising than at home in the barrio with his grandmother. During extensive interviews he explained how he arrived at the boulevard and the process by which he learned the rules of the streets. Like all the street boys,

Prince's story is both his own and every boy's. Especially his candid references to his initial fears, his sense of personal space, his initiation into the group, and his transgressions help put human faces on often dehumanized boys. His account explains how networks are established over a period of time and talks of the meaning of friendship.[20]

I arrived on the streets in the middle of 1987 and I was already walking like this. I arrived here by mistake, because I took a bus at a time when I did not know Caracas very well. I was crying. *Why were you crying?* Because of my mother. Well, I arrived at Chacaíto by mistake and I saw all those people and I was like the immigrant who thinks, "This will all be mine."

Did you have money with you? Yes, I had money because on that Sunday I had worked at the Guaicaipuro Market selling bags; I had 300 bolivares. At that time three hundred bolivares really meant something, and during that first week I lived the life of a Boulton [a very rich Venezuelan family], but afterward I had to sleep on the floor on top of cartons.

How was the first time sleeping on the streets? The first days I slept on restaurant chairs; otherwise I walked all night. More than once the police took me to that small detention center—not the big one, but the small one by Pida Pizza.

Who was the first person you met? Pechundío. That was because I had started to beg when I remembered what my grandmother had taught me. I thought, "This way I won't go hungry," and then Pechundío came up to me and said, "Hey, what are you doing around here?" and "That's a nice bag." He could see that I was all dirty and he asked, "Do you have a place to live?" "No, I don't, I left my home." "Ah! Do you want to go back?" "No, I don't, because my grandmother beats me a lot." "Well, come with me," and he took me to La Cortina. Later, I had been wearing the same clothes for more than a month and I had long hair like Marco Polo. Pechundío and I shared our profits from begging, but at first I ate by myself, saying, "I have to get to know how to do all of this alone." I got close to Pechundío, Nava, and Kilian and others who are no longer here and who escape my memory.

How old were you? About fourteen. *And how old was Pechundío?* About eleven or twelve. *Was he a glue sniffer?* I think he began to sniff when he came here from Los Caobos, where there was a place to sleep.

What type of things did you do? Well, some of us made knives out of empty cans and taught each other tricks such as how to grab someone like this—aghh! We did crab combats among ourselves, where you lie on the floor and count to five before fighting. This is a mean game—I learned it on the streets. At the count of five, you lie on the floor using one hand to hold on and the other to fight crab style, and the one who wins makes the other one pay the price. Someone always ends up getting fucked over. "Ah! For your punishment, you have to provide breakfast." *So it was a game?* Yes, but I used it a lot at the Playa Grande detention center to defend myself in fights. At the beach we did it a lot. Pechundío and I made sand traps.

Where did Pechundío come from? Did you know his family? I met his mother by chance, through Carmen who worked at the CONAC; his mother is fat and very friendly. *Why did he go to the streets? Do you ever talk about his family?* No, he would start crying. *Why?* I don't know. He left because he had problems communicating with his family; he would always say that his father was a drunk. Every time he's full of glue or drunk, he talks about his father.

What other things did you do? Later we would enforce the law of the group, like having to sleep at the cemetery. *And what happened?* All the new guys who left scared were not allowed to enter our group. There were about six kids who kept hanging around the gate, and we said, "Get in, get in or we'll throw you to the dogs."[21]

Prince tended to view the past with romantic nostalgia:

Before, groups were much more united. There were the "Antichrists," who didn't believe in Christ but who helped people. They lived like gypsies and slept everywhere. They showed Pechundío and me all the abandoned buildings in Caracas. *Where did this group come from?* It was a seventies group, they were all rockers. There was a guy named Leroy who is now a great baker. More than anything, he taught us how to be warriors. There's a bridge above the Guaire River where he made us compete by crossing it like soldiers—Pechundío, myself, and another guy. One time, someone fell and came out three days later really stinking. . . . One of my first robberies at a newsstand was with those guys. We had to cross that bridge with the bags; Nava and I were holding the money and the candy like this. . . . You had to steal something to be accepted. *How was it?* Terrible, I was very scared. *How many times did you do it?* About three times. Later, I had to do it out of hunger, because I was ashamed of begging; I went into the supermarket and stole cookies and fruit.

What happened after you joined the group? Well, Pechundío and Leroy taught us how to do things. Leroy was great at stealing caletas, breaking into cars with fake keys, and injecting water into the security systems of expensive cars. Pechundío still steals car stereos that way, because cars today have electronic security systems. He would sell the stereos in different businesses, and if he was broke, he'd say, "Let's talk like gentlemen." I like Pechundío: he says, "Let's talk like gentlemen" and then he hugs you saying, "My friend, my pal." When he hugs you and he wants something, he says, "Look, I'm hungry, I can give you this, let's talk, I have something for you, how much can you give me?" The other person always answers, "I can give you this much, plus food."

Once I robbed a store with him. I took three shirts, a pair of pants, and ugly shoes that made me look like the clown Cepillín. It was horrible. The thug stole a lot of stuff, which he put in a bag, and then the national guard caught us and said, "Stand still, what are you doing there?" and Pechundío said, "This is the trash, they pay us to pick up the trash here." We were standing next to a newsstand, and he grabbed one bag and opened it with his pocket knife, and what luck! It really was a bag full of garbage. Then we left and went inside a building. He started to burn himself with a piece of paper to warm himself up. It was later that he got the bad idea of carving tattoos on himself with a knife. Most of my adventures were with Pechundío.

How was your relationship with the police? There was repression. A street child could not be on the streets, because they would take you to an INAM center, but this is a global problem, abandoned children exist everywhere. *But how did the police and the community treat you?* The police were bad to us and the community treated us as if we didn't exist. There are more policemen now, but the majority have been malandros or have lived on the streets. They are like thieves, thinking, "Look here, if you have to eat I have to do it too: I won't take you to jail, but we have to do something about that, give me something and I'll let you go." It is like I told you, there are some policemen who grew up in the barrios just like us. . . .

I distanced myself from Pechundío in the middle of '89. I always told him, "Let's study," because I wanted to study and get away from this country. The problem is that I am slow. He was a great mimic and a clown. "Pecho, let's join a circus, we'll do fine." But he was pessimistic and always said no. When Zamora got killed, we split up. Zamora was a boy who lived on the streets and he got killed because of drugs. *Why did that separate you?* Pecho was a good friend of his and wanted to be in that world, but I didn't, so we went our separate ways. I told him we could still be friends, but we couldn't hang out together. Sometimes we see each other and eat together. Sometimes we teach other children [tricks for surviving on the streets]: Pechundío treats them like a father and says, "These kids don't want to learn" and beats them and I tell him not to hurt them.[22]

For Prince, home is the boulevard. It is there that he is loved and cared for by other booksellers and street merchants, who laugh at him for having his "office" in front of the fast-food place, the Tropy Burger. It is on the boulevard that he has acquired his education—not just learning new begging techniques but reading books and watching people. He is never short of a job but seems to shift often from one chamba to another, because like many other street children, he does not like to obey other people's rules.

I have met other people, perhaps less fortunate than Prince, who are even older—some in their forties and fifties. I met them on the Catia boulevard, not on Sabana Grande. In the 1960's and

1970's they were in INAM centers (which were then called Concejo Venezolano del Niño). Later they spent time in jails all over the country. Many who have survived life on the boulevard still get together there, drinking and talking. They feel, as one of them named Gurrundanga put it, pointing to his bottle of *aguardiente* (cane liquor) and looking at the boulevard, "This is what the government did to us—and now this is our home."

Street Children? Barrio Youth and the Struggle for Safe Places

For consumers, shop owners, and policemen, "street children," seen as invaders, are becoming the most difficult segment of the population to deal with. In Caracas, the origins of most children in downtown areas, their family situations, and the amount of time they actually spend on the streets remains unclear. In the institutional literature they are catalogued in several ways: as "niños de la calle" (children of the streets), "niños en la calle" (on the streets), "menores en situación de abandono" (abandoned minors), "menores en situación de peligro" (minors at risk), "menores en estrategias de supervivencia" (minors trying to survive), "menores infractores" (transgressors). Each of these terms carries a different connotation, ranging from the careful neutrality of the first two terms, to the sympathy of the next three, to the punitiveness of the last.

How people are placed in these categories can be a matter of convenience. For example, for a youngster catalogued as a "child of the streets," the street becomes the most defining aspect of his existence. These terms dissociate young people on the streets from their families and communities (Aptekar 1989). The Inter-NGO Programme on Street Children defines the street child this way: "Any girl or boy who has not reached adulthood, for whom the street—in the widest sense of the word, including unoccupied dwellings, wasteland, etc. has become his/her habitual abode and/or source of livelihood and who is inadequately protected, supervised or directed by responsible adults" (Inter-NGO Programme on Street Children and Street Youth 1983, 24, in Glasser 1994, 54).

The truth is that a whole range of lives converges on Sabana Grande to create these impressions. In Sabana Grande visible numbers of people spend the night there. Many more spend most of their days and nights on the boulevard but sleep somewhere else—at a rancho, an apartment, or a house. There are children who work with their parents, selling gadgets, books, roses, or hot dogs. Others work under the supervision of a parent, like one youth I've met who anxiously tries to sells flowers to the visitors while his mother watches from afar. Other youngsters clean shoes by day and go home at night to help their families.

Not all young people on the streets of Caracas fit into the category of "street children"; the label is only applied to those children who become defined as a visible problem to dominant groups. Many Venezuelan children (and adults too) spend more of their time outside than inside their homes and are not given this label. Laypeople and authorities alike apply the term exclusively to children living on particular streets in specific neighborhoods.

In Caracas many young people grow older on their own on the streets of their natal communities. The category "street children" as it is generally applied ignores the outdoor lives of many young people. For instance, four-year-old Hermes's mother had abandoned him on the streets of her old barrio before taking off with a lover. Although his great-grandmother occasionally took care of him, he spent most of his time on the barrio streets. Yet this child would not be considered a street child; a person becomes a street child only when he lives on downtown streets.

Although I do not pretend to give an extensive analysis of barrios in Caracas (see Bolívar 1993; Ontiveros 1989), in order to understand the phenomenon of youth on the streets I consider in this study two aspects that deeply affect barrio life—territoriality and violence. In most of the barrios I have visited, along with economic poverty, the crowdedness and the emerging territorial divisions are very striking. Not only are the ranchos close to one another, sometimes on top of one another, but often several people (five to twelve) live in one small house. Because so few spaces are left to gather or play in (when such spaces exist they are usually crammed with garbage), there is a great sense of territory, which often leads to violence among the inhabitants. Drug distribution is now often connected to violence as well. Young barrio people who sell and distribute drugs can make a good deal of money quickly, and they are willing to take the risks involved. Barrios are arbitrarily divided up into different zones by young people controlling the space through drug-related violence.

One barrio I visited several times is located alongside a stream that runs from the Avila Mountains for about a mile. The barrio is so rigidly divided into an upper, a middle, and a lower part that people, especially young people, cannot move freely from one zone to the other without running the risk of getting hurt or even killed. Every day the boundaries become more defined as more and more young people enter the drug economy and as more and more territorial culebras are made. Disputes among people in the three zones are further aggravated by the difficulties of accessing scarce resources, such as water. The structural limitations in each zone complicate social relations, such as searching for potential romantic partners and then discovering they are on the "wrong side." Under pressure and living where the public spaces of the barrio are so full of risks, many young people move to the major city streets for fun, to make a living, to play, to do sports, to hang out, or just to escape. Barrios have be-

come increasingly prisonlike. To experience "freedom," a person
has to move away from them. As another young member of Ma-
tias Camuñas's community says, "To live in the barrio . . . is prac-
tically like being in prison; you have to be aware of everything"
(Camuñas 1993, 3). (Camuñas is a well-known priest working in
several barrios in Petare.)

Young people in Caracas more and more use city streets as
centers for developing their informal, sometimes illegal, economy. In areas such as the Sabana Grande boulevard, the Bellas
Artes park, and the Nuevo Circo bus terminal, young people can
escape the crowdedness of the barrios. But those who are called
de la calle (of the streets) share similar experiences and lifestyles
with those who still live in their ranchos but spend most of their
time on the streets. The line between living in the shanties and
on the streets is sometimes a thin one.

Camuñas once quoted a young person speaking about life in a
barrio: "Our barrio life basically occurs on the streets, on corners,
on the stairs, at the entrances of grocery stores. We spend little
time at home. We go there to sleep and eat when we're hungry.
We go upstairs, eat, and then quickly go back down to our
friends" (Camuñas 1993, 4).

Since the Caracazo of February 1989, the threat of the barrios
appears more imminent to those who live outside them. Barrios
are perceived by the media and by the elite as the breeding
ground for delinquents and as the main source of violence. Furthermore, the triangle of youth-barrio-delinquency has led to
the localization and conceptualization of urban violence as an
exclusive problem of the barrios and quite unconnected with the
socioeconomic and political problems of the country. Barrios exist in the dominant social imaginary as a social problem and as a
growing cancer in the city (De Freitas 1993, 6). Young people on
the streets are the most visible reminders of the changing urban
landscape, and it is therefore assumed, especially by the media,

that because violent events happen in the barrios, those events are the sole responsibility of those who occupy those spaces. Accordingly, the state believes that it has the right to keep violence from spreading beyond the barrios by using violence; the state slogan has been "La toma de Caracas" (take back Caracas). Police operativos may vary in form, but they share the practice of penetrating and harassing barrios. For those who live in the barrios, death as the result of an operativo has become merely "terror as usual" (cf. Taussig 1987). Along with robberies and disputes, getting shot by stray bullets, which penetrate the fragile rancho walls and are often attributed to gang encounters, has become increasingly more common. The police add their drops to the mortal rain when they "take back Caracas" before others do— often they will enter a barrio and just start shooting out of fear.

At a conference I attended about violence in the city, a man named Jesús from the barrio San Agustín, explained that the community had created the movement La Calle es de los Niños (the street belongs to the children) as a response, among other things, to the fact that in 1992 alone 103 people suffered violent deaths in San Agustín and that the community was tired of police operativos. To regain control of their own streets, the barrio inhabitants organized an event in which six thousand people went on a peace march. In counterpoint to "toma de Caracas," the police force was invited to collaborate in this peaceful takeover, but they neglected to show up. Jesús posed this question to the audience of professional experts and police officers:

> Why do we have to tolerate police harassment? They come to San Agustín to attack and then say that it is a disarmament to be carried out in conjunction with the community. They just want to sabotage everything. They are not interested in the community's organization, because here there is a business with violence. Notice that here the minister of justice asks for justice because he does not know what happened with the narcotics amnesty. What they show

us is that Venezuela is no good. I saw some policemen who went up to Marín [a barrio next to San Agustín] and gave some weapons to two seventeen-year-olds. They are the ones generating violence.[23]

Another member of the barrio group, Oswaldo Páez, speaking very movingly at the conclusion of the conference, placed the phenomenon of violence beyond geographical boundaries. The effects of structural and political violence, he stated, are part of the human condition: in the context of everyday violence and increasing poverty, only violence is possible.

It is truly hard to talk about peace when one is violent. The truth is that I am a violent man. Poverty generates violence. We are not an isolated spot in the middle of so much violence. . . . Those responsible for it are the ones who have forgotten about us. There is no social justice. It is difficult to be a man of peace when children attend school underneath a bridge; we can't go to a theater like the Teresa Carreño Theater, which we are not allowed to enter because we are black, poor, and marginal. In a city in which there are horrible health centers, it is difficult to be a man of peace.[24]

Young Travelers: Views of the City

The young people I met during my fieldwork have their own ways of experiencing the city. These young people, in their movement throughout the city, are, in Michel De Certeau's words, "escaping the imaginary totalizations produced by the eye" (1984, 92): young people on the streets develop practices that are unrelated to the more theoretical constructions of urban space that only take into account the geometrical or geographical contours of a city. The picture is far more complex. Young people sleeping on the streets occupy spaces that are always contested. They have to move around the city, creating their own maps and searching for places to settle temporarily, to make a living, or to have fun. They create their own Caracas through their daily experiences.

Young people who arrive at the Sabana Grande boulevard can remain if they become part of local networks and group dynamics that will help them to shape their experience and bolster their awareness of what the city holds for them. Those without money and power have to find other ways to define their territorial privileges, and therefore the city marginals protect their turf by means of violence and seek to define collective spaces over which they will be able to exercise the strictest social control (Harvey 1985, 197). For many young people on the streets, the Sabana Grande boulevard is divided roughly into three areas: the western end called the Gran Café area, the middle area known as Sabana Grande, and the eastern extreme in the Chacaíto area. Glue sniffers along the boulevard seldom come into friendly contact with one another; if members of one group identify a boy as being from another area, they will often push him around. That is not to say that some boys, especially new ones, cannot move through the different areas, but in general the division of space on the boulevard is similar to the territorial divisions in the barrios, where zones are established based on networks, informal economic activities, and personal animosity.

The chupapegas that I met were those who lived between the Sabana Grande metro station and the Plaza Venezuela metro station—that is their territory. They do not go to Chacaíto, and the groups there do not come to Plaza Venezuela. Occasionally I encountered a boy who had moved between two territories, but it seemed to me that this happened only in certain areas and for short periods. Ruben, for example, had moved back and forth. He was ten years old, but looked two years younger. When I met him he had been on the streets for only a few months, and he did not sniff glue like the other chupapegas, which is most likely why he still looked so young. The first time I saw him was at an event organized by the Alcaldía de Chacao honoring a new program for street children. He was there watching the mayor (a former Miss Universe), screaming "mi reina, mi reina" (my queen, my queen) while stuffing himself with hotdogs. There were no other Plaza Venezuela (Gran Café) chupapegas there, despite the organization's efforts. The next time I saw him he was all the way up at the Gran Café area. He had stolen some books from a street bookseller and he tried to sell them to me. Policemen who were nearby looking for chupapegas did not yet recognize him, nor did street groups who might consider him a culebra. He was too new to the boulevard and considered too harmless to have to stay put in one area.

In the Gran Café area of the boulevard, the chupapega group led by the Gómez brothers attempts to control which of the younger ones, between the ages nine and thirteen, will be permitted to stay. The movement from one area to another also depends on whether one is "rayado en la zona" (respected in the area), that is, it depends on the reputation of an individual or his group in the eyes of the police. Once the police identify a group of transgressors, they can catch them at every opportunity and occasionally give them beatings just to keep them in their places. After a while the youngsters wisely consider it safer to move to another area rather than to continue being harassed by the police.

Wilson, who we met earlier in this chapter, used to sleep in the Nuevo Circo–Bellas Artes area. Along with other children, he would sleep close to the *machiques*, that is, indigenous people who have come to the city from remote areas and for lack of places to stay, end up living around the bus terminal. Wilson said that his group made a living by robbing people who went near an abandoned construction site in the Bellas Artes area. "Sometimes we got lazy and we would sleep in the Bellas Artes' caves." These so-called caves are immense concrete construction cylinders that have been there for more than a decade and have been used by generations of street people. Wilson's perception of the Bellas Artes zone, a museum area on the surface, was determined by his experiences at the caves and the "nightmare" he had there:

> I had to be careful with rapists while I slept. I carried a machete, just in case. One night a rapist came and touched my arm. As soon as I felt the guy's touch I grabbed the machete lying next to me. I got really scared when I heard the man screaming. I moved away deeper into the tunnel until I fell asleep again. The following morning I thought I had a nightmare. Then I got really scared when I found someone's finger. I was never able to sleep there again.

Young travelers, such as Wilson, Benjamín, and Edison, construct their own imaginary urban topographies based on their experiences of violence, in whatever forms it takes: scarcity, hunger, beatings, rapes, psychological abuse, and escape.

Once when I was with Benjamín he asked me to give him a ride in my car; he just wanted to tour the city. With some distrust, for I still did not know him very well, I told him to jump in. He said he loved to move around the city, that he knew the city like the palm of his hand. As we drove along the highway, Benjamín spoke of how he had become a street person, how his mother had died, and how his sisters did not want to help him. When we passed the imposing statue of María Lionza (the mythical Venezuelan indigenous queen), Benjamín told me that he sometimes came there to leave some coins for protection, since he had a lot of respect for the queen. He said that he once knew a man who was punished by María Lionza because he would come and take the money other people left and buy alcohol and drugs. One day this man fell asleep with his leg sticking out into the highway and a car smashed it. Benjamín thought the man had received the punishment he deserved.

A little farther on, Benjamín pointed out a bridge near Maxy's, a large department store. He said that two months before, he had almost gotten killed there. He and a homosexual friend were walking together, when a man named Julio and another man who lived under the highway attacked them because they thought they had come to steal from them. They gave the two boys what Benjamín described as "un cachazo en el güiro" (a knock on the head with the butt of a gun) and made them strip. The men then put pillows over their heads and yelled that they were going to shoot them, but just then two prostitutes showed up and the men got distracted. Benjamín started to run, and because he had neither clothes nor shoes, he hurt his foot. He looked at me and very matter-of-factly asked, "Hubiera sido una muerte muy fea, no crees?" (It would have been an ugly death, don't you think?)

As we got near Chacaíto, where I was going to drop him off, he pointed to the metal barriers along the highway and said, "Do you see those bars there? I used to pull them out to sell them for the aluminum." Then as he got out of the car he said, "See, I have been all over this city and I know it like the palm of my hand."

Contrary to popular belief, the ways in which people on the streets perceive and experience the city are not restricted to the geographical boundaries of what are considered marginal spaces, places of the poor. A majority of people on the streets move between the imaginary topographies of what is called the two Venezuelas, the rich and the poor. Every Tuesday and Friday the chupapegas of Sabana Grande go to the apartment of an upper-class man they call "el doctor," who decided to help them in his own way. Five or six street boys spend their afternoons in the rec room the doctor set up for them with Nintendo, video games, and a television set. The boys have a late lunch and dinner, and at the end of the day, the doctor's chauffeur returns them to the boulevard. The world of these children is not confined to the boulevard, to the barrio, to the Guaire River, and to state institutions. When the youngsters try to rob a house in a rich neighborhood or are invited into one, thanks to the charity of others, their mapping of Caracas is one of east and west, wealthy and poor, a Nintendo room and a hard cement floor. In other words, their geography is determined by their sophisticated understanding of the unequal configuration of Caracas.

Aquiles, a man in his thirties, provides an instructive example. He grew up on the streets near the boulevard and until recently had been in jail more often than not. He once asked me to introduce him to my family. So one afternoon, I arrived at Parque Central at around three o'clock. Aquiles was waiting for me outside the art gallery where he worked. When we got out to the parking lot, he was horrified and told me never to park there again. "It is a dangerous place, believe me, I know it is a dangerous place." When we got into the car, Aquiles told me how he had started on the streets at the age of eight, how he had joined a group of older youngsters and begun his life of drugs and delinquency. He truly did know what parts of the city were dangerous.

We arrived at my grandmother's house. The first thing Aquiles noticed was the outside wall, which he said was too low. It would be too easy to enter the house; for her safety, Aquiles argued, my grandmother should at least consider putting some broken glass on top of it. When we arrived at the house, he compared it to the house of Mrs. Rivas, who had an impressive art collection. To Aquiles's delight, my grandmother then led him to a room where she kept all her paintings. When Aquiles noticed her books, he asked her if she had *The Magic Mountain* by Thomas Mann. My grandmother, who was in shock, said she had it somewhere but did not know where. After that my grandmother offered him some coffee and cake and asked him questions about his life. She wanted to know where he lived. Aquiles told her, "I live here and there." When she insisted on knowing where he lived, Aquiles told her that he lived in a place called "el pasaje de la soledad" (solitude's boulevard). My grandmother did not know where that was in Caracas but did not press the issue further.

The use of private property to segment urban spaces into controlled zones comes into direct confrontation with the public's ability to appropriate space more freely (Harvey 1989, 185). Through their use of urban streets, young men and boys in Caracas remap the city on their own terms, transgressing spaces and challenging the social order. In their new urban topography, violence, creativity, and imagination mix freely with hunger, dreams, games, and wounds both physical and emotional.

Injured person at a disturbio (student protest), October 1997. Anonymous photographer.

Encapuchado (hooded person) running with empty soda bottles to be used as homemade bombs, January 1994. Anonymous photographer.

Johnny (Caracortada),
a chupapega from
the Sabana Grande
boulevard, April 1993.
Photo by the author.

Street child sleeping at
an abandoned site near
the Sabana Grande
boulevard, 1997.
Photo by another street
child, courtesy of
Rigoberto Rodríguez.

Benjamín visiting his younger brother (later killed in 1995) after becoming an evangelical Christian, November 1993. Photo by the author.

Gomita coming out of the hospital, February 1993. Photo by the author.

Youngster in his room at a state institution, August 1993. Photo by another youngster at the same institution.

Two woperós on the Sabana Grande boulevard, July 1998. Photo by María José Jijón.

3 · Young People and Family Life

In this chapter I will focus on the Venezuelan family which, right or wrong, is increasingly being held liable by the state and by the general public for the rise in youth violence. Those negative constructions of family forms hold that young people on the streets have unknowingly been put into a larger struggle among the disparate familial, cultural, and economic elements of the country (Aptekar 1988).

In Venezuela, as in many other countries today, there is a great difference between what is seen as the ideal family structure and what actually constitutes a "family." The nuclear family is the promoted ideal family type, but it is far from being the prevalent family structure (López-Sanz 1993). Venezuelan families, which are often extended and matrifocal, when compared by the state and mass media to the Western nuclear-family model, emerge as "in crisis" or "deviant."[1] Matrifocal families reproduced in *concubinato* (common-law marriage) are often considered "illegitimate"— from a legal or moral standpoint—or "atypical."

The state, mass media, and the general public all place some of the blame for current social problems such as juvenile delinquency and the prevalence of street children on common-law unions and their offspring (Campos and Colmenares 1991; Consejo Venezolano del Niño [CVN] 1973; Pinto Castro and Quijada 1980). As delinquency in Caracas grows to ever larger proportions, the responsibility is placed on the marginal family, particularly on women, who, as mothers and (re)producers of barrio children, are popularly considered accountable for youth violence and the chaos of modern Caracas.

The official discourse of state welfare organizations argues that the Venezuelan family is in the process of disintegrating, and that this disintegration is both changing the moral order and increasing the number of juvenile delinquents. Although the state attributes children categorized as dysfunctional or delinquent to so-called illegitimate families (see CVN 1973), seldom does it confront the problem of street children and youth violence in light of the immense social inequalities, political and economic corruption, and the ongoing collapse of state bureaucratic institutions.

In the popular imagination, street children exist as part of the urban landscape not only as products of deviant family dynamics but also because they are isolated from family systems. Yet to say that people of the streets live outside of any family system does not capture a more complicated and nuanced reality. In this chapter I will discuss ways in which young people on the streets perceive of family and family dynamics and how they create their own families while on the streets.

Double Standards and Stigmas in the Venezuelan Family

During the conquest of Latin America, the Spaniards often established sexual relationships (often extramarital) with indigenous and enslaved women. Many of these conquistadors maintained their legal families in Spain for as long as they could and formed new families with one or more native women. These unions were further promoted by the fact that single Spanish women were not permitted to come to the New World until the first half of the sixteenth century (Troconis de Veracoechea 1990).[2]

In Venezuela, emerging family structures were shaped by the mixing of different races. Over the centuries particular family forms were imposed and maintained by the Spanish and their descendants, the *criollo mantuanos* (the Venezuelan elite). The elite managed the collection and maintenance of colonial wealth, partly motivated by their desire to establish a family line (Lombardi 1976, 48).

In general, it can be said that the Spanish and their descendants maintained a sexual double standard with their two-family system. On one hand, the men—either criollo mantuanos or Spaniards—had a "legitimate family" consisting of their Spanish wife and children or of their union with an Indian woman and their offspring. On the other hand, there were also "illegitimate" families composed of the often nonlegal union of a Spaniard or mantuano with a black woman or with the "indias menos estimadas" (Indians of lower status) (Vethencourt 1974, 69). These categories did not include the family forms existing among the less powerful ethnic groups, and it was assumed by dominant groups that *mestizos* (people of mixed Spanish and Native American blood) and *pardos* (people of mixed Native American and Afro-American blood) adopted common-law marriage as an acceptable type of family organization (Ceballos 1983).

The different family forms were conditioned by the socioeconomic systems of both the elite and the nonelite that developed during the process of colonization (Ruiz de Mateo 1984; Vethencourt 1974). In general the systems of the elite were propagated and imposed on other groups. The two most common socioeconomic systems throughout Latin America, *encomiendas* and *haciendas*, allowed minority ethnic groups such as *indígenas* (Indians), mestizos (Indian and white), pardos (Indian and black), and *mulattos* (black and white) little access to land. Without land and economic stability it was difficult, if not impossible, for less powerful ethnic groups to maintain either their traditional forms of social organization or Spanish-style family structures. Although not an even process, the hacienda system in Venezuela played a more significant role in the evolution of present economic patterns (Arellano 1967; Ewell 1984; Carvallo 1994). The hacienda system gave control over large plots to one *hacendado*, who coerced the local peasants into peonage. It provided peons with land—which had been taken from the indigenous peoples—on which to live and raise small crops in exchange for a certain number of days' labor per year (Gibson 1966; Morner 1973). Peasants most often did not marry but lived in various forms of concubinato (Ruiz de Mateo 1984, 42). Both parents formed a working unit tied to the land, and both were responsible for their children. Because of existing social pressure, it was difficult for a peasant father to avoid his responsibility toward his children: neighbors all knew which children belonged to what father.

In colonial times, the economic system also facilitated abusive unions between mantuano men and their female slaves. The slave work of black females often included copulating with their owners, rendering "respectable" monogamous relationships effectively impossible (Troconis de Veracoechea, 1990).[3] The numerous children who were born out of these relationships between female slaves and mantuanos created a different family form, in which the mother was the sole head and the father seldom recognized the existence of the children.

José Luis Vethencourt, who has had great influence on the analysis of the Venezuelan family, sees the types of family that emerged in colonial times as very different from European models.[4] In his early work he classified them as less structured, and less desirable: "The type of colonization that produced the new Latin American nations did not permit the formation of typical family systems. The lack of property and the duty of adapting to a new monogamous marriage created as a result *an amorphous product, one which is undifferentiated and culturally weak in relation to the family group*" (Vethencourt 1974, 69; my emphasis). Vethencourt apparently does not believe that what he considers atypical family structures—those of the majority for several centuries—had legitimate dynamics and shapes of their own. According to his argument, then, a family made up of a black slave woman and her children is both culturally weak and a shameful anomaly.

Vethencourt's views are widely and uncritically quoted in Venezuelan family literature as fact (see Marrero 1988; Pinto Castro and Quijada 1980; Ruiz de Mateo 1984). Official discourse on the family has fallen back on his distinction between "typical" and "atypical" families and stigmatizes marginalized female-headed households. What Vethencourt seems to be ignoring is that families formed through legal marriage have not, until recently, been the norm in Venezuela. In the nineteenth century, despite the efforts of the Church, only half or fewer of the members of minority groups were legally married. Church records in Caracas from 1799 to 1809 show that only 43 percent of Indians, 36 percent of whites, 35 percent of pardos, 32 percent of free blacks, and 28 percent of slaves were married (Lombardi 1976, 82).[5] Even though President Guzmán Blanco's government (1870–88), attempted to control marital unions through law, the 1893 census shows that legal marriage was the norm for only 12 percent of the population in Venezuela. The illegitimacy rate was around 60 percent (Ewell 1984, 19). Another census in 1904 indicated that less than a quarter of the total population was legally married (Ruiz de Mateo 1984, 42).

In his effort to "civilize" and to Europeanize the country, President Guzmán Blanco also formally legalized civil marital unions, but he was motivated more by a desire to maintain the hegemonic structure of land and property inheritance and rights than by morality. The ordinance of 1876 declared civil marriage as the only legally recognizable marital form. This guaranteed a particular distribution of wealth among elite mantuano families, since only the descendants of legal marriages could inherit. The elites thus kept their control over Venezuela's economy and politics. Guzmán Blanco's resolution, however, had little influence on the rural population, which mostly maintained common-law marriages.

A lasting effect of Guzmán Blanco's edict was the reinforcement of the distinctions between a "legitimate" and "illegitimate" family types. As discussed above, the former was closely related to the family form idealized by the Spanish colonists and the latter to that of peasants. Among the wealthy groups, the "illegitimate" family was considered deviant, even though it was practiced among them, a hypocrisy inherited from the conquistadors. Many well-known powerful men in Venezuela still maintain more than one family or at least more than one woman.[6]

The civil code of 1942 reiterated the Guzmán Blanco decree that property and wealth would stay in the hands of the "legitimate" family. Until the reform of this civil code in 1982, clear distinctions existed between legitimate children, born out of the "legitimate" families, and illegitimate "natural" children born out of concubinage. From this distinction among children emerged an association of the "illegitimate" with the lower classes and potential delinquency. "Se dice que es un problema social porque la mayoría de los delincuentes (de todo tipo) provienen de familias concubinas" (It is said that it is a social problem because the majority of the families of delinquents [of all sorts] come from common-law families) (Pinto Castro and Quijada 1980, 32).

Starting early in the twentieth century with the growing oil industry, large peasant populations began migrating to cities, where men, and some women, became wage laborers.[7] This change resulted in a transformation of the family forms that had existed in rural areas. The peasant family was no longer a working unit, since the father was now a wage laborer working away from home, and without the common bond of the land, the father's responsibility toward his wife and children declined. Also, thrust among strangers in a large city, the father did not experience the same social pressure to care for his children—at least financially—that existed in rural towns. Men developed several relationships with different women, and women who were left alone developed new relationships with men. Now women took care of the children while continuing to work so that they could support them.

The increased responsibility of women was not unique to the migration process. During the colonizations and wars of the nineteenth century, the death rate among men was very high. Women took care of their households alone or with the help of their families. Perhaps more surprisingly, at the end of the nineteenth century, according to the Anuario Estadístico of 1894, a significant number of women worked as merchants, artisans, and public administrators (Ewell 1984, 19). This economic self-sufficiency among women, which was fostered by the upheaval of the nineteenth century, continues into the twentieth century in Venezuela.

Family Type, Women, and the (Re)production of Young "Delinquents"

The rapidly increasing juvenile crime rate in Venezuela in the last five years appears to suggest a direct correlation among poverty, the disintegration of the family, and delinquency. As discussed earlier, the family types formed by common-law marriages or single mothers are associated by the state, the mass media, the Church, and many researchers, including Vetherncourt, with the poor and the marginal. Vethencourt in particular stresses this simplistic connection between family type and delinquency: "It is in the lower strata of society, in the economic sense, that social scarcity is manifested in the structureless family life. We believe that in general the Venezuelan family is historically characterized by its incongruence, ambiguity, inconsistency, and instability" (Vethencourt 1974, 67). In other words, family forms among people with fewer economic resources, which differ from the idealized nuclear family, are a social problem. Vethencourt (1974, 1988) proposes *matricentrismo* and *machismo* as the two psychosocial phenomena that explain why the mother is often left alone with the responsibility of several children. Matricentrismo refers to the abandoned mother who is the head of household and who falls into a polyandry shaped by guilt and shame. Vethencourt calls these mothers, women of few economic resources, "primitive mothers" (1974, 69). It follows, then, in light of his widely used thesis, that young people living on the streets are the products of women who, on account of their "primitiveness," are not capable of being proper caretakers.[8]

Not only are "menores infractores," young people who transgress the established order, women's (pro)creation; the "irregular children," those who live away from home, are also the responsibility of women. The legal apparatus regarding young people is clearly female oriented. The judges in charge of determining the futures of minors are mostly female. Even the Ley tutelar de menores (Minors' code) is considered by newspaper reporters to be a female creation, and therefore its effectiveness is questioned even today: "The Ley tutelar de menores has a matriarchal influence. The judges dealing with minors and family matters are women. Even if this is not in the codes, it happens because of the extensive matriarchy that becomes manipulative and attributes the responsibility for the abandonment of children to fathers" (Kalinina Ortega, "Las leyes de menores no se ajustan a la realidad" [Minors's laws do not adjust to reality], *El Nacional*, October 7, 1990). It is easy to see that Vethencourt's popular views on the family and women have been appropriated by the state and the mass media and used as a blanket judgment on women, as both mothers and professionals. Female lawyers and judges are considered responsible for young transgressors not only because they are mothers but also because as professionals they are unable to deal with the problem through the law. They are blamed for both legal inefficiencies and for the inability of the judicial system to control young transgressors.

In this ongoing crisis, when more and more young people are living on the streets, protesting and rioting outside their schools, and robbing people, men—not women—are looked to as the ones capable of taking charge. The governor, the mayors, and especially the minister of interior affairs—all have their crusades to control young people. Their measures, supposedly unlike those of women, are oriented toward repression. Several governors and mayors have imposed a curfew on minors and increased the number of operativos in the barrios. The interior minister, for instance, has proposed an increase in the number of gun permits so that people can defend themselves; he has also created two special prevention agencies, both managed by men, for the purpose of involving the community in its "lucha contra la delincuencia" (fight against delinquency).

Clearly this intense focus on particular family forms and holding women responsible for youth transgressions and violence make it possible for the state to brush aside the all too real problems of public discontent and extreme socioeconomic inequality. The increasing crime rate of the last decade, and particularly of the last five years, have gone hand in hand with a worsening economic and political crisis. Young people steal and kill partly because they want to gain access to the wealth they observe only in certain parts of the city—wealth they see no other way of getting. But—as even Vethencourt recognizes—the most powerful models for criminal behavior are usually outside the family, even when the head of said family is the "primitive mother." These models include powerful figures who manipulate people and large amounts of resources for their own benefit, such as the popular former president who was imprisoned for corruption and released in 1997; a mayor, who after spending months in prison on charges of corruption, became a popular presidential candidate; and the well-known union leader, who after a year in jail for corruption, was treated by many like a hero upon his release. As Blas from the Carolina Center says about delinquency:

> Delinquency does not exist only in the barrios. Today 100 percent of minors are malandros, no matter what family they come from. If these malandros don't rob, then they smoke marijuana. Many malandros dress in suits, but those are congressmen. There are many people just like you sniffing coke. People from the east side come to the 23rd to buy cocaine. Joselo [an actor], colonels, and others go in their fancy cars to apartment complex 25 [a well-known place to buy cocaine].[9]

The State, the Family, and the Production of "Irregular Children"

The process of making the family the focal point of Western societies has resulted in the construction of positive stereotypes about children, upon whom the qualities of vulnerability, innocence, and fragility have been progressively imposed (Meyer

1977). In contrast, society has labeled "irregular" any family in which the offspring, because of poverty or cultural practices, are not the gravitational center and are not legally recognized. In the Western world this atomization of society into families has coincided with the emergence of the concept of the "maladjusted" child, whose irregular characteristics fall into a special category and who is constantly subjected to subtle definition by the state (Meyer 1977, 40).

In the specific case of young people living on the streets, the term "street children," as it is routinely used by the public and most professionals, implies that these children have no other place to live but on the streets and that their families are remiss (Aptekar 1989, 428). From the perspective of the state, their "ghost families," rather than socioeconomic and cultural conditions such as an unequal distribution of wealth and the collapse of social services, are to blame for the existence of increasing numbers of "abandoned" children.

As the populations of "irregular children" grow in number, the family as a basic unit no longer shows its allegiance to "traditional institutions," such as schools, the church, and so on. Therefore, when "irregular children" come under the surveillance of the state, the family also comes under inspection. Not coincidentally, the most recent minor's code (1980) is more concerned with the child in relationship to the family than were the previous codes in 1939 and 1949. In particular, the 1980 code included several dispositions related to what it regarded as family protection. The minor was no longer considered an isolated individual with problems but a member of a family with problems (Tudares de González 1989, 83). This change in the code essentially made the family responsible for the children's welfare but allowed the state to assume the role of official guardian for families with problems and especially of those minors considered "at risk."

In Venezuela, when a young person is first taken to an INAM

center, those who work at the center conduct a study of his or her antecedents, personality, and family—in other words, the child's environment. The environment within the household and the community is scrutinized by a specialized team of psychologists, psychiatrists, and social workers—what Franco Basaglia (1987) refers to as "social technicians." In many cases, the team finds the rancho, house, or apartment too small for the numerous family members. It is more or less assumed that under these circumstances, immorality and delinquency are a way of life and there can be few "good" children. At the INAM Carolina Center, which houses children between the ages of fourteen and eighteen, the specialized team of social technicians undertakes an inquiry into the minor's status, that is, into his economic and moral situation and that of his family, during which the family is measured against traditional criteria of public morality. The head of the household, his or her degree of formal education, the household's monthly income, and the condition of the living quarters are all duly noted.

The minor's institutional history actually begins in the womb. The woman's body, considered by the state as analyzable and passive, becomes, in the Foucaultian sense, the "object" of the INAM's inquiry. The team asks mothers visiting their children about all the events revolving around their pregnancies. If a mother admits that her child was unwanted for any reason, it is as if a red flag has been waved in the faces of the social technicians. It is as if the mother's rejection of the fetus, regardless of the reasons, had been transferred to it like a disease. Later on, according to this argument, the child infected with this disease will be capable only of rejecting the "good morals of society." Any indication the mother provides that the child was unwanted or that physical harm or illness occurred during pregnancy directs the technicians to find some deficiency, such as delinquency, in the minor.

In one case study I read, a mother explained that she had fallen while pregnant; the group of psychologists and social workers at the INAM center jumped at the chance to explain the relationship between the young person's act of homicide and his allegedly low intelligence level. His case file reads "nivel limítrofe, su capacidad de abstracción es limitada y se conforma con el evento concreto" (he has a low IQ and his capacity for abstract thinking is very limited). Essentially, the implication of the team's analysis was that the child's low IQ, which resulted from his mother's fall, did not allow him to distinguish between right and wrong.

The family's reaction to this official probing into their lives greatly influences how long the minor stays at the center and the terms of his sentence, which is arrived at only after the completion of the background study. Cooperative parents who answer the team's questions and regularly visit their child can thereby show allegiance to traditional patterns of family socialization; but they must be careful to provide the "right" answers.

Lendel was a seventeen-year-old youngster staying at INAM's Carolina Center for allegedly causing another adolescent to suffer from serious lesions. His grandmother, although very cooperative with the inquiries, hurt her grandson's case with some of her statements: she wouldn't admit that her grandson was guilty of anything. The case file says: "It is noticeable that the grandmother does not have a critical attitude toward the minor's problem: owing to her limited comprehension she tends to diminish the gravity of the situation." The grandmother had her reasons for supporting her grandson: even though Lendel was a drug dealer, he was a responsible provider. The report makes no mention of this constructive role, however.

Parents who provide admissible answers to the team's questions are portrayed as understanding the process of reeducation recommended for the minor. In those cases the minor is thought to have "un hogar estructurado" (a structured home) and a higher chance of returning home and complying with the conditions of their *libertad vigilada* (parole). For a young person living on the streets, this opportunity does not exist. He must pay his penance with detention at a closed center (where no leaving or visiting is allowed), even if his transgression is not considered serious enough to merit it.

At times, the institutional gaze extends to other relatives such as aunts, uncles, and cousins. Case files sometimes contain comments about alcoholic or schizophrenic relatives. The file on the personal history of Corazoncito—who had accidentally killed one of his friends while playing with a gun at the beach—contains this observation: "It is known that within his family circle there is a history of psychiatric pathology: two maternal uncles with diagnosis of schizophrenia, and an aunt and maternal grandparents with chronic alcoholism." Families that stray from the ideal nuclear family model are seen as unstructured, amoral, and improper. In Lendel's file the section about his personal history describes his family situation this way: "La madre lo abandona a los ocho meses de edad. Vive con abuelos y tía materna" (The mother abandons the son at eight months of age. He lives with his maternal grandparents and aunt). This assessment supports the following recommendation: "Taking into account that the minor lacks a positive structured and guided family group, that he is a school dropout, has no stable employment, and no consciousness of the situation, it is suggested to the magistrate that she recommend his admittance into an intensive closed center where he will receive orientation, training, and treatment." According to this logic, family groups with grandparents and a maternal aunt as heads of the household are not considered stable.

Felipe, another youngster at the Carolina Center, also had a "family problem." He had spent nine months at the center for evaluation, even though the maximum legal time was three months. The team of social technicians liked Felipe because of his good behavior and wrote a letter to the judge recommending his release rather than his transfer to another center. The judge is not obliged to follow the recommendation of the team and in this case he did not. Although Felipe had been accused of armed robbery, he had not been involved, like the majority of the young people at the center, in a homicide. But he was not released and was instead moved to another center for an additional six months. When I questioned this ruling, one of the psychologists at the center explained that the judge had not found Felipe's current family structure satisfactory. The boy had a Venezuelan father and a Colombian mother, who had left the home with her two other children. By the time Felipe had gotten caught for stealing, he was living in a low-income apartment project with his alcoholic father, his grandmother, and an uncle. The judge had considered it problematic that his mother was not there to guide him.

More often than not, however, the team shows little concern about the conditions in which this sort of family dynamics occurs. In this case, Felipe's own view of his family situation was never considered. When I asked him about it, Felipe explained that his transgressions were influenced by problems with his father and his longing for consumer goods. He was upset that his father pushed him to study all the time while not being able to give him money for shoes. As I explain further in Chapter 5, I asked the boys at the Carolina Center to write about their lives. Felipe wrote the following for me:

> When I was eight years old, my parents separated and I had to learn how to survive. My mother is Colombian, and she left, taking my two brothers with her. She asked me if I wanted to go with her, but I decided to stay because my father was lonely. Time went by, and little by little I distanced myself from the family. Everything they said bothered me, even though I knew they were right.

> I felt bad when my father was drinking and I couldn't stand being
> a hindrance to him. I continued to do what he wanted, which was
> to study. But studying was hard, because I wanted to be able to go
> to school wearing a nice pair of shoes. My father couldn't afford
> that kind of thing because of his budget, so because I didn't have
> expensive shoes, I decided not to go to school.[10]

The location and condition of a youngster's living quarters also affect the final judgment. In most cases, the houses are not considered big enough for all the family members. The team's analysis correlates particular spaces with deviant behavior. Elvis, for example, was categorized as a high social risk. The head of the household was his mother, about whom no information was recorded other than she had abandoned her husband seven years before because of physical abuse. The house was made of bricks and had an asbestos ceiling and cement floors, which was considered a decent rancho. There were only four rooms for eleven people, which although normal for the majority of people in Caracas, was judged as a condition leading to bad behavior and delinquency. Furthermore, what finally determined that Elvis was not safe in his community was not economic misery or that he had several culebras waiting to kill him. It was, according to the team, that the community "presenta un índice de contaminación moral-social" (presents a high rate of moral and social corruption).

This last phrase—moral corruption—appears again and again in the files. Not in a single official case file I read was there any indication of awareness that most minors and their families have limited choices in where they live. When a young person commits a homicide, often his entire family has to move from their community for fear of retaliation. Where are entire low-income families going to move in an instant? According to the team at the Carolina Center, families move to other corrupt communities, where crime and violence are a part of everyday life. But since crime and violence are a reality in most of Caracas's shantytowns, they can hardly be a justification for keeping a minor inside a state institution.

The narrow focus of the state's technicians regarding punishment is clearly evident in their analyses of entire families, which are measured against unrealistic standards. In their attempt to control "maladjusted" children, the state's bureaucratic gaze rests on the mothers, the family members with "deviant" behavior, the home situation, and the community. In many instances, the INAM centers have obviously gone to great lengths to fit the answers provided by parents and other family members into some preconceived notions about deviant behavior. The standard against which everything is measured is, inevitably, the idealized nuclear family model, which bears little relation to these families' everyday lives. Most critically, in the case files, the voices of the minors themselves have been silenced.

Young People and Family Dynamics

What has been the family experience of the young people I met on the streets and at the Carolina Center? How do they feel about their parents? Where and how have they grown older?

In Caracas, as in the rest of Venezuela, mothers are generally the focal point in family relations (Lopez-Sanz 1993). That is, regardless of whether a man is absent or present in the household, women represent emotionally, and often economically, the main pillar of the family. Contrary to popular belief, young people living on the streets of Caracas leave home gradually when changes occur in family dynamics; in most cases, as in Colombia, no sudden abandonment takes place (see Aptekar 1988). One of the major transformations of family dynamics occurs when the mother either dies or for other reasons is unable to care for the children. Benjamín, the sixteen-year-old I met on the Sabana Grande boulevard, moved to the streets gradually after his mother died. When I asked him why he had ended up on the streets, he said:

> Well, I left for the streets because I was studying and taking care of the house when my mother died. Then my sister rented the house, but she didn't collect a cent. Later she sold the house and I didn't get my half of the money she got for it. *How did your mother die?* She died because of a stone. *How did that happen?* Well, she fell and hit her stomach on a stone, you know? Then, after that she died. *Where does your dad live?* He lives in el Valle. *Was he still married to your mom?* No.
>
> *What happened after your mother died?* My sister sold the house to another sister who lives with a man. I was living on the streets then, and one day I told my sister that I was having a hard time.
>
> *How old were you?* Twelve. Then she told me that it was not her house, but Raulito's, her husband's. Well, then I thought, "If she is my sister she has no right to kick me out of the house." *How old was your sister?* Eighteen. I told her that I would never see them again, and I did not go back for three years. I came back when I was sixteen.[11]

In other cases the mother lives with her children but is unable to take care of them because of drug and alcohol addiction or because of work, as in the cases of Edison and Wilson, who gradually left their households. These young people realize that in order to survive they must leave.

For most of the youngsters I met, the move to the streets came when their mother lived with a man different from their biological father. In those situations, the child's relationship with his new stepfather becomes progressively unbearable, so that he is, at best, made to feel he is a burden to the family. Although the mother does not actively abandon her child, she passively chooses the new *marido* (husband), whom she thinks will support her, over her son. When mothers make decisions that leave some children out, the youngsters do not necessarily condemn them. The decision to leave is considered one of survival. The children make a choice which, under certain circumstances, makes sense to them and their mother remains the most important figure in their lives. These youngsters often try to regain their mother's affection while proving to her that they have been able to survive on their own.

The mother is in many cases the only thing a boy can hold on to at critical moments, such as when he is caught by the authorities and institutionalized. She symbolizes the possibility of freedom: she is the one who cries when they are caught, visits them at the centers, and does what she can to accelerate the judicial process.[12] Regardless of their relationship with their mothers before their incarceration, the youths at the centers constantly expressed the need to see them, or they worried about the great pain they must be causing their mothers by being there. It is particularly noticeable that those boys whose mothers did not visit them were the most likely to escape.

Though the mother may gradually have abandoned her son, she is still the only connection to idealized positive emotions that children in the *retenes* (juvenile centers) have. In moments of fear, solitude, and boredom at the center, many children, whatever the true relationship may have been, tend to idealize the mother figure as one of care and tenderness. For Blas at the Carolina Center, the most important thing in his life was to stop his mother's suffering. He was struggling over what to do. His brother had recently been killed, and Blas wanted to escape the Carolina to avenge his death. A while back Blas's culebra had shot his brother and wounded him, and Blas had shot the culebra; the culebra had survived but was left with a colostomy bag. Blas was taken to Center B and escaped because his mother had told him to. He was caught and taken to Center A, where he

stayed because his mother advised him to. Meanwhile, his
brother had been shot again by the same culebra and had died.
Blas could not decide what to do and was concerned that he did
not have much time, because he was almost eighteen years old
and the police would send him to La Planta. That would destroy
his mother; she would have one son dead and another in jail.

I asked him why he did not take revenge without anyone
knowing it was he who had done it—that way he would be
satisfied and his mom would be spared the pain of seeing him in
jail. But he replied, "No! [beating his breast]. Everyone has to
know it was me who did it. I can't go around as an *encapuchado*
[with a hood covering my head] to kill my culebra—that is for
cowards." Blas had to solve his conflict between his masculine
identity and his loyalty to his mother before he could act.

At the Carolina Center the people loved and repeatedly sang
salsa singer Hector Lavoe's version of an old tango, "Consejo de
oro" (Advice of gold). It was an anthem about the feelings that
Jerson and many others have for their mothers. But it was not
until I visited Edison's grandmother's house that I realized what
the song was about. I was sitting in their living room with all his
cousins, a hen, and a couple of dogs when Edison told me that he
was going to play his all-time favorite song, the one that had
helped him bear up during the few days he had spent at police
headquarters the previous Christmas. He asked one of his cousins
to play the song for him on the record player. The record was
scratched, but I was the only one who seemed to notice. All the
others joined in singing the lyrics, which they repeated at least
five times until they thought I had learned the words too. In the
song a man remembers his miserable childhood after his father
dies and his mother has to break her back washing other people's
clothes for a few pennies. In his youth the man seeks a life of easy
money until his best friend sells him out to the authorities and
he ends up in jail. Once in jail none of his alleged friends visit

him; only his mother comes to see him. The "advice of gold," then, is to realize that you can count only on your mother because she will always be there for you. Therefore, you should stop partying and trying to make money and take care of your mother. Otherwise, you will probably give her so much grief that she will eventually die and you will regret it for the rest of your life. Edison was determined that I should understand the lyrics, and after playing the song, he wanted me to meet his mother. He had to send one of his cousins to go fetch her at her house because he could not go there, though it was only three blocks away, for fear of meeting some of his culebras on the way.

Ester, Edison's mother, did not want to come, but after Edison sent a message that he would be very upset if she did not, she consented. Ester was quite young. She told me that she and her husband had separated after their second son was born. She decided to go to another city to work as a maid, but she could only take her younger son with her, so she sent Edison to live with his father. At the time Edison had already become an *azote de barrio* (a shantytown terror), and his father, and especially his father's new wife, did not like having him live there. After Edison stole an electric piano to buy drugs, his father kicked him out. When Ester came back to the barrio and learned that Edison was living on the streets, she tried to find him, but to no avail. That afternoon Edison tried hard to prove to his mother that he had changed and that soon he would be able to take care of her and his younger brother. He promised to buy his mother an apartment, but she did not pay much attention to him.

Prince also used to sing "Consejo de oro" while selling books on the Sabana Grande boulevard. When I asked him why he liked to sing that old song so much, he told me his family's story. His mother left him when he was little, and his father is "una leyenda" (a legend) (I gathered that he was talking about a ghost father because he never met him). Prince was raised by his maternal grandmother. At twenty-one, Prince still makes a continual effort to gain his mother's affection. When he was growing up he was hurt the most by his maternal grandmother. The pain came not from her blows, which were frequent enough, but from her comments about his mother. The doctors attribute Prince's deformed legs to undiagnosed polio, but his grandmother told him that his parents had dropped him on the floor when he was a baby. The grandmother spoke of his mother as "la muy puta" (the big whore) and told him, "Tu nunca vas a tener como pagarme lo que yo he hecho por tí porque tu mamá te dejó en un pipote de basura y yo te recogí, si no es por mi estuvieses muerto" (You will never be able to repay me for what I have done for you because your mother left you in a trash can and I picked you out. If it wasn't for me you would be dead).

Despite everything, Prince was always calling his mother and asking her to come see him on the boulevard. At Christmas he begged her to come, but she told him she was too busy cooking. He often phoned me to ask for advice about how to get his mother to care for him. After many years on the streets, Prince agrees with the authorities, believing that young people end up on the streets because they do not have fathers:

> All family problems emerge from the father's absence. I have corroborated this with my adoptive aunt. She says, "I have done so much for you because the bastard left you." Because the woman is alone, she has a double role, but a woman needs a man to provide moral support and she falls into the mistake of the stepfather—the intruder. Almost always the son of a bitch acts like a detective and communication stops and everyone becomes cross because he wants to impose his ways. Then from the mother's side there begins an unconscious blackmail toward her children: "I, who have given everything to you" or the method of beatings and word games, which is rough. After that the youngsters move to the streets—they cannot stand the image of the intruder. There are stepfathers who are very strict, but the real father, however mean

he might be, still spoils his own child. The stepfather begins with, "In my house I impose the rules," and he does not allow a boy of ten to sixteen years to seek his own image—he doesn't let him be. They go off to the streets and seek support. If they find a guy who says, "I am going to help you, but you also have to help me," the youngster ends up being a mule until he realizes what's going on, but that will only happens if he uses his head.[13]

Young People on the Streets and "Fictive Kinship"

"Tío, tío, tío . . . brindame el desayuno" (uncle, uncle, uncle . . . treat me to breakfast) yell young people living on the Sabana Grande boulevard to those policemen, waiters, merchants, and visitors who they know will occasionally help them with some money, food, clothes, or shelter. When young people leave their barrios to live on the streets of Caracas, they develop a set of social relations—sometimes very intimate ones—with people trying, in a variety of ways, to help them. These relationships not only indicate an important source of help but they also suggest why many children who appear abandoned are not without contacts and assistance or the means of securing some income (Aptekar 1989, 430).

On the city streets young people develop, with these relationships, their own forms of kinship. Many of the relationships constitute what Prince calls "familiazgo imaginario," or fictive kinship:

There is fictive kinship, because your own family does not give you moral support, and you say, "Shit, these strangers, they are so different in their social and religious ethics, and even though they're not very cultured, the guys are giving me the moral support that I have not found. It's a refuge—but a momentary one." However, one still has to imagine that one is a stranger wherever one goes.[14]

When the young person decides to spend time on the streets, he finds a group of other young people with similar situations.[15] They become friends, panas, or culebras. As Prince puts it:

> When you arrive for the first time on the boulevard, you have to associate with a group in order to be accepted. Then when you find somebody to guide you, he might be facing his own moral crisis, because he knows he can change but doesn't do anything about it. It is a moral crisis because he has it within himself and he reflects the global misery of his country, the lack of education, the lack of acceptance. When a youngster arrives on the streets, he has to put on his other face, his bad-person face, because otherwise he will be the laughingstock of society and among his peers. He has to appear to be a bad guy, and why not, he even steals, perhaps prostitutes his body, or else he falls into the trap of misery and becomes a beggar.[16]

In addition to peers, there are almost always *mayores*, or older people, drug dealers or former street children who are now adults who will further teach the group the rules of the game. This is not to say that there are no young teachers who are streetwise, but the one who is truly influential as a teacher, a tutor, or a father figure (or perhaps all three) for the individual or the group is someone they see as a man. In Chapter 2, I described how Prince had his friend Pechundío to protect and guide him on the streets (and also to cause mischief). But it was Barrabás, the pimp, whom Prince described as a mentor and as a *papá putativo* (substitute father) for both of them:

> You have to look for someone to train you during the first months, and then you can fend for yourself. Although Barrabás taught us how to steal, he also taught Pechundío, me, and four other kids to read. He would tell us about how they spoke in other places, and he would say, "See, in Colombia people steal in this way . . . " and things like that. "You don't need to be dirty in order to steal, the better you dress the less you will attract other

people's attention," and I thought, "Wow!" He taught us tons of things.[17]

This sort of association is common. Often an adult and a group of street youths develop a relationship of mutual help. But not all of these relationships are as tender and instructive as the one between Prince and Barrabás. Chita, another eighteen-year-old from the boulevard, and his group were associated in the past with an older man who got them a hotel room in exchange for money. The man coached them in how to steal, telling them, like Fagin, "See that old woman over there? Go get her bag and bring it here." Chita's group would do as he said and then get only 100 bolivares for food, while the man kept the rest.

This older man was hardly a guiding paternal figure, but perhaps he was no worse than the real fathers or stepfathers the kids left behind in the shantytowns. Chita (he was given that very racist nickname—Tarzan's chimpanzee's name in Spanish—because of his dark skin), for instance, left the barrio when he was twelve years old because he was tired of being mistreated by his father. He never learned how to read and write, because his father made him go to work at an early age selling food on the streets. Prince helped me realize that despite my romanticized ideas about father figures, most of the boys had not even known their fathers. Because I still did not understand the ambivalent nature of the youngsters' relationship with masculine role models, I asked Prince to explain whether he perceived Barrabás as a father figure: "Yes and no, because I knew what he did for a living. Barrabás was submerged in his own misery, and he wanted to change but he was a prisoner of himself. So I really don't have an image of a dedicated father. Barrabás was a good life guide."[18] As described earlier, young people on the streets establish fictive kinship relationships for support and help, whether they need assistance with an injury or just someone to phone them to check in. People working in the various organizations often stand in for the youngsters' fathers, mothers, uncles, sisters, brothers, and girlfriends, and playing these roles contributes to their success with getting through to the boys. Although young people on the streets rarely live in the ideal family portrayed, these ideal family figures are not unknown models to them, and they often structure their fictive relationships around their idealized fantasies rather than around their actual relationships with biological kin.

Sometimes organization members have naive ideas about how to help the youngsters. At the time of my research, the Association for Street Children had two active staff members—a middle-aged couple without children of their own. They had started the organization a few years before and at the time acted as president and treasurer. Though they said they wanted to be perceived as friends rather than as parents, they often acted like parent figures and tended to isolate any new volunteer who might threaten that image. The president took on all the "motherly" roles, such as giving advice and being nurturing, while the husband took on the "fatherly" roles, such as teaching and disciplining and participating in rough-and-tumble games.

At one point the association bought a house in a barrio, and the couple brought Wilson and Edison to live there. These well-meaning people immediately started acting like "parents," trying to get the boys to work and study and to dress and eat well. Edison and Wilson could not deal with the pressure "to be so good" all the time, and they kept stolen goods, brought in women, and smoked marijuana in the house. Although the entire barrio knew what was happening, the couple found out only when Edison could no longer stand lying to them. The two boys were promptly kicked out of the house. The couple later told me they felt like disappointed parents for several months. They had known Wilson and Edison for a long time—since they were eight and fourteen, respectively—and it was only after they brought the boys to live with them that they developed these kinds of expectations, thinking that their success in building a model of the stereotypical middle-class family would prove the success of the association. It is difficult to believe, however, that they did not realize how hard it would be to impose on the boys so suddenly such a different lifestyle.

In some cases those who extend help think of themselves more overtly as substitute family figures. "El doctor," the seventy-year-old medical doctor who visits the chupapegas on the boulevard and gives them money and clothes, takes them on short trips and treats their wounds. He thinks of himself as a father figure and is dedicated to the task of helping these fatherless nomads. Besides fixing up a room for them to give them a place to relax, he gives them a place to wash, clean clothes, and decent food. "El doctor" was interviewed on a recent TV program about street children, during which he was portrayed as someone who is actually doing something to alleviate the situation of these youngsters. For some of the boys, of course, he is less of a father figure (not always a very positive image) than a kind grandfather figure who spoils them.

Final Remarks

Young people on the streets of Caracas create their own sense of family. They possess the same ideas about family as society does, which they adapt to create meaning in their existence and to develop some sense of security. These youngsters often possess remarkable perspective about their lives. Edison summarized the interplay among family stereotypes, mothers, and young transgressors in a piece he wrote and I edited for the first issue of the

Association for Street Children's bulletin, "Nosotros tambien soñamos . . . " (We also dream . . .).

> You'll ask yourself, what does it feel like to live on the streets? It is like opening the door to another world of beings who are disliked by society, humiliated, scorned, made to grow up at a young age. It is like everything with its highs and its very low lows. Another question you might ask is, Why are they on the streets? Don't they have houses? Of course they have houses, but not all of them. The problem isn't that, but the relationship between father, mother, and son and also when there are family conflicts. That is, when the mother and the father leave each other or divorce, then there is a stepmother or a stepfather who seldom likes their stepchildren, and the innocent child takes the blame for everything. Or another case: the mother mistreats the son with or without reason, and the child, because of who he is, is affected and one day decides to leave the house. He does not know where to go, for maybe one or two days. During this time he walks by himself, without knowing anybody, and then he finds another child just like himself or with more experience on the streets or what looks like the free life. After that happens and one or two months have gone by, the mother decides to find her son. When she finds him, she speaks the street language. She whines, "Come with me because I love you." The child asks himself, If she truly loves me, why did she wait so long to come pick me up? Hatred builds inside him or maybe not so much. There are few cases where a child really hates his mother, but I should tell you that he cares very little if his mother looks for him or not, that is, he loses affection and any sentiments about returning home. So when his mother hugs him, he feels uncomfortable, they don't speak, he feels strange. And a worse case is that when children on the streets start to take drugs, it becomes even more difficult to leave the streets that are their new home, and they don't feel, or we don't feel (and I say this because I don't know whether I am a street child. Please don't ask me about that—let's go on) the same anymore. We consider ourselves a different species, like rebels with the capacity to survive, like warriors, and we are a family here. I speak for the youngsters who I know and have met.[19]

Edison is quite aware of the different entities that he simultaneously and confusedly constructs—the child, the warrior, the mother, the stepfather, the family, and the streets. On the one hand, Edison is a street person. On the other, he also speaks for the Association for Street Children. In his text, these two voices intermingle to evoke his complex relationship with a society that supposedly cares about him while at the same time humiliating him. In the end what Edison concludes, like Prince and many others, is that he has found his own sense of family on the streets.

Edison's text reflects how difficult it is to establish who the families of young people on the streets truly are. However, it is clear that whatever the structure of the family of origin is, it is ultimately the mother or the grandmother who carries the main responsibility, symbolic and material, in the household. It is the mother who, if anyone, will search for her son on the streets or bring him food in jail. Ironically, it is also the mother who is portrayed in official discourses as the one responsible for the increasing numbers of maladapted youth.

The young person in the barrios moves to the streets for a combination of reasons, such as lack of opportunities, problems in the community, and bad relationships with his parents or stepparents. Nevertheless, in many cases the youngster does not cut his ties with his family completely or permanently. On the contrary, youngsters will often try, at least from their point of view, to better their relationships with the family or to maintain some form of contact. At the same time, while they are living on the streets, these children survive by creating their own new sense of family, establishing diverse relationships with new acquaintances.

4 • *Guerra Contra el Hampa*: Control Through Media, Law, and the State

In a conversation with a group of four young people at the Carolina Center, I asked them if they felt protected because they were under eighteen years old. In Venezuela only persons who are older than eighteen can legally be considered criminal. My intention was to understand how the youngsters defined being a minor and how those definitions compared to those of the state.

> *Patricia.* How do you distinguish between being a delinquent and not being a delinquent?
>
> *Lendel.* What minors do is a transgression.
>
> *Patricia.* Do you believe that is what minors do?
>
> *Jerson.* It is a delinquent act, but they call it a transgression.
>
> *Patricia.* But do you believe that?
>
> *Felipe.* That is why they study us.
>
> *Lendel.* Here they study us and we pay with six months. If we were adults, we would pay with four years at the La Planta jail.
>
> *Patricia.* None of you sees yourself as a delinquent?
>
> *Lendel.* I don't.
>
> *Felipe.* I do, I am a delinquent. I like money, that is what a delinquent is [Jerson agrees with him]. A delinquent is put in a place of high security. This is not a high-security place only because we are minors.

Patricia. What is the difference between being a minor and an adult?

Lendel. Our minds are only fully developed after we're eighteen.

Patricia. Do you believe that?

Lendel. Of course not.

Patricia. So why did you say that?

Lendel. Because that is what the books say.

Patricia. Do you feel different after turning eighteen?

Jerson. Yes, because here you know that you are not risking your life. In Los Flores jail you can get killed. Here no one wants to go to La Planta jail, here you want to solve your problems.

This discussion shows that the youngsters are fully aware of the sanctioned opinion that defines them as minors not entirely capable of being responsible for their actions. At the same time the conversation points to the youngsters' own confusion and sense of urgency about their age. They know that being younger than eighteen gives them, if nothing else, a certain impunity; they know that regardless of the nature of their crime, most often they will not be treated as adult prisoners. After they turn eighteen, whatever their offense, they will no doubt be sent to adult jail, where the conditions are harsher and there is little chance of escape.

The youngsters express a fairly mature understanding of the complex dynamics behind the set of social categories that the state has created to control them. The state justifies its activities with the studies it conducts of the young inmates, that is, everything is done in the name of producing information. Lendel captures the circular irony of simultaneous state surveillance and management in his statement "that is what the books say."

The hypocrisy and contradictions inherent in the state's intentions are demonstrated in the legal and institutional control of those considered deviant children. My review of institutional records reveals how the state, in its claim of protecting young people, develops constructions of deviancy that are isolated from the reality of the environment the children are responding to. The media, the state, the technocrats, and the upper and middle classes refuse to acknowledge the logic behind the choices made by these young people, which allows them to justify using repressive measures to control particular kinds of transgressions. Furthermore, mass media's treatment of these issues reveals the ways in which prevailing attitudes about juvenile delinquency are developed in the national consciousness.

Mass Media, Choices, and Public Outrage

As I write, Venezuela has been receiving international attention not because of what it has been popularly known for—its oil production, its democracy, or its beautiful women—but because of its rising crime rate. An article in *The Economist* (October 1994) entitled "Crime Wave" took note of the fact that even though Venezuela's economy is in crisis, Venezuelans' main concern is its increasing crime rate. Violent deaths in Caracas have already reached intolerable proportions, with two hundred violent killings reported each month. The article quoted the minister of economic planning, Werner Corrales, as saying that Venezuela is sitting on a "social bomb."

It is also apparent, however, that although the Venezuelan mass media act as an agent in the onset of public outrage by sensationalizing criminal events, they also underplay the dimension of the problem to avoid disturbing the public. In fact, the violence in Caracas is much more serious than anything portrayed in the media. People of all social classes in Caracas know that violence is ever present—not just in the barrios but in all parts of the city. People are afraid to go out at night, to park their cars on the streets, or to leave their houses unoccupied. Even people who are better off are frightened, since violent and senseless deaths are no longer confined to the barrios. The memory of the events of February 27, 1989 conditions people's imagination. The economically powerful are afraid of young people who may perpetuate the popular violence of 1989. After all, it is the young with fewer resources who have continued to organize violent protests outside of schools and to trespass in wealthy neighborhoods to take cars, stereos, perhaps even lives.

The mass media attribute the collapse of the social system to violent crime, and to this end they take all current political, economic, and social issues and turn them into a steady reporting of sensational crimes and grisly deaths. As a consequence, there is finger-pointing from all sides at the most vulnerable perpetrators of crime: young marginals.

In *Folk Devils and Moral Panic*, Stan Cohen developed a useful concept of moral panic:

> Societies appear to be subject, every now and then, to periods of moral panic. A condition, episode, person or group of persons emerges to become defined as a threat to societal values and interest; its nature is presented in a stylized and stereo-typical fashion by the mass media; the moral barricades are manned by editors, bishops, politicians and other right thinking people; socially accredited experts pronounce their diagnoses and solutions; ways of coping are evolved or (more often) resorted to; the condition then disappears, submerges or deteriorates and becomes more visible. Sometimes the object of the panic is quite novel and at other times it is something which has been in existence long enough, but suddenly appears in the limelight. ([1972] 1980, 9)

Phenomena that have always existed suddenly become visible and the objects of fear. As Cohen nicely puts it, out of moral panic emerge "folk devils," or negative models. In *Policing the Crisis*, Stuart Hall et al. (1978) used Cohen's concept to show

how British society entered into a moral panic about mugging in the 1970's. The authors regarded mugging as a social phenomenon rather than as a particular form of street crime, and they concluded that society has come to perceive crime in general primarily as an index of the disintegration of the social order. They further found that the sense of disintegration had to be embodied; there had to be a scapegoat. They examined extensively how in the early 1970's mugging had come to be identified with black youth.

The same type of scapegoating is typical of the Venezuelan mass media, which misguide the public about the conditions that generate different types of violence and about who the perpetuators of violence really are. In general, the media focus on petty crime independent of violence as a whole. If anything, the mass media, tightly woven into the social fabric, participate in silencing the general discontent, thereby providing an opportunity for politicians and those in power to talk about the crime situation and potential solutions. And without qualifications, they always end up placing the blame on the same group: marginal young people. The young emerge as the "folk devils." The problems that drive chupapegas, malandros, and others to live on the streets, to steal a pair of shoes, or to kill for a leather jacket, are ignored or, if taken note of, superficially discussed. Instead, the focus is generally on the sensational and the gruesome. One newspaper article bore this typical headline: "Another bloodbath left by the hampa in Caracas over the weekend: fifty dead, more than in a war" (Miguel Arcángel and Armando Rangel, "Otro baño de sangre deja el hampa este fin de semana," *El Mundo*, January 11, 1994).

Although I do not intend to imply a simple correlation between consumer desire and increasing crime rates, as I have shown earlier in this study, desires and ambition generated by propaganda have inspired many young people to acts of transgression. They follow powerful authoritative role models of taking what you can, such as that of the impeached former president Carlos Andrés Pérez, who was imprisoned for mismanaging of public finances. In the past twenty years, levels of white-collar corruption have risen enormously in Venezuela. Most amazing, though, has been the continuing acceptance of corruption at all levels. The war on corruption is focused on only a few people like Pérez, while the war on crime is focused on all the people of the barrio.

The way the media constructed the case of Darwin reveals the biased representations permeating the crime sections of a great many newspapers. Darwin was a seventeen-year-old high school student killed by a culebra who lived in a nearby barrio. The newspaper accounts did not pose the questions of how it was that a boy could have a mortal enemy at such a young age or why their quarrel wasn't worked out some other way. Instead, the stories dwelled on the details of Darwin's gruesome death. He was shot eight times at eight A.M. in his own house. He was killed by a sixteen-year-old boy whose seventeen-year-old girlfriend Darwin had been seeing; the upset lover and the girl had a ten-month-old baby. The young man entered Darwin's home and shot him without saying much. Then he dragged him outside and took his shoes and wallet to make it look like a common robbery.

Darwin's death was not an isolated incident. Many young people in the barrios and on the streets die because of a conflict with another person. A culebra, who in some cases dies not even knowing why he and his adversary are enemies, fires his gun before he himself gets killed. Whether disputes are between individuals or groups, the verbal exchange usually revolves around the weapons and the act of killing. The people involved move fast to take revenge, to hide, to kill, and to run.

What is most shocking to those reading the newspaper, listening to the radio, and watching television is that the frequent deaths seem so senseless. Reading a headline in *El Nacional* such as "Bloody aspect of the weekend: another high school student gets killed for his shoes" is a common and disturbing reality. Nike shoes and Chicago Bulls jackets have become invitations for being shot at. Anyone can be killed for a pair of shoes, which have become a symbol of manhood, status, and fashion. Style has become an everyday cause of death; the life of another seems to be worth less than a pair of fashionable tennis shoes. It is very difficult to understand what style means to young people and why so many are willing to die and to kill in its name.

The upper classes, although aware that this sort of violence exists in the barrios, are of course most outraged when it is directed at them. The social conscience of those in power is most shaken when those they see as innocent victims and/or the rich are killed. Cases such as the murder of former dictator Perez Jiménez's brother in the country club neighborhood sparked, once more, the desire for a *guerra contra el hampa* (a war against the hampa).[1] The upper classes demand safety and put pressure on the state to control the segment of the population that does not participate in traditional youth institutions such as schools, Boy Scouts, sports, and so forth. Repressive measures are then taken, and talk begins of creating militarized centers for young delinquents or of the need for more "operatives" in which police enter the barrios to collect, harass, and torture people.

Juvenile Crime as Current Debate

Today one of the major public debates orchestrated in the Venezuelan media, among others concerned with youth, is one that started in the 1960's when there was guerrilla fighting, a time the young also seemed "out of control."[2] The types of debate the media engages in—rather than focusing on practical preventive solutions—are about the age of responsibility and whether it should be lowered from eighteen to sixteen. Some participants in these debates want to reconsider whether the illegal acts of Caracas children and adolescents should continue to be called transgressions instead of crimes, whether children who kill should be considered delinquents. And with the current panic about rising crime rates, the debate is growing desperate.

Propositions of this nature date to the turn of the century, when children could legally be considered criminals. One of the most recent visible figures in this debate was the governor of Caracas in 1993, Asdrúbal Aguiar, who often appeared in the media proposing to modify the penal code to lower the age of legal adulthood from eighteen to fifteen years. Aguiar also reinstituted the curfew for minors, making it illegal for them to be on the streets without their parents or a guardian after 11:00 P.M. or before 6:00 A.M.[3]

Debates occurring in the media and new propositions are based on two main perspectives regarding those young people who transgress the established order. On the one hand, there is the perspective of the marginality and the abandonment of children and adolescents, in which case the state's discourse involves protection. On the other, there is the perspective of the violence of which these youths are capable. In Venezuela, the two perspectives compete with each other to justify "tighter justice" for abandoned, marginal, yet violent youth. There is, in Sartre's terms, a show of "bad faith" (cited in Scheper-Hughes 1992, 209) in the everyday remarks, comments, rumors, and debates about these people of the streets. In a recent newspaper article, for example, a chief of police asked himself whether a minor who has done something premeditated can really be acting without judgment: "Can a minor act without judgment when he wakes up at ten in the morning and begins to plan the day's work with his four buddies, splitting the job, evaluating it, and then executing it? And when he gets caught he says with irony: 'I'm a minor'" (Humberto Jaimes, "Las tumbas son pa' los muertos y yo de muerto no tengo na" [Graves are for the dead and I am not dead], *El Universal*, December, 10, 1993). The police chief goes on to argue that the law is not socially responsible since it does not deal with the great pain minors are causing "the family" in Venezuela. Nowhere in the article does he show any concern for the daily hardships of the young people he condemns. This kind of article has the effect of galvanizing the public into solidarity in the repression of the youths on the streets.

Young barrio people are generally portrayed as out of control, as in the chief of police's statement, independent of the general chaos and the collapse of social services such as hospitals and schools. His accusation disguises the real dimensions of everyday structural and political violence—the impossibility of obtaining health care, job discrimination, the lack of educational opportunities—and instead singles out the traditionally guilty group, those with few economic resources. And though violence and crime are said to emanate from lower-class sectors, government violence, manifested in corruption, lack of services, and inefficient bureaucracy, continues unprosecuted. And yet the perpetrators of this political violence emphasize through media, policies, decrees, and conferences the all-too-real problem of juvenile transgressions. Young transgressors, mainly minors, are suddenly responsible not only for the degraded state of personal safety but also for the collapse of the family, the community, and social services. Many, like the police chief, would declare a war against the young as their knee-jerk response to social disintegration.

The priority of the recently elected government to provide safety to the public translates into a war against the hampa, the hampa being an objectified and evil entity that, as an enemy of the real Venezuelan, has to be wiped out. The hampa is regarded as an alien invader, entitling the authorities to do a "toma de Caracas."[4] Police chronicles characterize delinquents as an enemy with a dark-skinned face, belonging to a strange underworld dangerous to society (see Gingold 1992, 114). The hampa image is exploited in the media through its association with the sinister mano peluda, a group blamed for popular protests; it is also associated with undesired Colombian, Ecuadoran, and Peruvian immigrants. The ministry of the interior publicly accepts this view, declaring "We will return the streets to honest Venezuelans" (Jesús Eduardo Brando, "Escovar Salom en la Comisión Nacional de Policía: 'Devolveremos las calles a los venezolanos honestos'," *El Nacional*, February 9, 1994).

Statistics: Another Battle Over Representation

Historically, statistics on young people have been used uncritically to justify state policies and programs. These statistics have a definite ideological function in Venezuela: they turn free-floating and controversial impressions into hard incontrovertible numbers, for which both the media and the public have enormous respect. These numbers end up displacing children's voices and supporting the state's representations. However, in Caracas, institutions such as the police and the INAM cannot even agree on numerical data they've gathered about crime patterns; the contradictions in their numbers point out their individual biases. Yet although many of the statistics on crime in Caracas are not totally reliable, they are of use in indicating the dimensions of the problem and can be thought-provoking.[5]

For example, one of the most recent statistical studies published was produced by the Ministry of the Family, the "Encuesta Nacional de la Juventud (ENJUVE)" (1993). The numbers point to the number of young Venezuelans growing up too quickly in an era of unemployment, violence, high rates of inflation, and wide-spread corruption. According to the report, four million out of a total of 21 million Venezuelans are between fifteen and twenty-four years old. People in this age group can face demanding responsibilities: approximately 900,000 already have children, and 200,000 are heads of households. However, 2.3 million people between fifteen and twenty-four years old are not studying, and 65,000 people in that age group have never gone to school. This research indicates that young people have started to drop out of school at earlier ages, since 750,000 between the ages of ten and fourteen have already quit school.

What is not measured, but only rumored, is the quality of the education these youths are receiving or the jobs they hold; the statistics do not indicate the options left to young people or the choices they make. What choices are left to young people at this time of changing opportunities and fewer resources? And most crucial, what are all these young people doing if they are neither studying nor formally working?[6]

When the public vociferously complains about poor economic conditions and violent disorder, law enforcement and social-control agencies such as the police and the INAM increase their activity, produce reports and programs, and generate numbers.[7] To explain the situation and justify their actions, these organizations produce statistics—"hard facts"—about the problem of juvenile crime and the amount of care young people are receiving. However, as we have seen, statistics can be contradictory and are not always representative of increased criminal activity. For instance, no statistics exist on the number of street children in limited areas, such as the Sabana Grande boulevard, and there are no statistics on the specific transgressions of the people living there.

The police, the heads of NGO's, and journalists expressing concern for these children often come up with their own fictitious numbers, which range all the way from a group of 35 to one thousand children.[8]

The INAM claims that there was an increase in the total number of minors under its care from 10,404 in 1991 to 15,618 in 1992 (Jaimes, "Las tumbas"). The significance of this increase remains unclear: Does it indicate an increase in rates of juvenile crime or a change in the rates of arrest and internment, unrelated to actual criminal activity? In other words, the increase in custody rates could be a reflection of a change in the definitions of illegal activity, a willingness on the part of legal authorities to intern youths, or other factors related more to institutional politics than to the behavior of the targeted population of street youths.

Although various sources disagree about the details, they all agree that the number of juvenile transgressions has risen sharply in the past five years and that juveniles are increasingly involved in more serious crimes. Fifty years ago, juvenile transgressions consisted mostly of damage to property, fights, drug use, and theft (Baiz 1944). At present young people's transgressions go beyond mere damage to property or public disturbance, and the incidence of homicide appears to be increasing drastically. Diverse institutions may come up with different statistics, but they do agree that crime is on the rise. Some recent estimates indicate that 80 percent of all criminal acts involve people who are under age eighteen; others indicate only 20 percent (Jaimes, "Las tumbas").[9] Regardless of the actual numbers, what remains clear, as the Monday papers indicate, is that juvenile crime and death rates are reaching high proportions. What also remains clear is this: there seems to be a greater willingness, on the part of the government, to use deadly force. Whether this willingness is in response to a change in technology (the higher number of youths owning guns) or to something else remains to be seen.

The Policía Técnica Judicial (PTJ) and the INAM cannot agree on what specific types of juvenile crimes are increasing. And police officers admit that they are not even able to register all the transgressions (*faltas*) committed by people on the streets. Their statistics reflect only the tip of the iceberg—those who get caught. These differing records of youth crimes indicate how each institution constructs patterns of juvenile crime based on its own reified social categories. In 1992, the INAM and the PTJ reported that they received 15,618 and 14,852 juvenile transgressors, respectively. The INAM recorded 1,628 crimes causing personal injuries; the PTJ recorded 2,795. Similarly, the INAM listed 3,469 for *hurto* (theft), while the PTJ listed 4,663 (Jaimes, "Las tumbas"). Another striking difference between INAM and PTJ reports was the number of categories describing youth transgression: INAM listed 21 categories, the PTJ only twelve.

The Social Construction of Transgressors

It was not until I began my research on street children in 1993 that I heard people being called *menores* (minors) so often. When I attended private school in Caracas, none of my classmates was given that label. We were called "niño" (boy), "niña" (girl), "muchacho" (kid), or even "burro" (dunce), but never "menor." In contrast, at the Carolina Center, all the young people are called minors—personnel most often did not know their names. Occasionally the youngsters also refer to one another this way, calling out, "*¡Epa! Menor*" (Hey, minor!). Becoming a "minor" is part of the increasing criminalization of the young in Caracas, who go from being young human beings to becoming defined solely in legal terms.

Mary Ana Beloff (1994, 107–8) argues that the distinction between those considered children or minors in Latin America follows Philippe Aries's classical historical argument (1961). Aries begins with the claim that there was no place for children in medieval society, and that not until the seventeenth century did a concept of children as beings in need of "coddling" emerge. It was at this point that the image of children as innocent and precious human beings within the family circle was firmly established. At the same time, a different notion of childhood was held by churchmen and moralists, who were eager to ensure that children were disciplined to be rational beings and taught manners. In this case, children were perceived in terms of their psychological and moral malleability. With the advent of the modern state in the eighteenth century, ideas of children as innocent and moral beings were coupled with concerns about hygiene, physical health, and discipline.[10]

In the nineteenth century, European societies began separating young people into two categories: children, who went to school, and minors, who went to the reformatory. Beloff explains that the division between children and minors became more of a global phenomenon beginning in 1899, when the first court designated specifically for minors was established in Illinois (1994, 106). This was followed by England's 1908 minor's code called "Children's Act."[11]

Beloff further argues that in this century, Western penal laws have been applied to children and adolescents in spite of the euphemisms that are used to disguise them. Names for the different forms of control have been changed: institutes instead of jail, reeducation instead of penalty, protection instead of repression. But no matter what name they go by, in the end they are all strategies of social control intended to transform minors into objects and to deny them their rights as subjects and as human beings (1994, 107–8).

The Development of Juvenile Laws in Venezuela

Venezuela's legal system has been influenced by the development of European and North American laws. During the first quarter of the nineteenth century, before the wars of independence, elite groups of Spanish and criollos mantuanos developed *ordenanzas* (codes) to control those people whom they considered threatening to the moral standards of society. Police force and ordinances were regarded as necessary to control beggars, petty thieves, and whores. The ordinances appeared arbitrary. For instance, one ordinance in the early 1800's declared, "Control over idleness, vagrancy, and bad women through police commissaries and officers has been established," which left it to the police to decide who exactly should be controlled (Kalinina Ortega, "Cronología del delito" [Chronology of crime], *El Nacional*, October 5, 1990).[12]

The need to develop laws controlling those who defied an established moral order also concerned the safety of the young. In the middle of the nineteenth century, the first laws were created to protect so-called abandoned children and those considered to be in danger. Then, as now, the terms "abandoned" and "at risk" were ambiguously defined or simply left to the interpretation of decision makers. In the penal code of 1863, minors were included in two main laws. One was a law dealing with theft, the "ley sobre juicio y pena en las causas de hurto" (law regarding the causes of theft), and the other was the "ley sobre procedimiento y pena contra los vagos y malentendidos" (law against vagrants and rogues). The latter law was applied to "the sons of families and orphans who shocked people through their bad habits and their lack of respect for their parents, mentors, or tutors." The punishment for those offenses committed by minors older than fourteen was a fine of one hundred bolivares or two to fifteen months in jail (Ortega, "Cronología"). These laws defined youthful disrespect, independence, and idleness as criminal but did not mention personal or violent crime.

The code also stipulated that those who were older than ten and a half and younger than seventeen who "wander around without a career or an occupation" had to "serve as a servant or an apprentice for two years with a salary fixed by a judge" (Ortega, "Cronología"). That law bears a significant similarity to the modern assumption that vagrants are lower class and that their adaptation to society should be through work proper to their status—that is, a low income. No minor from the upper classes was ever sent to work as a servant, nor are most woperós seen at the INAM centers.

According to this first penal code of 1863, people under the age of nine bore no responsibility for their acts.[13] The age of responsibility went up to fifteen if the person acted without discernment. Those who were older than fifteen but under eighteen were still treated as incapable of being completely responsible for their transgressions; that is, people in that age group were considered incapable of clearly understanding the consequences of their actions. However, they still had to go to jail.

In 1873, under the government of President Guzmán Blanco, which promoted free and obligatory education for all children in Venezuela, there was a push to reeducate minors who had committed transgressions. This reeducation could be conducted with the family or at special centers, where the youngster could remain until he was fifteen years old. For those between the ages of fifteen and eighteen, the code of 1873 remained the same as the previous one. In 1898, under President Joaquín Crespo, the permission to be controlled at home was revoked as being too lax: the minor had to be sent to a reeducational establishment. When it became apparent that there were too few of these establishments, the next government, that of President Cipriano Castro, reinstated family control in 1904. The dictatorship of Juan Vicente Gómez, which lasted for twenty-seven years, succeeded Castro's eight-year administration. Gómez's totalitarian regime promoted several codes involving minors. The code of 1916 extended the age of irresponsibility to twelve years old. If the child was between the ages of twelve and fifteen, his sentence was reduced to half if he was considered to have acted without judgment. The magistrate, using the penal code of 1926, was to determine the sentence as if the crime had been committed by an adult and then reduce it by half. The juvenile laws of 1911, and later of 1926, were concerned with minors, but they were still part of the penal code, and they helped to maintain Gómez's dictatorship because they were often applied to young students. Under Gómez, protests ended with many young people in prison.

When special juvenile courts were set up in the West at the turn of the twentieth century to deal with "deviant" children, Venezuela began to develop its own special code for minors. After Gómez's death in 1935, the new era of increasing oil wealth made possible a democratic process and a modern state, complete with sped-up urbanization and increased services. In 1939, during the government of López Contreras, the *Código de menores* (Minors' Code) was approved, and a juvenile court was created. This was partially an effort to exempt abandoned children, who were many, from the penal code of 1926. However, transgressors, if they were between twelve and eighteen years old, were still punished. Because it was assumed that as youngsters got older they acted with more discernment, their age was considered an important factor. During this period, the transgressions of minors involved mainly vandalism to private property and street fights (Beroes 1938, 28).

The Código de menores of 1939 asserted the authority of the new modern state over minors, establishing that it was the state's duty "to assume the tutelage, education, and protection of those minors under eighteen years of age who have been abandoned or have committed an offense." When in 1948 a military regime was imposed under the command of Marcos Pérez Jiménez, the state considered a different approach to youth. In 1949 the *Estatuto de menores* replaced the old Código de menores. This new set of laws provided young people with the right to not serve a sentence for acts judged to have been committed without discernment. These new laws changed the role of the punitive judge, since he no longer operated under the penal code. Theoretically, the judge's orientation had to be toward promoting re-education instead of punishment (Salazar 1993).

The categories applied to youths in the Estatuto de menores differed from the three categories established in the Código de menores of ten years earlier: "abandoned minors," those "at risk," and "delinquents." The new legislation kept the first two categories and replaced the third ("delinquent") with the phrase "those with an 'irregular situation,'" thereby attempting to develop a protectionist role. The young, regardless of the circumstances, did not have to be incarcerated in the same places as adults. Under the new law, each minor who committed an illegal act was considered in need of individual psychological treatment. In this sense the code constituted an advance, because it focused on exploring the causes of crime, but this preoccupation about the individual transgressor soon led to the establishment of an expensive and inefficient bureaucratic apparatus, in which the interests of the minor were completely disregarded (Romero Salazar 1993). In practice, social conflict involving minors was solved by ignoring the true causes and by using repression.

The Estatuto de menores of 1949 was modified in the 1970's to take the changing times into account. The changes led to the most recent set of juvenile laws, the Ley tutelar de menores, in 1980. This legislation established the concept that minors cannot be deprived of their freedom. A judge decides whether there has been a transgression; if it is found that there has been one, the minor is sent to a reeducation center. Although the judges who give the sentences do not think of the centers as diminishing the minor's freedom, certainly most minors feel that the reeducation centers are the places that most deprive them of their personal freedom (Romero Salazar 1993, 54). This new set of laws maintained the previous two categories of minors, "abandoned" and "at risk," and added that of "transgressor" (*menor infractor*). Schooling, professional training, and recreation became mandatory for all the centers.

Like earlier laws, the Ley tutelar de menores of 1980 associates poor minors with vagrants and potential delinquents (Romero Salazar 1993, 36). For example, article 85 establishes that the minors considered "at risk" are, among other things, those who "frecuenten la compañía de malvivientes o vivan con ellos" (who keep company with lowlifes) or those who "se encuentren en cualquier otra situación que pueda constituir riesgo inminente para su salud, su vida o su moralidad" (find themselves in any situation that could be hazardous to their health, life, or morals). The implication is that those who are surrounded by the poor, in this case by the *malvivientes* (the lowlifes), are at risk. But in reality, any person, young or old, who lives in a rancho on top of a crowded hill without basic services will obviously be at a health risk. In a country in which approximately 40 percent of the population lives in abject poverty, it seems there are too many minors "at risk" for the state to take care of.

Laws and Life on the Streets

Juvenile laws in Venezuela appear to legitimize the power structure by regulating the poor (see Piven and Cloward 1971). Even though juvenile laws are theoretically supposed to protect minors, in practice they are used to control young persons, who for various reasons, mostly linked to poverty, do not follow the established and accepted patterns of socialization. The law does not necessarily help the poor young person on the streets, but it certainly stigmatizes him with legal categories. Laws regarding minors maintain order by facilitating the placement of undesired minors in reeducational institutions. They do not protect the minor against hunger and abuse. On the contrary, they protect the wealthy from having to deal with the conditions that induce increasing numbers of children to live on the streets.

My friend Prince of Sabana Grande was criminalized for being on the streets, for being an "abandoned" and "at risk" minor. When he was about fifteen years old, he left his grandmother's house because he could no longer stand her abuse. He lived in Chacaíto, where he made many friends. Prince had met a man who sold hot dogs at the corner of his old school. As time went by, the man and his wife helped Prince by letting him shower and stay occasionally at their home. One day his grandmother found him there and became very upset. Prince's grandmother, his biological mother, and the woman who was helping him got into a judicial dispute over Prince, which resulted in all three being sent to jail for a short time, two of them—his grandmother and his mother—for abuse and the other for "corrupting a minor." Meanwhile, Prince was sent to two INAM institutions, where he was deemed better off than when he was with any of the women or when he was on the streets. The following is from an interview with Prince:

At Los Chorros I stayed two weeks because of my handicap, and in Caracas Uno I stayed for three weeks. Then I escaped and after they brought me back I stayed for three more weeks. Then I was sent to Los Chorros, where they made up a special letter for me so that I could get a scholarship to study and they took me to the

> Francisco de Miranda in Los Teques, which was worse. I got there in '88 and I stayed for two weeks. I noticed that my section had boys older than me and they fought and stole other people's belongings. The guards ignored it and I thought, "If on Sabana Grande I did not get corrupted, here I will because these guys are not going to treat me with the softness of my friend Pechundío."[14]

In another instance the police arrested Prince and his friend Pechundío and others of the boulevard for vagrancy. Prince and Pechundío were sent to police headquarters called Zona Siete, because they had been taken to the small police station El Recreo at the boulevard too many times.

> There were a couple of policemen named Barriento and Malagón, who on account of the neighbors' complaints about us entering their shops and taking clean clothes, as well as the fact that we slept in those shops, were after us like the black hand of Brazil. After so many entrances to the police station, El Recreo, they said to us, "Now you'll go to Zona Siete." I was very scared because I had done nothing wrong and I asked, "What is that?" Pechundío, who had been there before, said, "Don't worry. It is like this place, they put us in a cell just for minors." "Are you sure?" "Yes, don't worry."[15]

Although Prince was aware that theft is illegal, because he was in such need, he did not regard breaking into a store in search of food or clean clothes as wrong. In the case presented above, Prince did not feel he deserved to be taken to police headquarters, where he knew that harmful things such as rape, injuries, or police abuse could happen to him (especially if Pechundío was not in the same cell to protect him). As noted earlier, one of the reasons Prince and Pechundío stopped seeing each other regularly was that Prince did not approve of Pechundío's behavior; he did not support stealing done solely to obtain money to buy drugs. The moral standing on theft varies among young people on the streets. Several of the youngsters I met on the Sabana Grande boulevard preferred to beg, and they stole only when in need. However, neither the police nor the state institutions show much understanding of these distinctions.

For the Welfare of Children

A year after the dictator Gómez died in 1935, the new government, under the supervision of a group of medical doctors and education specialists, created the Consejo Venezolano del Niño (CVN). This new institution, part of the Ministry of Health, was to have the specific purpose of "coordinating official and private organizations working on the protection of mothers and children" (Gaceta oficial 19027, 1936). In 1939, the same group of doctors organized the First Venezuelan Conference on Children, at which the Código de menores and the CVN were presented as indicators of a state preoccupied with youth affairs. In practice, a long history of insufficient budgets started here. After the congress, the responsibilities of the CVN were increased to deal with infant mortality and abandoned children, but the budget was not increased to reflect these changes.

From the beginning, the CVN developed a predominantly medical (*médico-asistencialista*) and pedagogical approach to solving the problems of abandoned children or those considered by the Código de menores to be "at risk" or "delinquent" (Castillo and Castillo 1994, 6). Among the group of doctors who participated in the development of the CVN was Dr. Rafael Vegas. Drawing on his vast experience with children, he formulated a proposal to create a network of institutions with a medical and pedagogical approach known as the "Plan Vegas." His proposal pushed for the study of the child and his sociocultural environment. Long before anyone else, he wrote extensively on the need to study children in street jobs, in gangs, or living on the streets (see Salgado 1985). In the case of "delinquent children," he insisted that society should be concerned not with the crime but with the person who had committed the crime.

Dr. Vegas proposed five types of institutions, precursors to current ones: psychiatric asylums, *casas de observación* (observation houses), *casas hogares* (family houses), *institutos de preorientación* (preorientation institutes), and *internados de readaptación* (reeducation centers). In all these institutions, children were to be observed individually. The observation houses were designed as centers for the study of children, or as Vegas said, *dispensarios de higiene mental* (centers of mental hygiene) (in Salgado 1985, 20). Family houses were shelters for small groups of children (no more than twenty). These houses were to look like other houses in city neighborhoods and were managed by couples (usually teachers). Depending on his age, the child was supposed to work and provide a percentage of his income to the maintenance of the family house. The preorientation institutes were for children under twelve years of age who were "mentalmente sanos, pero socialmente enfermos" (mentally healthy, but socially ill) (cited in Montero 1992, 3). Finally, the reeducation centers were for those older than twelve who had what were considered behavioral problems.

The Plan Vegas, often misinterpreted, influenced national policies on children for several decades, and it had a broad impact in Latin America; it was widely recommended at the Ninth Pan-American Conference on Children in 1940, where it was proposed as a model for dealing with abandoned children and juvenile delinquency throughout the continent. At least in Venezuela, although interpretations of the Plan Vegas have varied, its name has been invoked to justify the establishment of various correctional institutions (M. Coronil 1977, 16). For instance, one of the first *internados de readaptaciónes* opened in the country was erected on La Isla de Tacarigua in 1947, which has had a long history of repressive brutality. The structure was built on what was formerly a jail for adults with an infrastructure designed for the punishment of the individual (Colomine 1974, 79).

In the 1950's, during the military regime of Jiménez, some of Dr. Vegas's ideas and those of other men concerned with children's health such as Gustavo Machado and Pastor Oropeza were considered in the new Estatuto de menores. Minors could no longer be called delinquents or be punished by the law. The new laws also emphasized the reeducation of children. For the most part, however, the new regime reacted to this need for reeducation by constructing enormous buildings for the housing of minors. A new type of institution called the *albergue* (shelter) was developed to provide immediate, short-term (up to a month) custody of minors between the ages of seven and eighteen who were in "irregular situations." The idea was to separate minors from adult prisoners. The minors, however, ended up staying much longer at the shelters than the maximum time allowed. A 1955 report indicates that the main reason minors stayed at the shelters for longer periods was that judges refused to release them, fearing that no one would hire or accept them into schools after they got out of such places (Montero 1992, 11). The state felt the shelters were a better alternative. To protect meant, as it still does, to intern, guard, and confine.

In 1959, the Policía Técnica Judicial (PTJ) also created a División de Menores (Minors' Division) to "protect" young transgressors from adult delinquents. It had been proposed with the idea that transgressors should be prepared before going to the shelters. However, today the División is the minors' worst nightmare, since the police do not appear to respect any of their civil rights.

Minors not only were made to stay at the shelters longer than stipulated but they sometimes were left alone for long periods of time. In some cases, parents had to beg to see their children under the tutelage of the state. For example, Nancy Montero (1992, 3) tells of a note found at the CVN, dated April 29, 1955, saying that Mrs. M. R. had been asking repeatedly for an audience with the president of the institution. The woman had a daughter who had been at the Luisa Cáceres de Arismendi shelter for two years, during which time the mother had not been allowed to see her. The mother was requesting permission to visit her daughter and to let her come home for Christmas. Another report, from 1961, exposed how the shelters functioned repressively, confining and isolating minors. The report noted that retenes, as the shelters were popularly known, were not used for "at risk" minors or "transgressors"; most of the minors were there because their mothers had left them there, even if it was not legally necessary (1992, 9).[16]

Such repressive practices in state-controlled shelters continued through the 1970's. An analysis of shelters in 1975 revealed that little had changed; if anything, they were getting worse (M. Coronil 1977). Problems such as frequent reentries and escapes, slow discharges, overcrowded centers, inadequate space, and inefficient follow-up of cases were continually revealed to the public. This led to new demands, and after a superficial revision of the institution in 1978, the old CVN was changed into the Instituto Nacional del Menor (INAM). The changes were supposed to stop the growing trend toward an excessive and inefficient centralization of administration and services. But in practice, the INAM, in its operations and philosophy, was simply the old system with a new façade. Albano, a former employee, described the new INAM designs this way: "When the old shelters were transformed into centers for immediate attention and then into centers for initial evaluation, it was only a change of name. The concepts of diagnosis and classification stayed the same" (Albano 1992, 4). No matter what the centers call themselves, they are still repressive and inefficient, as the number of minors on the streets and the crime rate continue to increase. After five decades, the Plan Vegas has turned into a system in which repressive institutions based on a model of punishing adult criminality have been copied to institutionalize poor children, resulting not in the state-as-fathers-and-educators as Vegas had envisioned, but in the state-as-punisher-and-controller.

Everyone recognizes the failure of INAM centers to reeducate transgressors. As the public increasingly demands safety, the state, with its inefficient bureaucracies, insufficient budgets, and poorly trained personnel develops systems of confinement that are more and more repressive. In 1995, for instance, INAM's budget represented only .18 percent of the total national budget, and salaries in the public sector were approximately 50 percent lower than in the private sector (De la Cruz and Márquez 1996). How, then, can INAM possibly offer any opportunities to an increasing population of barrio youth on the streets who transgress—sometimes very violently—the social order?

In response to public demands for safety, more and more young people under eighteen are being sent to adult jails, as with Benjamín's case, described in Chapter 2. Adolescents are being legally "disappeared." When a young person is sent to jail, the INAM abdicates its responsibility, since adult jails are under the auspices of the Ministry of Justice. And the Ministry washes its hands of responsibility because the children and adolescents are not in the adult jails legally. In other words, these minors do not exist except in the minds of their families and friends or in the occasional newspaper report about the increasing presence of minors in adult jails.

   "83 minors staying at La Planta" ("83 menores están en La Planta," *Ultimas Noticias*, September 23, 1991)

"Ten highly dangerous minors who have escaped repeatedly will be sent to La Planta" ("Diez menores de alta peligrosidad y con varias fugas serán trasladados a La Planta," *El Nacional*, June 21,1992)

"Because of crowding: 15 injured in a minors' riot at La Planta" (Adela Leal, "A causa de hacinamiento 15 heridos dejó motín de menores en La Planta," *El Nacional*, August 27, 1993)

Article 103 and the Blessings (Curses?) of Being Under Eighteen Years Old

Article 103 of the Ley tutelar de menores embodies the contradictory constructions of what it means to be a minor for people on different sides of the system. Article 103, also known as the *cientotres*, is, at best, ambiguous, because its application by the INAM personnel can be seen either as a blessing—because it keeps minors out of adult jails (at least in theory)—or as a curse because it subjects young people to a set of studies used by the state to construct legal terms and definitions that can be as confining as the jails. Article 103 is also the only article in the Minors' Code that young people appear to already know about.

It is a common belief among authorities that young people, especially transgressors, know that the Ley tutelar de menores "protects" them. In the circuit of those working with minors, the basic argument is that the young, regardless of the falta committed, know that all that can happen to them is a few months at an INAM center and "a 103"—as the application of article 103 is popularly known. As a consequence, article 103 embodies for the young the leniency and protection offered by the law. For the authorities, article 103 and a few months of limited freedom are not considered to be real punishment.

Article 103 establishes that

the judge, by observing a minor at open or closed institutions, should determine the following:

1. the minor's personality
2. family and social factors
3. the minor's behavior and the circumstances in which it occurs

However, in some cases, the judge could ask for the study of only some of these aspects.

Most of the young people I talked to on the streets, the barrios, or the centers did not truly understand the 103 until they got caught and sent to INAM centers. What they do know about it is that, in theory, they cannot be sent to adult jails and that they spend much less time at INAM centers than adults spend in jail. Also, unlike adults, they will have no record. They are well aware of the difference: the INAM centers, although certainly not paradise, do not experience the constant violence of jails like La Planta and Los Flores (Retén de Catia).[17] But young people are mostly unaware of their other rights as expressed in the Ley tutelar de menores: they did not know, for example, that they are neither to be called nor considered delinquents. Yet at the police's Division de Menores, young people are certainly treated as delinquents; they are referred to in negative terms, such as malandro, *delincuente* (delinquent), *carajito* (little prick), and *coño'emadre* (similar to motherfucker). The nature of the state's protection again becomes very questionable.

I will discuss the violence at institutions created for the welfare of children in the next chapter. Here I want to discuss the hidden violence done to the young through article 103. I am convinced that the professionally supported analysis of the minors' personality and crimes has become a means of controlling a generation of economically deprived people. Through biased probing of the minors' lives, the state transforms these young people into social bodies in which only aberrations, pathologies, and criminality can exist.

The application of article 103 at the INAM centers results in the creation of individual case files on the minor's psychosocial history. I read several of these case files after explaining to the personnel at the Carolina Center that I wanted to compare transgressions committed in 1987 and in 1993. I was very surprised that I was permitted to read them with such freedom, since this was not in line with the usual INAM secrecy. The more I read, the more appalling the facts became. Out of the 27 cases from 1987 that I examined, only one person was accused of committing a homicide; out of the 25 in 1993, ten were accused of homicide. As I read the 1993 cases, I recognized the stories and the people involved, even though I knew most of the minors only by nicknames or first names. Those case files did not just contain another version of what transgression the minors had committed or how they had ended up at the center. Rather, they contained a total dismantling of each person into antisocial acts. Often nothing positive was said about the minor under study other than that occasionally it was stated that he had dressed well for the interview.

I do not question the good intentions of the team in charge of the 103 at the center, which was composed of a psychiatrist, psychologists, and social workers. Albeit uncritically, these people were doing their jobs. The institution had developed a set of formulas by which they were to catalogue minors, and they followed the formulas. They were, to use Michel Foucault's term, the "technicians of discipline" (1979). To give the benefit of the doubt, however, I assume that the team did not fully realize just how much stereotyping went into their analyses.

The team conducts the 103 while the minor is at a Center for Immediate Attention (CAI), one of the facilities at INAM centers, where he spends between three to nine months (if he does not escape). The center's team studies the minor during the first few weeks, and the results are gathered in a three-to-four-page typewritten report that provides a version of the events leading up to the minor's admission, previous records, personal history, results from the mental examination, psychiatric diagnosis, psychological evaluation, and conclusions. The results are then sent to the court, where the judge decides whether to send the minor home under *libertad vigilada* or to send him to a more intensive center.

After eight months at the Carolina Center, I concluded that the team and I were looking at different people. Whereas as they saw typical juvenile transgressors, I saw Oveiwin, Lendel, Felipe, Jerson, and Corazoncito, each with their own story.[18] Oveiwin's story is particularly instructive. Through the differences between his version of events and the team's conclusions, we can see how, by ignoring the social, cultural, economic, and political contexts of the acts that brought youths like Oveiwin into state custody, the 103 team distorts the nature and significance of those acts.

The Construction of Pathologies

Oveiwin was sixteen years old when I met him in May 1993, when he started to come to group activities. He seemed one of the quietest boys in the group, though he could act up, and when things did not go his way he left the room. But he participated in discussions and liked to do manual activities. When I asked Oveiwin why he was at the center, he told me he had killed a minor in his barrio. He and the deceased boy, Freddy, had grown up together, but Freddy had gone the wrong way. In particular, he constantly harassed Oveiwin and his girlfriend. Oveiwin was most upset about the fact that Freddy insulted and threatened his girlfriend as well. Oveiwin's patience slowly wore out, until finally he got a gun and killed Freddy.

Oveiwin wanted to take responsibility for his actions by staying at the center for as long as the staff and the judge thought

necessary. Yet at the same time, Oveiwin did not feel he had
done anything terrible, because in his mind, there was no other
way out of his problem. In the course of our conversation, Oveiwin expressed little regret over the killing. There had been no
place for him to go to escape Freddy's tauntings. What hurt him
the most was that because of him, his sister also got involved in
the dispute; just why was not clear to me, but she was sent to La
Planta, and his family had to move out of the barrio. Oveiwin
worried about what had happened to his family. The 103 report
on Oveiwin indicated that this was the first time he had been
caught by the authorities and confined to an INAM center.

Oveiwin's case file at the Carolina reported his version of the
events as follows:

There was a guy whose name was Freddy, alias "Aldillón." When
we were kids we lived in the same barrio and we fought twice.
Later he moved to the barrio San José, then he became a malandro
and came to my barrio. He did drugs, had a gun, and he liked to
make little kids suck his cock. One time when he was on drugs he
told me to stand still on the corner, where he was going to make
me do it, and I started to run. He told me to do it four times, and
every time I ran away.

One day I was leaving a party with my girlfriend, and when we
were near my house he came running. My girlfriend and I began
to run and he caught us and asked, "Why did you run?" and I told
him, "I am a man and you want me to suck your cock." Then he
said, "No, I will not do that because you are with your girlfriend,"
and I said, "Hey, chill out and put down your gun—you could
shoot somebody." He uncocked the gun and hit me with it on my
head and my chest. Then he started to harass my girlfriend and I
said, "Leave her alone," and he answered, "Shut up, because I
might explode," and then he said, "Take off, witch" and he kicked
me. He told my girlfriend, "Watch out, *mamita*—you're going to
be mine."

Later, on Friday at around 2:00 P.M., he saw me at the matinee,
and he said, "Do you want to see how I can blow you away right

here?" and then he said to my girlfriend, "You look sexy, I want to make love to you," and then he left because a malandro called him. They had a stolen motorcycle and they were riding here and there, shooting into the air. Then they came back and he started to humiliate me again, he slapped me twice. I was so ashamed that I left the party.

Around four I began to shoot baskets and then around six a guy came who told me someone was selling a gun, and I asked who it was. He said that he didn't know, and I said that even if it belonged to a policeman I was going to take the risk so I could scare Freddy, who was driving me crazy with so much humiliation.

That night at around 8:30 P.M., I was coming from my girlfriend's house and when I got near the school, he was standing there saying that this time I did have to suck his cock, that he was going to kill me. I told him that it was all right, that I was going to stay there a while. He was eating a hamburger and he said, "Follow me." He was taking me to the place where he took his little loves to suck his cock. When we got there, he finished his hamburger and went to pull out his gun. When I saw it, I got scared and I pulled out my gun and shot him in the chest. Then he started to run, and I thought that his entire family of malandros was going to come after me and kill me. So I shot him two more times—I hit him by chance—and then I ran and threw the gun into the Guaire River.[19]

Oveiwin provided more details about what happened than anyone else featured in the case files I read at the Carolina Center. Also, unlike many other transgressors, who said they had not done what they were accused of, he accepted sole responsibility for the murder. Freddy had publicly insulted Oveiwin's masculinity and offended and threatened his girlfriend with sexual invitations. Oveiwin tried to reason with Freddy, telling him several times to stop. Freddy's response was to pistol-whip Oveiwin on his forehead and chest.

I concluded that Oveiwin could no longer stand the abuse and that he had nowhere to go. Therefore, he used barrio gun justice, even though he was not a malandro. To his panas at the center, Oveiwin embodied someone who doesn't take any abuse. They respected him. All his friends agreed he had done the right thing, that there had been no other way to solve the problem.

The group of psychologists and social workers at the center saw something very different in Oveiwin's story. According to their analysis, his entire persona was built on his deviant sexuality: "This person denies that he masturbates." A short paragraph about his personality said this: "Hay en el deficiente identificación sexual, tensión masturbatoria" (He has a deficient sexual identification, masturbatory tension). The staff's recommendation to the judge was a "center for treating his castration complex as well as his obsessive and psychopathic characteristics. Socially he shows little interest in other people and does not participate much in the group."

Because of the sexual details involved in his case, the official account transformed Oveiwin into a sixteen-year-old sociopath with a high social risk. If the professional team came to their conclusions about his sexuality based on something else entirely, the account does not say so, so I can only assume that their interpretation was based on the story I presented earlier. Strikingly absent is any consideration that Oveiwin acted out of self-defense. And his aggressor's sexual insults are portrayed as Oveiwin's fault, not as Freddy's aggression. The fact that Oveiwin's family moved to another barrio strengthened the technicians' recommendation to send him to a closed intensive center such as Carolina 3. The family had moved to a barrio described in the file as a "comunidad muy contaminada con la presencia de personas transgresoras" (a community highly contaminated by the presence of transgressors). The reality that most barrios in Caracas are dangerous did not stop the team from using this argument to support their case. As I explained in Chapter 3, INAM personnel referred to these communities as centers of "moral corruption."

In most case files, the personalities of the young people at the center are portrayed as highly defective. Despite the influence the 103 has on the judge's decision, I have never read anything positive about any minor's personality. The mental condition of the analyzed subject justifies the institution's further legal intervention. Meyer (1977) described how French institutions for minors similarly legitimize legal intervention by three methods. The first is to suggest that the child is mentally defective to explain his behavior, the second is to suggest that he is developmentally delayed, and the third is to devalue and blame his family through an analysis of the interrelations among its members (1977, 66).

Here is a case in point. Felipe, whom I considered one of the most intelligent of the group, is labeled in his 103 file in the following way: "He has an emotional type that indicates that he reacts with difficulty to the stimuli of the inside and outside world. He presents psychological blocks, reduced affection, instability, infantilism, immaturity, masturbation guilt, lack of orientation and clear goals in life, and the desire to compensate for corporeal insufficiencies."[20] The file did allow that he was well dressed and fairly receptive at the interviews. There were no notes on the fact that he was interested in the few books that were available and that he was trying to learn English.

Lack of education also shapes the young person's identity as a transgressor, or more correctly, as a malandro. In "antecedentes transgresionales" (transgressional history), their delinquency is reaffirmed as the majority of minors are described by the following line: a "vocabulario cargado de clichés propios del argot transgresional" (a vocabulary full of clichés typical of the trangressor's argot).

Further negative judgment appears in the case files in relation to the youngster's discomfort with the center. Corazoncito, who had killed a young woman while playing with a gun, was, like the rest of the group, upset about being at the center. In his 103, the team explained that emotionally he "se muestra ansioso ante su estadía en la institución, posee tendencia a la participación social pero reprimida" (he appears anxious with his stay at the institution, he is restrained in his social participation). This statement implies that a psychological disorder—not just plain juvenile stupidity—motivated him to play with a gun.

The ways in which the state assumes tutelage of young transgressors, usually people living on the streets or in the barrios, use specific negative constructions of crime, youth, and mental and social health. Even though the latest Ley tutelar de menores claims a protective role in its interpretation, actual practices appear punitive and repressive. Through article 103, those young, who for a variety of reasons fall under the supervision of state welfare institutions, are analyzed and labeled with psychosocial clichés that ignore the real dynamics of these young peoples' everyday lives. Article 103 disguises the state's criminalization of marginal youth by focusing on individual and collective pathologies that appear to exist independently of the overall system.

The Social Technicians

Often the director, the guides, and the psychologists at INAM centers are frustrated and, at the same time, because they are part of the system, they are unwilling or incapable of being critical of the centers. Since many of them come from lower economic strata of society, they are as marginalized by the system as some of the youngsters. In fact, some of them, such as Raymond, a psychologist at the Carolina Center, live in the same low-income apartment buildings (*bloques*) as several of the kids. Very few staff members even have their own cars. They are thwarted by having to work with so few resources and at such meager salaries. Morale can be very low. In general, the staff members feel as forgotten as the youngsters, and, like the youngsters, they believe their lives are slowly passing them by within the yellowing walls of the center. Under these conditions, some shirk their duties—coming whenever they want to, working for only four hours of an eight-hour shift, justifying their actions by saying they are not paid enough to work so hard. They harbor no illusions about being able to present young transgressors with acceptable job opportunities or trying to give them even the most basic education, such as teaching them to read and write. Even though the technicians are peripheral to the INAM institution and hardly participate in any top decisions, they experience constant pressure from the public to "readapt" (in their terms), to "contain" (in mine), young transgressors. At the same time they share with the general public ambivalent feelings about the minors at the Carolina and Los Chorros. And they clearly suffer from burnout induced by their impossible situations.

The director of the CAI at the Carolina Center, who had worked at various INAM centers for 25 years, exemplifies the general ambivalence of the staff toward these young people. I had several long discussions with him. He saw himself as a liberal teacher who understood young people's troubles and as a manager of socially created deviants, and in his day-to-day work he seemed to be concerned for the youth at his place. Yet at the same time he dismissed the young as being simply part of that objectified group called the hampa. At times he was proud to point out how well he treated the boys, such as when he calls them "hijo" instead of "minor." He intellectualized and justified his relationship to the youngsters by claiming that his pedagogical philosophy was based on Anton Makarenko's writing.[21]

The director did acknowledge that the Carolina is an outpost for marginals, where the contradictions of society, embodied in the existence of large numbers of young transgressors who crowd the center, are temporarily hidden from public view. He perceived the youngsters as victims of governments that have forgotten them since they do not vote. Occasionally, we discussed the conditions at the center—to open the classroom door he had to carry the doorknob, long since broken, from his office—and what was expected of him by the main INAM office. We laughed at the absurdity of certain INAM strategies, such as sending cheap plastic toys for the young during Christmas. "Patricia, what am I supposed to do with these? Can you imagine what the youngsters will say when I give them these silly things?"

However, although the director acknowledged that they were victims of the system, at times he saw the people at the center as young criminals. He often said that he had given up all hope of anything decent coming from these young people. For all his good intentions, he shifted the responsibility from an unequal and unfair Venezuelan system to the youngsters, whom he characterized as having a "desesperanza aprendida" (learned hopelessness). While we were chatting one day, I mentioned that the youngsters in my group told me they were afraid of escaping by way of the mountain surrounding the Carolina because they feared the people from the barrio. His reply was, "Ay mija, serán ellos los que asaltan a los del barrio" (Oh, my dear, it's probably the youngsters who assault those from the barrio).

One afternoon as I was leaving, the psychologist from Carolina 3 came to the CAI asking for Raymond. There was a minor who had "hurt himself," and they wanted Raymond to give them a ride to the hospital. The CAI director told me to go with them to see what was going on. We found a youngster sitting on the floor of the patio of Carolina 3; he had some blood on his shirt and shorts, and there was more blood on the floor. A woman, who claimed to be a self-taught nurse, was washing his wounds while the staff team was standing around. As soon as we approached the young man, the team told us that he had cut himself with a tile. The youngster had a long, deep cut along his left arm that ran from his wrist to his shoulder. He had other smaller wounds on his chest and one approximately ten centimeters long on his abdomen. The wounds did not appear to be self-inflicted. The team told Raymond they did not need to find him a ride anymore because they had managed to get hold of Ayuda Juvenil.[22] When I asked how long it would take them to get there, Raymond replied, "Como una hora, tú sabes como son esas cosas" (About an hour, you know how things are). The director told us he thought the cut on the boy's arm would require at least 30 stitches.

A few days later, I met the psychologist from Carolina 3 and asked him how the boy was doing. He said that the hospital had refused to stitch up the wound because it would take too long. "We came back here and applied Mercurochrome and placed him away from the others so the wound would not get infected. The doctor at the CAI saw him today and said he will be all right." The message is clear: this youngster does not merit any time or attention.

5 • The Institutionalization of Violence

Occasionally the chupapegas on Sabana Grande and other people on the streets disappear from the boulevard for several days, sometimes even for months. In many cases these young people have been caught by the police or the national guard and placed at police headquarters or at centers run by the National Institute for the Welfare of the Minor (INAM).

In this chapter I will discuss the two primary INAM institutions for minors, Los Chorros and the Carolina, as representative of the ways in which the state deals with youth violence in Caracas. I intend for my ethnographic accounts of the daily lives of young people at the INAM centers to capture the state's desperate and disorganized attempt to contain street children and others catalogued as "delinquents." I also wish to reveal the particular practices state welfare institutions such as Los Chorros and the Carolina develop for groups of youngsters based on their ages and the stereotypes that go along with these young people's life stages.

Current national politics toward delinquent youngsters translate into repressive and often brutal incarceration. However, INAM's repressive strategies are increasingly becoming a matter of public embarrassment because of the ineffectiveness of their rehabilitation program; indeed, a great majority of people in Caracas believe young transgressors should be severely punished instead of simply sent to centers such as INAM. Some critics have pointed out the inefficiencies of INAM's increasingly chaotic bureaucracy, but the INAM justifies its disorganization by stating that it is the result of budget cuts and the increasing number of young people with which it has to contend.

Furthermore, the INAM is constantly ridiculed in public by the same young people it has to "hide," "punish," and "discipline." The youngsters go in and out of these centers as they please, ignoring the underpaid guards and counselors, and inside the centers they create a violent dynamic of their own that is all too frequently beyond the control of the INAM staff.

I shall examine the daily experiences of young people at these two centers as they relate to the institutional setting and to the staff members. Young people's own accounts reveal the complex social relations established among themselves while at INAM centers; they explain the ways in which the social structure outside the cell is negotiated to produce dynamics that are simultaneously violent and supportive inside the cell. I also seek to understand the position of the social technicians—the psychologists, social workers, and counselors—who, as a result of the economic, social, and cultural constraints on their own lives, are often unaware of the violence they reproduce. Many of these social technicians recognize the illogical and disorganized state of the INAM bureaucracy, but because they feel they have no control over the system, they continue to rely on INAM's outdated psychological tests to create absurd case files and to follow rules that in the end only harm their charges.

From the very start of my research at Los Chorros and the Carolina, I got a sense of the absurdity of the INAM structure. In detailing the many difficulties I encountered, my purpose will be to show the anthropologist's experience of the bureaucratic inertia that permeates the welfare system—an experience that is very frustrating, to say the least. It is also my intention to show my own fear of pushing certain issues and entering supposedly forbidden spaces, the whole time struggling between what I had learned in the United States about ethics and what my Venezuelan instinct told me to forge on and discover.

Los Chorros and the Carolina

In Caracas, the two main INAM centers where the young males of the boulevard are placed are Los Chorros and the Carolina. Because I did extensive fieldwork at the Carolina Center, my experiences there will be the focus of this discussion. However, several visits to Los Chorros and conversations with children who had been there and with former staff members provide insights for points of comparison between the two places. The dynamics at the two centers are clearly shaped and determined by the power relations between the young people and the psychologists, social workers, educators, and psychiatrists. In Los Chorros and the Carolina Center, punishment of the minors is the end result of the relationships and practices that develop in the context of run-down and inadequate buildings, lack of resources, and apathetic and uncritical professionals. The generally poor conditions of the buildings, the blasting music, the oppressive smell of urine, the unpalatable and insufficient food, and the tedious routines are all too effective in transforming the bodies and souls of the young people staying in these places.

Los Chorros is a center for (certain) boys between the ages of seven and thirteen and girls between the ages of nine to seventeen; the Carolina is for boys between the ages of fourteen and eighteen. The boys at Los Chorros are treated as children who are vulnerable but who embody the potential for delinquency. These children, because of their youth, are smaller, weaker, and less symbolically and physically threatening than those at the Carolina. The young people at the Carolina are perceived as "almost men" (since they are almost eighteen). Though they are between fourteen and eighteen years old, they are already perceived, treated, and feared as criminals who legally—to the despair of many, who would like to see them in jail—cannot be considered as such.

The young at Los Chorros are usually put there for vagrancy or petty theft or because they have been abandoned. As might be expected, the social technicians look upon these children as more treatable than the older boys, many of whom have committed homicides or caused serious physical injuries to others. Yet the psychologists, social workers, and counselors at Los Chorros often show a lack of respect for the children's humanity. The young person, because he is considered a child, is also assumed to be more easily intimidated by overt physical and psychological abuse.

At the Carolina, however, the unequal power in the relationships between the youngsters and the social technicians is obvious. Both groups are influenced by fear—the youngsters fear the environment at the center, which they have heard of or experienced before, and the technicians fear what these adolescents are capable of doing to one another or, what is worse, to the technicians themselves. At this institution, staff members, although they are often authoritative, interact with young people from a position of cautious power, knowing that they will eventually be released and can retaliate.[1] Yet although they impose their rules and examinations with fear, they are also capable of showing occasional affection and concern for the youngsters.

The INAM Bureaucratic Labyrinth

In the early stage of my research, Los Chorros seemed not only less threatening as a place to work than the Carolina because of the age of its inhabitants but also because of its location: Los Chorros is situated in the wealthier east side of the city, whereas the Carolina is on the west side and surrounded by barrios. It also seemed less threatening because the younger chupapegas on the boulevard are taken to centers more often than the older malandros and monos. Like the upper-middle-class women who occasionally visited the center to bring candy and toys, I found Los Chorros more comfortable.

Once the director and staff at Los Chorros discovered that I was not there to donate anything to the center—like a refrigerator, for example—they became suspicious of my visits and tried to prevent me from spending much time with the boys except on the basketball court, where it was difficult to engage in long discussions. However, the fact that the chupapegas went in and out of the place with regularity allowed me to follow the dynamics at Los Chorros throughout the year. The youngsters sometimes spent as little as a few hours at the center, taking the first chance they got to escape.[2]

Most of my difficulties in conducting research at Los Chorros came from the INAM main offices downtown—difficulties in obtaining a research permit or in getting my questions answered because of confidentiality: although the INAM claimed they were protecting the minors' privacy, to me they appeared to be protecting their own privacy because of the ineffective way in which the centers were operating. In order to observe and participate in activities other than the regular Sunday basketball games, I decided to ask for a part-time job as a "counselor." This idea had been suggested by the director himself of Los Chorros, who desperately needed more personnel at his center. Many days my patience was tried by my visits to the INAM main offices on the forty-second floor of one of the tallest buildings in Caracas. Finally, after interviews, several psychology tests with 1959 copyrights, and my insistence, I was told that I could start working at Los Chorros. However, the director insisted that I work lengthy shifts, which would have necessitated my staying until late at night. Given the unreasonable nature of his demand, I decided to consider a different center.[3] The only other similar center for males in Caracas was the Carolina. I went back to the forty-second floor to a new office. Then, despite advice from a friend in the know, I told INAM exactly what I wanted to do: undertake research on my own schedule. I expected them to say no. Surprisingly, they gave me a permit to do research at the Carolina.

Was the INAM losing its well-known fear of outsiders who might reveal their secrets? Or did I just get lucky because the boss was too busy to read my project and because the secretary thought I looked harmless? Only with time did I realize that the people at INAM never considered even the remote possibility that they might be included in any published findings about the daily lives of young people in their institutions. They assumed that I would write about the violence among the young but not about the innate violence of the institutions themselves. In the minds of the social technicians, the behavior of the children was totally separate from their own.

Los Chorros: Discipline Among the Mango Trees

Imagine a large field at the foot of the Avila Mountains covered in mango trees, in the middle of one of Caracas's upper-class neighborhoods.[4] Los Chorros, as it is popularly known (*chorros* means river rapids), looks like a nice place to first-time visitors, with its three large buildings, plentiful trees, and basketball courts.[5] It even has a swimming pool, which gives the center the air of a country club—until one gets close enough to see the color of the water.

At first the visitor asks herself why a reeducation center for children sounds so eerily quiet from the outside. Then one notices that all three sickly yellow buildings have barred windows. What goes on in a place where the mango trees can only be seen through institutional barriers?

When the chupapegas first arrive at Los Chorros, they are sent to the middle building, the CAI. In theory, the boys are required to spend two to three months at the CAI, where they are evaluated by the staff. After this procedure, they are sent to a longer-term institution, often outside Caracas, or to their homes. However, at the Carolina Center, as at other INAM institutions, theory is reshaped by practice—the inefficient bureaucracy and a generalized apathy toward the well-being of marginal children. Many youngsters who do not have anywhere to go or who are tired of living on the streets can spend as long as eight months waiting to be relocated. As I have stated earlier, most of the chupapegas do not stay long; they can easily escape, even through the main doors.

At the CAI, young people converge regardless of the reasons for their being there. Children left by relatives who could not or did not want to take care of them share space with those who live on the streets or who have committed transgressions. The center's attitude is that all the young people share a common marginal background. As a consequence, in Los Chorros, Gómez, a chupapega, ends up in the same group with Victor, a developmentally delayed boy whom no other institution wanted.

The INAM tries to make the children look the same as well, by issuing all of them old shorts, shirts, and cheap recycled shoes.[6] The whole atmosphere of the place reinforces one's impression that the children are unwanted—by their families, by the barrio, by the streets, by society in general, and certainly by the staff at Los Chorros, many of whom are also lower-middle class or even from the barrios. In words and deeds, the counselors constantly make it clear to these young people that they are a burden both inside and outside the walls.[7] Their rejection of the children is manifested in the staff's neglect, insults, and physical punishment. Almost with malice, counselors, psychologists, and social workers at Los Chorros direct their resentments at the children, whom they consider transgressors and potential criminals.

These forms of violence and exclusion are justified by the staff as the necessary consequence of legitimate educational goals or regulatory functions (Basaglia 1987, 61). The chupapegas say that in Los Chorros all they do is "pagar plantón," which consists of standing in front of a wall or underneath a mango tree for several hours at a time. On one of my first visits to Los Chorros, Roy from Sabana Grande was standing with two other boys under a mango tree. He waved at me to come over, and then the small group anxiously told me their own version of what they were doing there while other boys were playing basketball. The counselor had punished them for fighting, and now they had to sit there for a few hours, even though they had already been there for almost three hours. They were not permitted to move beyond the shade of the tree or to take any of the mangoes. Roy muttered that he was going to escape and that it was unfair to make him go hungry sitting beneath a tree full of mangoes. He resented the fact that he had to sit in one place for several hours without food just because he fought with another boy on the basketball court.

The public holds the social technicians at Los Chorros—even though they are poorly trained and underpaid—ultimately responsible for the children's continuing involvement in illegal activities such as prostitution, petty theft, glue sniffing, and drug distribution. The staff is sensitive to the criticism, which is further reason for the counselors, psychologists, and social workers to take out their frustrations on the children. The staff recognizes that they lack status, that society and the main INAM do not appreciate their dedication to the job of reeducating these young but potentially dangerous people. On top of this, the children appear ungrateful, with their misbehavior and constant attempts at escape.

Although Los Chorros is designed as an evaluation and reeducation institution, it does not fulfill either of those functions; the staff there does not even teach the youngsters to read and write. As far as the INAM staff is concerned, the young people at Los Chorros do not need more than a bed and food three times a day. In other words, the staff feels it is doing the young a favor by letting them stay there and by protecting them from poverty. If it weren't for their centers, the INAM argues, those minors would be in poverty-ridden barrios or on the violent streets. What these bureaucrats refuse to acknowledge is that everyday life in the barrios and on the streets can actually be of a higher quality than life at Los Chorros. From the moment a young person enters the place, he is made aware of his potential as a delinquent, even if he is developmentally delayed like Victor.

The rejection and mistreatment of youngsters at INAM centers is nothing new. These practices are not the product of a recent deterioration of social relations caused by the current socio-economic crisis. R. A. Rodríguez, who published a book in the early 1970's about his experiences at reeducational institutions as a youth, described his first entrance to the equivalent of Los Chorros center. In the late 1950's, his mother left him at the center because she was kicked out of the house by her landlord. He describes the sentences with which he was welcomed: "Look, you little shit, you are new here. You are not in your own house. And just so you know, and don't forget it, you better be pretty careful around here! And if you slip up, you better watch your butt!" (Rodríguez 1974, 22).[8] Much of the physical violence and emotional abuse experienced by the children—shocking and nerve-racking to me as an observer—can be interpreted as "common-sensical" by the children themselves. In some ways, they consider violence, especially physical punishment, part of the same cycle to which they are accustomed in the barrios and on the streets, with the exception that at Los Chorros there is limited space to run and hide. I resented the sense of horror and impotence that flooded me whenever I witnessed the children's screams of resistance and pain. On one visit I heard terrific shrieks coming from inside the CAI. Gustavo and I were on the baseball/soccer field applying medicine to Gomita's wounded leg. When he saw my reaction, Gomita said matter-of-factly, "Es la señorita Milagros, que le gusta pegarle a uno" (that is the counselor Milagros who likes to beat us). Gomita dealt with the counselor by avoiding her when he could or by acting so violent that he frightened her.

Punishment: Surviving Los Chorros

I understood what was behind the punishment of the children at Los Chorros through the events surrounding Gomita's leg wound. The way in which his wound became infected became for me the ultimate metaphor for the collapse of the very institutions meant to protect young people. Gomita's pain and the means used to relieve it reveal the existence of a morality that regards marginal children as disposable (see Scheper-Hughes and Hoffman 1994). The episode of Gomita's injury demonstrates the ways in which the institution, the hospitals, and the family overtly reject Gomita and his suffering, simultaneously pointing out his potential "delinquency" and vulnerability.

I first met Gomita on the Sabana Grande boulevard during the summer of 1992. He was a great trickster, at that time about eleven years old, with a captivating smile. When I returned to Caracas in January 1993, I visited Gomita at Los Chorros. He had a cast on his left leg, because only nine days before he had escaped the center and a car had run him over. The police had to try several hospitals before he received treatment—the nurses said, "We don't treat this type of injury here" or "We can't offer that type of service right now"—but eventually the wound was treated, and the police took the injured boy back to Los Chorros. Nine days after this incident, of which we knew nothing, my friend Gustavo and I went to visit Gomita at the center. Gomita's wound had been left unattended all this time. The cast was filthy and covered with dried blood. No one at the center seemed at all concerned about Gomita's need for further treatment; obviously, the staff saw him as a nuisance since he was always coming in and out of the center.

Gustavo and I took Gomita to the hospital, where we had to argue about a special code in the Ley tutelar de menores before we could be admitted. The nurse almost fainted at the sight and the smell of the infected wound. I did not want to look, but I know the wound must have been very bad from Gomita's screams and his cries for his mother. The wound had been left unattended too long and was festering with pus. After cleaning up the mess, the doctors said the boy must go to the Children's Hospital at least every other day to continue the treatment. He needed antibiotics, vitamins, and above all, rest.

Gustavo and I returned to the center two days later on a Friday afternoon. All the children were locked up, while the secretary and the counselors were chatting among themselves and reading the newspaper. When we told them that the doctors had suggested rest for Gomita, one of them replied, "But that child is so restless," thereby placing the responsibility for the state of his leg entirely on Gomita.

The director of Los Chorros, upon hearing the conversation, immediately came in from the next office and said, "And as soon as his leg heals he will escape." He was annoyed by the fact that Gomita needed to be taken every other day to the hospital (the staff took him only once during the two months of treatment, leaving the task entirely to Gustavo and me). The Association for Street Children had to pay for Gomita's medicine. The director insisted that the care could be given at the center, even though they did not even have a complete first-aid kit. He continued that a boy had once come to the center with a bullet in his lung and that "nothing had happened to him." And with that, the director pointed at Gomita and with disdain repeated, "I know that as soon as you feel better you will go back to the streets."

The director was angry with the child for being such an inconvenience and for not acknowledging that indeed, as soon as he could walk again, he would escape. Rather than being concerned for the boy, the director was frustrated over having to deal with the main INAM offices, which he knew would not be very helpful in providing transportation for the child and even less in supplying the money needed to pay for the medicine. In other words, the director felt that his job was to run what I call a "depósito de muchachos" (deposit of children), not to go out of his way to take care of them.

The Carolina Center

The Carolina Center, located in the western part of the city, is surrounded by a hillside barrio; unlike Los Chorros, it is seldom visited by female charity workers with their candy bags (instead, it is visited on Sundays by evangelicals).[9] The Carolina Center is divided into three separate structures that share a central courtyard with a greenish swimming pool and a set of parallel bars. Two of the units are CAI's. The third one, the most feared unit, is the Carolina 3, a center for intensive treatment, where those considered by the 103 and the judges to be most dangerous may be placed after preliminary evaluation at one of the CAI's.

The two CAI's are called the Carolina 1 and 2. These two sub-centers, designed for the observation of those young people "at risk" or of transgressors, each contain an average of 30 young people. The youngsters theoretically spend a maximum of three months in these places, during which a specialized team of psychologists, psychiatrists, and social workers carries out a psychosocial evaluation before the youngsters are released or sent to Carolina 3—or sometimes to the adult jail, La Planta. However, just as in Los Chorros, youngsters can spend up to nine months at the CAI before they are released or sent elsewhere—unless they escape or unless a judge quickly establishes that they have not committed a transgression. Unfortunately for the young, legal processes in Venezuela are continually delayed by bureaucratic inertia of the center itself, the main INAM, and the courts, which are often on strike.[10]

When I finally obtained the research permit to work at the Carolina, I expected to find restrictions similar to those at Los Chorros. There is a general sense that INAM centers are filled with secrecy and that they are not to be scrutinized, especially when there has been rioting or when one of the boys has died. I found, however, that the director and other personnel at the Carolina were very generous with their time and gave me room to work with the youngsters. Not to diminish the staff's generosity, but this openness no doubt served two practical purposes: first, I was providing an activity for the group, even if it was dangerous; second, I was relieving the staff of some of its burden; most of the ten or so social technicians at the center admitted to being tired of working in such mean conditions.

My research at the Carolina Center was focused primarily on a group of young people I met at one of the two CAI's between

April 1993 and February 1994. During my first weeks there, I sat in a filthy bare room called a library with a group of eight adolescents. They told me stories; sometimes they begged to talk. I learned about their daily lives from our conversations and my observations. I also asked them to write something for me about their lives. The center did not allow the use of tape recorders, and it was hard to follow their stories since they were always coming and going in and out of the room; I just could not manage to write down everything they said. Because I was perceived as a kind of teacher, although I told the youngsters many times that I was an anthropologist, I had luck asking them to write their stories as assignments.

At first I did not get much out of the boys until I complained to them that they were not helping me with my thesis. Corazoncito, whom we met earlier, replied that he had done his homework.[11] After that many others began to write, persuaded in part by the nice typed booklike version I produced out of Corazoncito's story. Corazoncito chose to write about his encounter with the teacher-anthropologist: "That same afternoon I met a young woman named Patricia, who always comes to teach us about things like the environment, fauna, animals, mountains, etc. She's writing a book and she asked me to write something about my life, and so I did. She is very intellectual and the only entertainment the minors in this place have."[12]

Within the Walls: Salsa, Concrete, and the Initial Phase

The entrance to one of the two CAI's is a large iron gate painted in "school blue," with a small window for screening visitors. Inside, there is a large corridor with a patio converted into half a basketball court. The corridor has a large cement bench, where many of the youngsters talk and listen to the salsa music coming out of two powerful speakers. Toward one side are the staff offices, and at the far end is a playroom that contains mainly an old set of weights and a classroom covered in spiderwebs and what looked like animal waste.

On the second floor is a long dark hall painted in the same shade of yellow as the rest of the building. The hall branches into three sections, each closed by an iron gate. The first section is called the *fase inicial* (initial phase). The youngsters, regardless of why they were admitted or where they come from, are placed there for one week as part of the process of adapting to a new place. In this section there are two rooms, where all the young people arriving from all parts of Caracas are left for a week. There the boys have mattresses on the floor, occasionally a pen with which to write on the walls, one another's company, and plenty of idle time.

The institutional logic behind setting these young people apart this way is that the initial phase constitutes a passage into institutional discipline. Erving Goffman (1961) compared the induction into institutions to rites of passage. In his model, these procedures, such as stripping the boys of their possessions and subjecting them to an initial medical examination, are intended to be identity-fixing events for both the incoming person and his keepers, a performance that establishes the standard of discipline in the institution. The initial phase, in this model, is an unavoidable rite of defilement for the new person, who is stripped of much of what constituted his preinstitutional identity. In many instances, the incoming person, once bereft of these identity components, has very few resources left with which to counter this massive socializing onslaught (Goffman 1961, 18–30; Feldman 1991, 131).

Induction into the Carolina seems to have been designed in much the same way: to show the young person the rigorous discipline that awaits him. The initial phase is really an attempt to control by creating a fear of what will come next. However, the young people who enter the Carolina are not completely stripped of their preinstitutional identity. In fact, the institution sets up conditions that reproduce a variety of their everyday practices (such as fighting for shoes to demonstrate masculinity), but now within the context of the center's ubiquitous yellow walls.

Fear mounts as the young watch one another's faces, trying to recognize friends and foes, or as they wait to attack or to be attacked. There is also the uncertainty about what will happen during a week of hanging out on their mattresses. The youngsters establish contests of masculinity as defined by physical strength, fieriness, and the ability to disguise fear. Their weapon of survival, since there are no guns, is precisely their preinstitutional identity, which will allow them to establish in one way or another their position within the group. When the initial phase ends, every young person will emerge with a sense of the others in the group. He will have carved out an identity for himself as the *arrecho* (brave one), as a malandro or someone who "se las tira de malandro" (poses as a malandro), as a *chiguire* (someone who works for others), as a *maquive* (a person who boasts of incredible deeds), as a *becerro* (a cocksucker), and so forth. Rules have been clearly established that will guide further interactions.

During this initial phase the psychologists, social workers, and guides mostly ignore the incoming group of minors, arguing that the confinement will teach them the rules of the game. However, Raymond, the psychologist, revealed a more practical reason for the design of the initial phase. On one occasion I saw two newly arrived youngsters run out the front and down the street when the caretaker was distracted. Jackson, one of the counselors, came in later saying he had seen two youths running and that one of them had even waved good-bye. When I asked why he had not tried to stop them, he replied, "I was too tired to run after them."

Raymond added that he was actually glad the boys had left, because with the ten whom had been released from initial phase that morning, it meant twelve fewer boys to deal with. Noticing my amazement, Jackson and Raymond said that I just did not understand what it was like when the place was crowded. What the staff at the Carolina truly hope for is that many of the minors will not be able to stand it and will leave the center, making less work for them. Many youngsters do escape during this phase or as soon as they are released into the next stage, group one, where they enjoy more physical freedom. The initial-phase rooms have to be regularly repaired because of holes in the walls or broken locks.

Security at the center is nonexistent except for a guard, who also ignores escaping youths because he is not willing to risk his life, and a stray dog that always chases after cars. The staff feels it is dangerous when there are too many boys at the center. Sometimes people from the outside get in through the roof to bring alcohol and drugs or to rescue their friends. "One time," Jackson told me, "a group of young people even cut the phone lines, but one of the counselors had already called the police."

Staff members are fully aware of the discomfort suffered by the youngsters going through the initial phase for an entire week. They try not to leave a person alone in one of the two initial-phase rooms, because if they do, the consequences can be tragic. In February 1994, a child who had been transferred (rejected) from Los Chorros—Los Chorros argued they had proved the boy was fourteen and not thirteen, as he had claimed—hanged himself with a sheet when he was left alone for a few hours. His suicide brought serious consequences to the Carolina technicians, because it meant being blamed by INAM headquarters, and depending on the media coverage, possible dismissals of low-ranking personnel.

Time passes slowly in these rooms. The way the youngsters experience this slow-moving time is beautifully described in Jacobo Timerman's description of his ordeal in an Argentine cell during the "dirty war." A guard had left a peephole open, and Timerman was able to see: "Indeed, I have full view of two doors. What a sensation of freedom! An entire universe added to my Time, that elongated time which hovers over me oppressively in the cell. Time, that dangerous enemy of man, when its existence, duration, an eternity are virtually palpable" (1981, 5).

In his writings, Corazoncito described, better than I could, the anguish he experienced during the initial phase.

Tuesday, May 4.   2:00 P.M.

They brought me up to initial phase, where I had the worst day of my life. I was really scared and in the room where they put me was a really big guy named Oweivin, and also the guy I met when I was in Division and another minor. Then I ate and there wasn't any fighting, but I knew that soon enough I would have to fight somebody. The worst thing occurred the night the counselor on guard brought us cookies and then left. Oveiwin rushed up to me and tried to hit me several times. I told him to go ahead and fight. Immediately León, who was the other person I knew, joined in and they both started to punch me. I told them again that if they wanted to fight, fine, but first one and then the other. So it happened this way: when I was fighting with León, Oveiwin threw himself at me because I was winning. That night and four more nights were full of bitterness and sorrow. Later, I was changed to room A of initial phase. There I met many minors like Lendel, Gonzalo, and others.[13]

Eventually Corazoncito and Oveiwin emerged from the initial phase as friends. Amid the torment of the initial phase, they had developed strategies to survive the week, they had influenced each other's plans of escape, and they had decided who was a culebra or who was not.[14]

Whatever relationships developed among Corazoncito, Oveiwin, and the other youngsters came from the cultural meanings and practices of their street life. For example, shoes are a recurrent and common theme among the boys. On the streets, shoes are markers of strength and masculinity and the ability to procure expensive goods, and one way to prove yourself is through your ability to hold onto them. Corazoncito wrote in his diary/assignment:

Tuesday, May 11. 11:00 A.M.

We went upstairs and they locked us up. When I got to the room I saw a guy lying on his mattress. I asked him where he was from.
—From Propatria.
—Why are you here?
—Because I killed two guys who were driving me crazy.
—What's your name?
—Orlando. They call me El Chivo [the goat].
At that moment, Eric, a guy from group two, came to initial phase and told El Chivo to give him his shoes, but El Chivo didn't want to. I told him to give over the shoes, because just as they had found the key to the door to initial phase, they could get the key to the rooms. El Chivo gave up his shoes. Now supposedly the group two morning counselor, Guariguata, has El Chivo's shoes. El Chivo was a good guy but I didn't trust him or anybody else.[15]

Lendel, another boy in the group, described his experiences during initial phase to me. The first time he was placed at one of the two CAI's, he escaped after a few days. Then he got caught again after a month and sent to the other CAI. After his evaluation, Lendel was sent next door to Carolina 3, where he had to go through the initial phase once more. The justification for putting him in initial phase again was "he has to get used to the rules." Lendel had learn to overcome his boredom, which led him to miss his old life on the streets. Again and again, he had to fight his immense urge to escape:

When I got there they took me upstairs to a room where you have to stay for eight days before you're allowed to go to the courtyard.

During those eight days I had a problem with another minor, Felipe, who wanted to stab me and I thought, "Go ahead, I will take care of myself and make you respect me." A night went by and I felt repentant, alone, and sad, and I couldn't sleep because I was thinking about all sorts of things: whether I should take off or stay. The next morning Felipe called me over and told me that I was in trouble with a cousin of his, and he tried to stab me, and we fought until he realized that it wouldn't be easy to stab me. I wasn't worried about Felipe, but I was worried about the problems waiting for me in the courtyard, and I could not stop thinking about escaping. On April 28, my mother came to visit and I saw that she was suffering because of my situation. I decided to stay and face my problem no matter what happened. After the eight days, I went to the courtyard and found minors who were there for a variety of reasons, and some became my friends because of my clothes. One of them, who was bigger than me, invited me to fight for my shoes and I had to fight, even though I was very scared. I lost the fight and the guy took my shoes. All of a sudden, another minor whom I knew from the barrio showed up, and I spoke with him and told him that he knew me, and they came to an arrangement and gave me my shoes back. I spent the rest of the day talking and making friends.[16]

The process is repeated in Carolina 3:

After I found myself at the center, they locked me up in a small room, where I had to stay for the next five days. It was another experience, and once again I had the urge to escape, but knowing that I would not solve my problem by escaping, I decided to stay. I had no problems there because several of my friends were there. Now I have been here for nine months. I am almost eighteen years old and waiting for my freedom.[17]

The easiness with which young people at the Carolina escape, even through the main doors, is one more example of the chaos of the INAM centers. The fact that young inmates are left on their own for an entire week, with nothing to do but harass one another, speaks of the informality with which INAM expects to discipline lower-class young people. This disorganization results in a brand of inertia and indifference toward the young, which in itself becomes a form of punishment.

Terror as Punishment

At the CAI, isolation cells are in the third hall. They are the most feared rooms in the entire building—not necessarily because of what happens there now, since they are seldom used, but because of what has transpired there in the recent past. A collective memory of what has happened in those cells exists among the minors on the streets. I visited the isolation cells with a visiting movie director, Raymond the psychologist, and a bunch of youngsters who were following us, all the while making remarks and cracking jokes about the "dungeon." Only Jerson refused to follow us in, because he knew that "menores se han tostado allá adentro" (minors have gotten roasted in there).

In the middle of the hall there were two cells, perhaps four square meters in size, with built-in cement beds. At the end of the hall were two blackened cells where as recently as 1991 youngsters had been burned alive. Over the last four years there have been a series of episodes at both CAI's in which youngsters had burned themselves in the cells. After the burnings of 1991, the newspaper printed a three-day series introducing the isolation cell with the following description: "Isolation cells are dark rooms of four square meters where they can place up to nine minors at the same time. There are no bathrooms, no water, and the stench, along with the solitude, can drive anyone crazy" (Aliana González, "El terror impera en las 'cárceles' de niños (I): tres menores quemados en extrañas circunstancias" (Terror within

"jails" for children (I): three minors burnt under strange circumstances), *El Nacional*, September 9, 1991).

The youngsters started a fire to force the counselors to take
them out of the cell, but because the paint on the walls was flam-
mable, the flames got out of control; in a matter of seconds the
youngsters were burned badly, and one died. Raymond admitted
that the cell was not an inviting place, but maintained that the
burning had been ultimately the youngsters' fault because they
were forbidden to smoke while in solitary confinement and had
ignored the rules. He essentially ignored the fact that the fire had
nothing to do with smoking. Then he told me that he had
rushed the minor who had died to the hospital, but he was already dead when they got there.

Alberto, a sixteen-year-old who was involved in this episode,
was interviewed by a newspaper reporter while he was in the hospital being treated for second- and third-degree burns. This is
how he explained what happened: "One guy who was with me
asked for some matches and started to light the mattresses; he
said that way we could get out sooner. I wanted to hit him to stop
him from doing it, but the flames began to burn me and I cried in
anguish. The counselors, however, did not seem to notice. It took
them twelve minutes to pull me out." From his hospital bed, and
in great physical pain, Alberto continued his story to say that
what hurt him the most was the reason he was in isolation at the
time of the incident. He had decided to escape the center because
he had lost some evaluation points that he had needed to get a
weekend permit to go home. Later he returned because his
mother had told him to: "This happened to me because I came
back to the center; I did it for my mother, who was worried. In
court they had promised not to place me in the isolation cells,
but they lied." In his conversation with the reporter, the director
blamed the burning entirely on the youngsters. This exchange
reminded me of the Los Chorros director who had blamed Go-

mita for his infected wound. The process of isolation itself could not be at fault—it was a just a way of enforcing the rules.

The reporter asked the director about Alberto's case in particular. The director answered that the minor was brought to the Carolina by his mother (implying that the mother had forced him to return rather than having persuaded him into coming, as Alberto suggested). He went on to say that there were guidelines explicitly stating that when a young person escaped from an institution, he had to spend twenty-four hours in isolation. When the journalist asked, "But, is it logical from a psychological point of view to place someone who has escaped the center in isolation for twenty-four hours?" the director brushed aside the question, saying, "All these criteria have been studied by the specialists. It makes sense from the point of view that the youngster has to feel that he has broken one of the institution's rules. They are youngsters who over the years have broken all the rules. The fact that society in general is responsible for this is not our problem" (González, "El terror").

The social technicians do not accept responsibility for the tragic outcomes to their enforcement of the rules. Apparently, their job is not to analyze whether these outdated rules still make sense, but to blindly follow them to hold onto their jobs. Whenever the center's policies go wrong, staff members blame not only the youngsters themselves but also society as a whole; rarely do they hold themselves or even the INAM responsible.

No repairs were made to the third hall after the fire. It stands as a powerful symbol of the INAM's institutional chaos and its apathy toward these young people. That the third hall, with its isolation cells, has been allowed to stand at all is in itself a form of punishment, an implied threat that inspires the youngsters' fear of being sent to the terrible place where children were burned. It is not physical punishment, but it is punishment nonetheless.

Rodríguez, in his autobiographical account of his numerous stays at INAM centers (then Concejo Venezolano del Niño) in the 1950's and 1960's, compares the terror he experienced in *aislamiento* (isolation cell) with that suffered by the independence heroine Luisa Cáceres de Arismendi in the Santa Rosa castle.[18] Rodríguez was placed in the isolation cell every time he escaped, and every time he asked himself, "Whom have I killed, what sort of dark heinous crime have I committed to deserve being locked up in this tortuous prison away from my family?" (Rodríguez 1974, 22). After one of his escapes, he was returned to the isolation cell in the center of La Isla del Burro (an adult prison that was used as a juvenile center in the 1950's). In his desperation to get even and to terrorize the guards, counselors, and teachers who were watching him, he cut himself with a piece of glass, using his body, which was all he had, to shock his captors (priests) into questioning their punishment:

> Once in the cell I started to yell all sorts of obsenities at my torturers. My screams did not move them, but then, possessed by some type of suicidal energy, I took one of my shoes off and threw it at the lightbulb, which fell into pieces. I took a piece of glass and began cutting myself like a madman, making all sorts of wounds all over my body. So much blood was running that all the witnesses were running around without knowing what to do. The smartest one called the director. The latter was horrified and was also unable to help me—what am I saying! He wasn't even able to talk to me. (Rodríguez 1974, 161)

Institutional Routine and Everyday Life

Every day at the center unfolds in a series of routines, in the middle of which many interesting or unanticipated things occur, such as fights, games, discussions, examinations, special trips to the museum—and the visits of an anthropologist. The only reason the youngsters comply with the routines is that by doing so they stand a better chance of earning the points they need to qualify for weekend permits, which allow the youngsters to visit their families and to get a glimpse of the outside world. Corazoncito's first written assignments included a detailed record of the points he scored:

Tuesday, May 18.   3:00 P.M.

All the youngsters who are transferred to a group are taught in the initial phase that they have to do their chores, that is, cleaning the place assigned by the teacher and waking up at 7:00 A.M. to sing the national anthem and at 7:30 going to the dining room wearing the uniform: blue jeans, a white T-shirt, and normal shoes, preferably not name-brand ones, to avoid making the minors envious. My first job was to clean the stairs, and my first grade was 450 points. The counselor did the evaluation. My second and third jobs were also cleaning the stairs, and I scored 570 and 578 points. Then on the third and the fifth, I scored 597 and 585.[19]

The daily routine is boring, and the youngsters often wish for more interesting things to do. Ironically, even with all the cleaning, the center always looks dirty and smells of urine because of the water shortage (a problem throughout the city). According to the staff, employing the boys in this way is not only good discipline, it also keeps maintenance costs down. Here again the logic seems to be that, after all, they are taking care of young marginals, murderers, and drug addicts whom nobody else wants, so the boys should be grateful for whatever they get.

The food at the centers also reflects the institution's attitude: since the boys are marginals, they can eat "poor people's food." Eating at the center, which the youngsters at Los Chorros do soley to stave off starvation, becomes just one more frustrating chore for them. While I was there, I observed the boys going for their early dinner and always returning angry and still hungry. The lucky ones ran up to their rooms to fill their stomachs with snacks brought by their relatives. Meals at the center consist mostly of sardines, pasta, rice, and *arepas* (Venezuelan cornbread), and only some street children are satisfied. Whenever the boys could, they brought me their food trays to illustrate their stories of how badly they were being fed.[20] Furthermore, the dining rooms were infested with cockroaches, which did nothing to make meals more appetizing. Lendel demonstrated his attitude toward meals at the center by throwing his food at the ceiling and concluding: "Nobody can eat food that when you throw it on the ceiling you still find it there the next day!"

In the midst of the daily routine the counselors allow the youngsters to develop their own dynamics based on their street culture—up to a point. The staff members exercise their authority when they think things have gotten out of control. The young people at the Carolina watch hours of television, smoke cigarettes, do drugs, drink alcohol, play dominoes, produce *chusos* (homemade weapons), and fight. In their everyday social relations, there is a high degree of physical violence, which, oddly, is often condoned by the staff. Most organized fights in which youngsters from the two CAI resolve old disputes happen with the consent of the counselors, who in this way are relieved of the responsibility of resolving the conflicts. Once again, Corazoncito provides a snapshot of everyday life at the center:

> I am living unforgettable moments here at the center, with its riots and fights. I don't remember the dates of all these things, with the exception of one insurrection. All of us from Center A were at the pool, and some youngsters from Center B were hanging out nearby. They asked counselor William to give them a *cancha* (court, meaning a space for a fight). We waited a while until night, and the counselor took Asdrúbal and Yoris to the outside corridor, and they started to fight with the boys in B. Because Asdrúbal was winning the fight, the group B guys pulled out their homemade knives. We were inside, but when we saw that those guys were pulling out their knives, we pushed at the door and took out some

> bats. We ran after the guys until we got to the street. Several guys
> were injured, and the next day we had a meeting with the direc-
> tors and the staff. The incident did not make it to court, because it
> was not convenient for the directors. And in this way many days
> went by and many things happened. Few were released and many
> escaped because they were going to be transferred. My brother-in-
> law would come and bring me food. One time my girlfriend
> brought me drugs, but not because she wanted to. She did it be-
> cause I asked her to and told her that if she didn't, some guys were
> going to beat me up, but that was all bull, because if I told her that
> they were for me, she wouldn't bring it. In that way I smoked
> drugs, took pills, and drank anise liquor every day.[21]

This fight clearly took place with the consent, indeed, the collaboration, of the staff, who were too lazy to help the boys resolve
their problem and who never imagined the fight would get so
out of their control.

Often violence that is so frequently blamed on the lower
classes is in fact pervasive at all levels of society and occurs with
the tacit permission of the upper classes. When violence erupts
in the barrios—among malandros—it is not as disturbing to the
upper classes as when it is directed at them. Some people argue
that when malandros solve their conflicts violently, "they take
care of each other" (meaning they kill one another off). Similarly, when the youngsters at the Carolina Center are allowed to
fight and physically hurt one another, the institution's personnel
is relieved of resolving the rivalries exacerbated by the confinement and the lack of constructive activities.

Institutions of Welfare

In *Brazil: War on Children*, Gilberto Dimenstein asserts solid evidence that institutions that are supposed to take care of children

only succeed in turning them into hardened criminals. Many youngsters end up joining gangs in the institution, just as they did in the barrios. Moreover, the use of violence in these places as a means of discipline only encourages violent behavior among inmates (Dimenstein 1991, 40). Although I basically agree with Dimenstein's premise, the relationship between young people and the many levels of the welfare institution in Caracas is, I think, too complex to fix the production of "hardened criminals" on a single structure. The young encounter practices of violence in the centers that are not totally unlike what they encountered before entering those places. Violence forms part of the culture of the streets they come from and return to.

Ramón Brizuela, who spent a large part of his life in and out of centers like the ones described and later in jail, wrote:

> I have lived longer in prisons than in freedom, and even the freedom that I have enjoyed I have had to steal. Therefore, I can say with all that I have inside me that all you learn in prison is pure evil, and you have to forget about fear and consideration to survive. Here you have to create a reputation of being bad and dangerous so you are respected and don't get killed by other inmates or the caretakers. (Brizuela 1974, 245)

Young inmates' punishment includes the frustration and anger they feel in response to the dated psychological evaluations of the ill-trained staff. The staff's preoccupation with discovering sexual deviations, their insistence on the madness of their young charges, their disregard of the conditions of youngsters' lives both inside and outside the institution devalues, depersonalizes, and stifles the children and adolescents they evaluate.

I find that equally crushing to the spirits of the young people in the centers is the pressure to feel grateful to the state for the chance it is giving them to become "better citizens." The fact that they are forced to sing the national anthem every morning is another reminder that they are expected to feel patriotic and grateful for the dregs they receive—another example of how the institution perpetuates their degradation under the guise of alleviating it. The young are perceptive of the institutional discourse on the inevitability of their marginality. They know that the structural and professional decadence of the institution is justified by the argument that the young who attend these centers are "used to it" (economic poverty); after all, INAM workers say, these young people come primarily from barrios.

The resentment that builds in the youngsters at the center also comes from all the waiting required of them: they wait for answers to their questions, they wait to see their mothers (which for the lucky ones happens twice a week), they wait for news from the courts. And equally painful is the impotence of knowing that life goes on without them—the death of a brother, the birth of a baby, or a holiday—while for them time ticks away slowly inside the ugly yellow walls where there is nothing to do. The waiting only emphasizes that their time is worthless.

The disciplinary (mis)treatment of marginalized youth in Venezuela concurs with Foucault's fairly Eurocentric analysis of the modern disciplinary power of the state (1979). Although state bureaucracies are not organized enough to manage surveillance and disciplinary institutions such as the Carolina in the way that modern European institutions do (see Foucault 1979), at INAM detention centers, a certain kind of discipline emerges out of the minute control of some activities, repetitive exercises, detailed hierarchies, and normalized judgments. For young people on the streets of Caracas, the only way to get released from an institution is to accept the hegemonic model of normalcy and to cooperate with it.

Corazoncito ends his powerful account of life in the Carolina with some thoughts about his own transformation:

Today, Monday, August 2, I am still here and I feel like another person. I have learned many things, good and bad. In two days I will have been here for three months, but besides that it will be my birthday and I am very sad that I will have to spend it here. The courts are still on strike, and I don't know how long I'll be here. I want to leave here as a normal person, working and studying. I think I'll be able to do that, but I also want the Bladimir that I was to live again, because I consider him dead. I am not the same, my thoughts are based on taking revenge for nothing, and I know I am not doing well. Therefore I ask God to help me find that happy guy I was and not this one, who only thinks about killing person X. I have faith that the Bladimir I was will come back. And I have faith that this new Bladimir will want to make something of himself in this life. Therefore, I say that everyone should have faith in God since he knows and sees everything, because with God nothing is impossible. I bid farewell, saying that it is not easy to live with the torment of killing someone you didn't even want to kill. I dedicate my story to[22]

Carmen Gregoria "Gollita"
Q.E.P.D. (Rest in peace)[23]

6 · Stories in/on Style: Consumption, Language, and Violence

My lowlife as a malandro began approximately two years ago, when I used to tell my father that I wanted a pair of Nike shoes that cost 8,000 bolivares and he wouldn't give them to me. My father spent everything on horse races and alcohol. I was upset when a friend asked me if I wanted to have money. I told him, "Yes, I want to buy a pair of shoes and my father won't give me the money for them." The guy started to give me drugs to hide and he gave me 2,000 bolivares a week for doing it. As soon as I realized that everything was working well, I bought the shoes I wanted and I always had money in my pockets. Later, I got to know another guy, and the two of us began to keep drugs until one day the other guy lost his and left the shantytown. I was alone to deal with the problem. I hid from the guy I was keeping the drugs for because he wanted to kill me. One unexpected day the guy grabbed me from behind and hit me while saying, "I won't kill you because you are a minor and you are only starting on the 'malandreo.'" At that moment I decided not to keep drugs for others but to sell them myself. Others gave them to me and later I would pay them. Little by little my business grew until I had good money and could buy some clothes.[1]

In this narrative, Felipe, a seventeen-year-old from the Carolina Center, writes about his experience of becoming a malandro. His transformation into a malandro and the life of malandreo implies a complex interplay of consumption, language, and the body. His account illustrates how the identities of displaced youth in Caracas are negotiated within a context of scarcity and violence. It points out the resourceful ways that young people find to gain material wealth and to create meaning in their lives—and the risks they are willing to take.

In this final chapter I will focus on the stories, songs, rumors, dreams, and fantasies of young people along the Sabana Grande boulevard and at the Carolina Center. I will also focus on consumption, language, and the body as they reflect the meaning and creation of style, both personal and social, and its relation to violence. These stories, both short and long, written and discussed, show how these young people in Caracas define, live, and experience violence in the midst of larger global and transnational events.

My examination of these phenomena partially follows Dick Hebdige's analysis of British youth subcultures: "I have sought, in Sartre's words, to acknowledge the right of the subordinate class (the young, the black, the working class) to 'make something of what is made of (them)'—to embellish, decorate, parody and wherever possible to recognize and rise above a subordinate position which was never of their choosing" (Hebdige 1979, 139). The youngsters' tactics can be considered "weapons of the weak," in James Scott's (1985) use of the word *tactics* to mean resistance to the established order. In this chapter I will demonstrate practices of style to be partial acts of resistance to the sociocultural, politic, and economic conditions of young men's lives.

However, youth styles in Caracas do not emerge as merely a response of one oppositional subculture to another or resistance to the dominant culture; they are also a demonstration of the extent to which transnational cultures are embodied and lived. Styles are created and contested not solely in relation to domination and resistance but also to new ideas about the media and transnational and global processes. My particular interest is in understanding what style means in the lives of young people and how and why it turns into an interplay between subjugation and resistance to a dominant hegemonic order. Style in this sense reflects a private world within a larger culture, a world that allows young people to bring to their lives some vividness and focus. Youth styles embody the positive and meaningful emotions and rhythms of young people, while expressing the fluidity of class structures. Furthermore, street children negotiate styles as a further strategy for defending themselves.

Subcultures and Style: Trends in Analysis

Youth styles in the Western world are almost always studied as part of the development of youth subcultures as generational and class-mediated phenomena. Most studies of subcultures emphasize style as communication of what constitutes the particular youth subculture. Style, then, is pivotal to understanding the so-called subcultures of the punks, skinheads, and mods in England. Different youth styles are constructed and reified as subsets of the broader working-class culture, which is then constructed as subordinate to a hegemonic middle-class culture in most industrialized Western countries.

In the United States, classic analyses of youth subcultures portray them as stemming from the frustration of working-class youth, who are continually confronted with unequal opportunities. Cloward and Ohlin (1960) state that working-class youngsters feel at a disadvantage in the general race to achieve valued commodities and prestige. Daunted by the prospect of trying to succeed, working-class youth veer toward alternatives, creating three subcultural options: "the criminal subculture," gaining money through illegal means; "the conflict subculture," gaining status and reputation by fighting; and "the retreatist subculture," withdrawing completely and indulging in sex, alcohol, and drugs. Albert Cohen (1955) sees working-class subcultures as inversions of middle-class standards. The value of these studies lies in their identifying the significance of social inequality in the lives of these youngsters and their understanding of the styles and postures of young people not as spontaneous whims but as part of a response to social conditions (Cashmore 1984, 16).

The British school has also produced extensive analyses of male subcultures as style mediated and class structured (see Hall and Jefferson 1976; Hebdige 1979; S. Cohen 1972; Willis 1977; Cashmore 1984). In general, these analyses show British working-class youth as inhabiting particular structural and cultural milieus that are defined by territory, objects, relations, and institutional and social practices. According to this theory, although they are born into and live within a subordinate culture, young working-class people come into contact with the dominant culture in schools, in jobs, and through the media. As youth subcultures emerge from the ranks of young, urban working-class people, they tell us something profound about the society in which they grow up and mature (Cashmore 1984, 18).

Hall and Jefferson's *Resistance through Rituals*, which traces the history of subcultures in postwar Britain, finds that they "appear only at particular historical moments: they become visible, are identified and labeled (either by themselves or others)" (1976, 14). In this model, youth subcultures attempt to resolve problems in class relations by what the authors call an "imaginary relation" that inverts the "real relations" that working-class youth cannot otherwise transcend. Again, subcultures appear as resistance to the dominant culture, primarily that of the middle class, while simultaneously aspiring to copy some aspects of that culture. Subcultures are shaped by youth, for people abandon them as they grow older and come to realize that the conditions of their lives most likely will not change.

All these Western models, however, are not applicable to societies in which no clear distinctions exist among the working, middle, and upper classes and in which, as in most of Latin America, hegemonic classes or states do not always remain static over a period of time. In the case of Venezuela, under the military and democratic governments of the twentieth century, the control of state resources and power has shifted among different groups of people (Carvallo, 1994; Coppedge 1994). A middle class has existed in some periods and not others, and the identity of this intermittent class has changed several times in response to political and economic change.

During the last three decades of democracy, state control has been held periodically by two political parties, the Acción Democrática (AD) and the Comité de Organización Política Electoral Independiente (COPEI). The growth of rampant corruption and the creation of a huge bureaucracy under these alternate ruling governments gave new meaning to the formation and fluidity of class structures. Venezuelan writer Elisa Lerner colorfully presents the formation of social classes:

> Our society is not chastised by the tight empire of old last names of the conquest and colonial times. Social classes are open windows, moved by the fast oscillation of political luck. Each party in power, each government—whether a democracy or a dictatorship—makes in its own way its own bourgeoisie. For example, the people from yesterday's government of Fulano are gone. Today you are a member of the bourgeoisie within the ruling period of Zutano. (Lerner 1995, 11)

In the last 30 years, Venezuela has seen periods of great economic wealth resulting from the increase in oil prices in the

1970's and times of crisis brought on by falling oil prices and the mismanagement of resources. In the Venezuela of the 1970's, various groups of people rose almost overnight to positions of economic and political power, and during the socioeconomic crisis of the past decade, class structures have undergone great changes. What was once considered, by Venezuelan standards, to be the middle class seems to be rapidly disappearing. This fluidity of class relations is a recent phenomenon in Caracas, and youth groups exemplify a different kind of class consciousness embedded in the social structure of the country.

In Venezuela it is very difficult to separate different youth styles into subsets of a single "culture" neatly bounded by class, age, and racial differences. Though people may have similar economic backgrounds and skin color, and though they may live close to one another, they do not necessarily think of themselves as the same people. Rather than identifying themselves with the dominant culture, they identify with different style groups. Hegemonic culture, in the last decade of the twentieth century, is not a single middle-class entity but, rather, contested, global, and transnational.

The development of style creates a space for opposition and resistance only to the extent that it recognizes the symbolic elaboration of contradictions, of transactions between forces that cannot be reconciled in reality. Styles in Caracas are not just expressions of subculture or rituals of resistance but idioms of the contradictions of society. They are about imaginary transcendence in the larger context of a violent city. A young man from a barrio sees that white-collar corruption is accepted and often praised; when the white-collar man is released from jail, he becomes a presidential candidate or he returns to his high-power job. The same young person believes that women want a man with a car, or at least a motorcycle. He thinks he looks cool—international—in his designer jeans. And he searches for ways to obtain what has become important to him without, in most cases, attempting to fight the structural order of things.

Monos and Woperós

As I discussed in Chapter 2, there are many different groups of young people on the Sabana Grande boulevard who occasionally converge at the Los Chorros or the Carolina centers. On Sabana Grande, the chupapegas are easily recognized by their ragged appearance and cans of glue; the monos (now also called jordans) and malandros have been recently associated with Nike shoes and NBA haircuts; and the woperós hanging outside the record stores are seen as clowns because of their long hair, baggy clothes, and wide belts. These groups of people have many things in common, starting with being young Venezuelans and spending a lot of time on the boulevard. The young people on the boulevard possess particular styles created and contested in the context of, to quote Arjun Appadurai, "a global cultural order, a world of many kinds of realism, some magical, some socialist, some capitalist, and some that are yet to be named" (Appadurai 1991, 197). These many realisms are presented through the mass media and processed through the imaginations of the young.

The diverse youth styles—personal and social—constitute a vocabulary of embodied class and race differences that many Venezuelans are unwilling to recognize. Young people on the streets shape and negotiate their self-representations through the symbolic capital of consumer goods available to them. The two woperós I met at the Carolina, Edwin and Gabriel (nicknamed Gabriela by the monos because of his long hair), acted very superior toward the rest of the group. Although they were at a detention center for reasons similar to those that brought in the rest of the youngsters, they continually argued that they were neither criminals nor monos like the rest of the guys there and they refused to participate in group activities except baseball, in which Edwin excelled.

It is clear that being categorized according to a particular style that defines itself through a collective identity emerges from the very nature of hegemonic culture. In such a culture, "The distance between classes and between societies on the fundamental question of ownership and control of the means of production does not disappear, but a dream is created that everyone can, actually or potentially, enjoy the superiority of the dominant culture" (García Canclini 1993, 8). This is a different situation from the one described in Hall and Jefferson's (1976) study of British youth subcultures, in which working-class youth want to be part of, but at the same time despise, middle-class culture. But, as the authors indicate, neither is it like the opposite case, in which the hippies went to the ghettos or tried to appropriate practices they associated with the working class.

Youth style in Caracas resides partly in the realm of fantasy, lived through the imaginations of the young. For young people in Caracas, style creates a powerful habitus (see Bourdieu 1977). The different groups have different dreams of domination and prosperity, contesting through dress, mannerisms, and statements what, for them, constitutes being superior. For woperós like Edwin and Gabriel, superiority is related, among other things, to knowledge of technomusic, love of ecology talk, and heavy black boots. For the monos at the Carolina, superiority relates to salsa music, Nike shoes, and familiarity with the lives of basketball heroes in the United States.

To the majority of the youngsters I met, I represented the more upper-class group, the woperós. In fact, they called me "Patricia Woper" and sometimes "gringuita." Although I dressed simply in Converse sneakers, jeans, a wide belt, and leotard-type shirts, because I thought they were appropriate for walking in the city, in the eyes of the youngsters on the boulevard and at the Carolina, these clothes defined me as a woperó. The young I worked with constantly pointed out that I lived in the east side of the city, drove a car (a 1983 Chevette), and supposedly liked woperó music.

On the boulevard the woperós sit outside the Recordland store, where they mumble the lyrics of English-language pop songs, such as Scorpion's "Winds of Change." They are interested in and usually have money with which to buy compact discs. If they go to educational institutions in the morning, they gather on the boulevard in the afternoons. Several woperós whom I met on the boulevard were school dropouts who had jobs handing out advertisements for stores selling "woperó" clothes. Woperós also hang out at university campuses or around the more upper-class malls.

Practices and the New Force of the Imagination

The monos I met listened primarily to salsa music, taking pride in their knowledge of salsa history, their records, and their pirated tapes. Those in the Carolina waited outside the supervisor's office to ask to get their tapes played so that their music could be heard coming out of the two powerful speakers.

When I asked them to write about their heroes, they all named salsa singers (except for one youngster, who put down Isaac Newton). They sang Jerry Rivera's songs and asked me to write down fragments they had memorized from Tito Rojas's lyrics for them, which they later sent to their girlfriends as additions to their love letters. Salsa songs provide young listeners at

the Carolina and along the boulevard with a set of public discourses (about emotional or romantic relationships, for example)
that both play back to them their own situations and experiences and provide a means of interpreting those experiences (cf.
Willis 1990, 69).

Felipe at the Carolina Center was the semiofficial writer of
love letters; his pals all asked him to write their letters for them.
Once he asked me to type Tito Rojas's lyrics to the song "¿Por qué
la vida es así?" (Why is life like this?) to add it to the letter he was
sending to one of his girlfriends, who was pregnant. A paragraph
of Felipe's letter reveals how, as Paul Willis states, young people
use song narratives as a conversational resource and to make
sense of their everyday lives (Willis 1990, 69):

> Sweetie, do you remember this song "Why Is Life Like This?"? I
> think you must. It means that since you and I have made several
> mistakes, we should forgive each other. Mamita, do you remember
> the letter you wrote to me in which you said that the heart of the
> beloved sought to feel with the other's heart? That is where I want
> to go, that is, to the deep wound I gave you so I can clean it with
> all the tears that are running down my face, which is the price for
> all the tears I made you shed. Joselyn, forgive me, because I never
> wanted to cause you such pain, I feel like the most despicable per-
> son in the whole world. You might say I'm exaggerating, but the
> truth is that I also caused myself immense pain. If you don't be-
> lieve me, I will show you next time we see each other. I hope there
> is a next time because I love you and you love me. We also have a
> mutual responsibility for "our beautiful son." You might say I am
> distrustful, but I truly love you and am jealous of all the people
> near you. Please, understand me, I am like a boy who dreams that
> you are mine and nothing else.[2]

For the monos at the Carolina, their imagined lives are related,
among other things, to salsa singers, North American basketball
players, and Venezuelan baseball figures. At the young age of

nineteen, Jerry Rivera, a Puerto Rican salsa singer, is famous in-
ternationally. His salsa songs about love constitute an imagined
life of quick success. In them he has money, fame, even a wife
and a baby. These songs are part of what Appadurai describes as
the new force of the social imagination that enables more people
in more parts of the world to consider a wider set of "possible"
lives than they could before (1991, 197).

During their stays at the Carolina Center, very few youngsters
relinquished their street styles, even though the consequences of
possessing certain items like expensive shoes could be dangerous. The youngsters even hired someone's mother, who was a
hairdresser, to come to the center and maintain their haircuts.
The meanings behind their styles were theirs, but the images
came from record companies, movies, and the NBA and its cor-
porate spin-offs. The possibility of attaining wealth and fame
through a sport, basketball, did not seem that distant to the
youngsters (even though in Venezuela few athletes become famous). In other words, these young people borrow the success of
others. Globally, more and more people are able to see their own
lives through the prism of possible lives offered by mass media,
communications, and commodities: "That is, fantasy is now a
social practice; it enters in a host of ways, into the fabrication of
social life many people form in many societies" (Appadurai
1990, 197). But this fantasy world, Appadurai cautions, does not
offer more "choices" (in the utilitarian sense) to more people or
more mobility and more "happy endings."

Radio Rochela, a humor television program that has been
shown for twenty-five years in Venezuela, continually recreates,
while making fun of, popular images of politicians, actors, delinquents, and so on.[3] This popular program describes and reinforces the images of both the mono and woperó groups. Two
very successful sketches created in 1993 examined woperós and
monos/jordans, from the point of view of their style, class, and

race. Closer examination of these sketches proves to be instructive. In the woperó sketch, a pair of male comedians (one of them the famous actor Emilio Lovera), with light skin and long haircuts, danced onto the scene to the rhythm of technomusic, wearing loose jeans and T-shirts with messages (usually ecological) or with the face of a classical composer such as Beethoven. The two woperós proceeded to make intellectual-sounding remarks—about their grief over Fellini's death and their concerns about the environment. Next a policeman named Matute came in to caution them about disturbing the peace, but the woperós managed to intimidate him by whispering in his ear about their influential relatives.[4] In the sketch, the woperós outsmart and make fun of Matute, who is presented as a charming fool.

The jordan sketch followed the successful woperó sketch. "Jordan" is the television name for monos and malandros, who sport NBA haircuts, Nike shoes, and Chicago Bulls jackets. Emilio Lovera also starred in this sketch, and when I visited the television station to see the filming, I watched him undergo an identity transformation from woperó to jordan in the makeup room. In this sketch, Lovera and his friend had blackened dark skin and the typical jordan style of clothing and hair. A policeman also appeared in this sketch, but this time to harass the jordans, who then made a statement about white-collar corruption and human rights. The sketch ended with the two jordans dancing off to the rhythm of salsa music.

These sketches were not just about superficial styles; they distinguished clearly between the woperó style with its implicit success as a transitional fashion and the jordan look as a lifestyle. For the upper-middle classes, the jordan sketch brought out the "otherness" of the monos. In the context of high delinquency rates and a state "war against the hampa," a "barbaric other" becomes popularized as the mono-malandro-jordan. In other words, being identified as a mono-malandro-jordan by the authorities parallels being considered the other, the delinquent, the one on whom the state and the dominant classes have declared a war.

On the boulevard, it is the monos who are stopped and harassed by the police. They cannot intimidate a policemen by whispering the name of an important relative in his ear. As Blas at the Carolina Center said about the police, "Just like the woperó, because they dress that way, they tell us that we are monos because we dress in brand-name clothes. A policeman sees you dressed in designer clothes and he stops you, saying to himself, 'This is a malandro.' Many malandros wear suits, but that guy happens to be a congressman."[5] For many youngsters, the mono-malandro-jordan styles—not mutually exclusive—are a way of living. Mono style is, above all, a source of status and identity in the context of the barrios and the city streets. Style plays different roles in the lives of youngsters. The woperós flaunt their funny dance, but many other resources for attaining prestige and status are available to them. As they grow older, they can move into positions of power like their parents, becoming bank clerks, businessmen, engineers, or lawyers. However, the general public assumes that when jordans grow older they will just continue to be monos. They will still look for chambas (odd jobs) in their informal economy and survive as best they can.

Consumption and Commodities of Violence

The monos-malandros-jordans of Sabana Grande and the Carolina Center acquire their symbolic capital through the commodities that are available to them. In a kind of bricolage, the monos pull together elements of material culture that are popularized by the mass media but that also allow for personal taste.

The interconnections can appear odd, as Japanese-owned North American basketball culture intermingles with the Venezuelan lower-class culture.

Style is also defined in relation to distinctive rituals of consumption. Human consumption clearly does not simply repeat the patterns of production; interpretation, symbolic action, and creativity are also part of consumption. And consumption, pleasurable and vital, is a creative process that involves a wide range of aesthetic considerations (Willis 1990, 21). For the monos, consumption is a physical action, involving transactions that are often violent. If we understand consumption as the overall effect of the appropriation of products (Castells 1980, 499, in García Canclini 1988), how do young people on the streets of Caracas formulate what commodities mean to them while developing their own identities in the process? What sorts of aspirations and dreams are constructed through the circulation of commodities? What social relations are mediated through commodities and consumption?

During my fieldwork, I was struck by the meanings those living on the streets attached to particular objects. Although many of these young people have few material possessions, they still manage to find objects that define them or perhaps remind them of who they are or want to be. When I first met Benjamín on the streets, he was always dirty from collecting cans and he had a serious bazuko addiction. He said that what served as a constant reminder that he could still get off the streets was the black plastic comb he kept in his back pocket. The comb was his sole material possession, and it embodied for him the possibility of a future as a clean and respectable citizen.

In some cases, as with Benjamín, commodities reflect the possibility of breaking with street life. What appear to be ordinary objects can spark transformations from street life to one that is more protected and intellectual. Edison, a street child since he was fourteen, made his transition at age seventeen to a respectable young man and advocate for children on the streets through a pair of glasses. Edison used to spend most of his days on the boulevard. When he decided to get off the streets, he tried to join the navy, but he was not yet eighteen. So he decided to change his image.

One day he came to an Association for Street Children's meeting wearing a pair of round intellectual-looking reading glasses. I told him he looked good in those glasses and asked him where he had gotten them. Edison replied that he got them at one of the video stores along Casanova Avenue: "They are reading glasses. A kid was wearing them and I asked him for them. He said he would lend them to me if I got him a hot dog." (Edison neither went back to the video store with the hot dog nor returned the glasses.)

Edison's stolen glasses symbolized for him his new attitude toward life as an intellectual educated young person. And his new persona also changed how others treated him. He often commented that the police did not stop him that often anymore now that he was well dressed in his work uniform and glasses. In the public light, he had become a different kind of citizen. When he gave speeches for the association, he looked very charismatic and quite convincing as a representative of the "good" way a street child could go. Edison explained his transformation when he and I were visiting his mother. He told us he felt as if he were from another world, that one night while he was looking at the stars a UFO landed and changed his old personality into the new one, the one with the glasses. Now everyone in the barrio said hello to him. Edison's mother agreed that the glasses had helped to give him his new image; somehow they made him look respectable. Neighbors would tell her they had seen Meliton, as they called him in the barrio, and that he had changed and now looked very serious.

Most the young people, however, were more concerned with the commodities related to the jordan style. The shoes, jackets, and jeans played important symbolic roles in their lives, and there is a surreal quality to this world of shoes and fashion in the midst of violence. In a group discussion at the Carolina I asked Lendel, a drug dealer, about how he was going to maintain his style when he got out of the center.

Lendel. By working

Patricia. Ay! Honestly, how much money do you think you will earn working?

Jerson. Nine thousand bolivares—fifty American dollars.

Lendel. Well, what can I do if I got used to living well?

Patricia. But you won't live with a lot of luxury earning nine thousand bolivares.

Jerson. You are always going to cause mischief because you are used to dressing in brand names.

Lendel. You can always sell drugs on the side.

Patricia. Ah, but that's illegal.

Lendel. Well, you can smuggle clothes.

Patricia. That is also illegal.

Felipe. If you have a good system, you can get the money to set up a clothes stand.

Patricia. So then, how do you see your options? How are you going to save to buy a pair of shoes that cost ten thousand bolivares if you will earn nine thousand?

Jerson. They cost seventeen thousand.

Felipe. If someone wants a pair of shoes that cost fifteen and a pair of pants, one has to fight for that.

Lendel. That is why you have delinquency.

What was most striking about this conversation was the young men's matter-of-factness. For these young people, the boundaries between legal and illegal acts were shaped by the scarcity in their lives. It is difficult, but important, to understand just what the young are willing to undertake and the boundaries they will transcend to obtain what they desire or consider a necessity. The numbers of young people ready to die defending their shoes or to kill to get other people's shoes in Caracas is shocking.[6]

It does not need to be stated that most young people in Caracas do not have the money to get what they want legally. They take risks to obtain the money or the things they want, risks that often go beyond what we could easily imagine. Obtaining money or goods often involves life-and-death situations. Stories of shoe-related deaths crop up in the early-morning news, at parties, and in conversations at the Carolina. What is shocking is that so many people are in a general sense of despair over the fact that anyone can be killed at any time for a pair of shoes. Even more startling, and a step further into the surreal, is the fact that so many youngsters would rather die than give up their shoes. Whether these acts are heroic or foolish begs the real question: Is life so valueless that it is worth giving up over a pair of Nikes?

The tragedies pile up. A mother, with immense sacrifice, provides money for her son's stylish shoes, and he gets killed for them. Pedro Guevara, at sixteen years old, was killed in January 1994, after being robbed two weeks before. The newspaper account says: "On December 24, the youngster had received a warning from a group who had tried to rob him of another pair of shoes. On that occasion, they only hit him with the butt of the gun. On this Wednesday afternoon, however, when the youngster ran away, the group fired the shot that hours later caused his death" (Aliana González, "Vivimos en una sociedad en donde parece normal que se mate por un par de zapatos" (We live in a society were it seems normal to kill for a pair of shoes), *El Nacional*, March 9, 1994). The mother, who had given him some money so that he could buy another pair of shoes for New Year's Eve, was most angry at the fact that he would have lived had he not lost so much blood after being turned away from so many hospitals.

These shoe-related tragedies reveal far deeper problems within the community. Disputes over territory and over women, for example, are mediated through shoes. Objects such as Nike shoes have become a form of dialogue and of violent exchange out of which new definitions of honor and life values are emerging. People who grew up a few houses from each other are now fighting and killing each other for shoes. In his diary, Elvis at the Carolina Center described how violent social relations are mediated through shoes.[7]

It was on April 16 of this year when because of an argument with some kids in my neighborhood, I had to make the biggest mistake of my life. That mistake was to kill one of the kids from the group who was bothering me and my compadre, a friend named Jhon.[8] Well, it all started when every time they saw me they tried to rob and humiliate me in front of whoever was around. It was then that I wanted revenge and I started to save money to buy a weapon to defend myself. Not many days went by before they found me with my friend and his brother and said:

—Take off your shoes and your jacket.

And my compadre said:

—Why are you going to rob my compadre?

And they said:

—Don't get involved Jhon, because this has nothing to do with you.

I said, "Look, I am not going to give you anything because I don't like it when someone tries to rob me," and one of the guys put a .38 to my stomach and said,

—Take off your shoes because I'm going to shoot you.

Then my friend said:

—Shoot me.

And he said:

—Not you, because I've known you since we were kids.

I got really upset and told them:

—Well, if you're going to do it, do it now, because I'm not going to give you my things.

Then the guy put the .38 even closer to me:

—Do you want to see how I'll shoot you?

—Well, just do it.

For a moment he was thoughtful, and then he shot me, and I started to move back and so did he, while saying:

—Guys, let's go. This guy is lucky.

As soon as I realized that the gun had misfired, I hid behind a car and they started to shoot again. Then I ran to the Plan. My compadre, who was all scared, arrived later and asked me if they had shot me, and I said no, and at that moment I wanted to buy a gun even more.[9]

Keeping your shoes, as in Elvis's case and in other cases at the Carolina Center, is proof of your masculinity and your toughness.

As with Elvis, certain commodities generate envy and resentment among those who do not have them. Jerson referred to the resentment directed at those capable of obtaining particular commodities as *rescordia*, a new word for envy:

Rescordia—they have rescordia of us. The place where we lived was a good place, but then we started to get money. We all had guns, and people envied us. We had bought a car; we had motorcycles and women. However, there was always the tough guy who had to shoot at us. Even when I'm in the mood to be left alone, there's always somebody saying, "Look at that guy on a motorcycle, he must have money. Let's get him."[10]

Gun Fetishism

On one occasion I brought a couple of art books to the Carolina Center, hoping to provoke some discussions. I asked a group of eight youngsters what they thought art was. Felipe answered that art was something one saw at a museum. El Chivo said that it was sculpture. But the rest of the group rapidly insisted that art was guns, that guns were pieces of art. Jerson said that guns were more than art to him and that he was "enamorado de su nueve" (in love with his nine-millimeter). In other discussions it appeared that guns could have personalities of their own. Not only could guns be the object of love, they could also be held accountable for a person's death. When a gun has been used to kill someone, the young men say "llevan un muerto encima" (they carry a dead person), as if the murder had been the gun's doing. By placing the responsibility of a crime on the gun, the youngsters deny their participation in violent events, which often do not make complete sense to them—the accidental shooting of a friend while playing with a gun, the killing of another youngster who constantly threatened you, and so forth.

Interest in guns and weapons in general is strong among young barrio people and those living on the streets. The knowledge these youngsters have about weapons is extensive and precise. They know which weapons are the most effective and which are considered most "masculine."[11] They can tell you what all the different guns cost and how to obtain them, and they also know what types of armaments police and national guards use and what weapons those authorities sell.

For young barrio people, having a gun in their hands can represent ideal manhood. Having or using a gun marks a transition from being an insignificant person or the "good boy" into a "real man." The gun itself provides not just status but also the possibility of obtaining the commodities needed to feel important: motorcycles, shoes, clothes, and so on. More than that, possessing a gun helps a young person feel he is "somebody" and to assert his identity as such in a society in which he is marginalized. Especially with guns such as the nine-millimeter, young individuals acquire a sense of power over others. But the power they have over others is very real and very frightful: armed youngsters, with their exchange of flying bullets, impose daily curfews on the public; people have to be told when to go inside so they won't be killed. In the same manner, guns empower young people to divide community spaces at will.

The youngsters I met at the Carolina believed that using guns was the only way for them to gain respect. Some of them even suggested that this was a universal belief because they had seen it in foreign movies. They felt that using guns was the only option for young people like themselves with few opportunities to have the privileged life of the wealthy. The "logic" that guns are ultimately the only resource for the everyday survival of the "good barrio boy" surfaced in a conversation I had with the Carolina group.

> *Lendel.* What I'm saying is that the good guy doesn't make it in our world.
>
> *Jerson.* People used to harass me, but after I bought the gun no one did anymore.
>
> *Patricia.* Why did they harass you?
>
> *Jerson.* Ah! Because I was a good guy, I didn't bother anyone. When they saw that I had a gun, they said, "I won't bother that guy because he can kill me."
>
> *Lendel.* Didn't I tell you the good person cannot live in this world?
>
> *Patricia.* Do you think all the good people are dead?
>
> *Lendel.* Those who live at the barrio are. When you are young you cannot be so innocent, because there is always someone who wants to humiliate you.
>
> *Jerson.* Yes, they always want to humiliate you.
>
> *Lendel.* It is like what happened to Oveiwin. He was good worker who had to realize he couldn't continue to be that way.

When youngsters cannot see any way to solve a problem or to avoid harassment, they feel a gun provides the only hope. Furthermore, it is a resource that is approved and admired and considered macho. Most youths consider firearms their only guarantee of surviving on the streets of Caracas.

For the youngsters living on the boulevard, especially the

younger chupapegas, the weapon of survival is the Gillette razor blade cut in half. They carry both halves inside their mouths. I always felt sick watching them talk, sometimes eat, while wiggling the blades inside their mouths. When the boys encounter a culebra on the boulevard with whom they have to fight, they put on a fighting performance. They pull out the blades and lower themselves, moving their flexed arms up and down and striking a blow whenever possible. Edison explained that in a razor-blade fight the right side of your chest faces your opponent's, since you have to guard your "clock" (heart). Edison carries his blades every time he goes to the boulevard because he feels there are many *equivodados* (mistaken ones) hanging put there. The equivocados often think that because Edison is clean and well dressed, he is an easy target for assault.

It is important to note that the culture of weapons spreads beyond groups of youngsters of few economic resources. Today in Venezuela, there is an increasing obsession with owning weapons as a matter of personal safety—"just in case"—and there are promotions to join shooting centers. Thus the shootings spread.

Style and the Use of Language

The young people I worked with use language very creatively. Language functions as a kind cultural marker that situates speakers for themselves, for their peers, and for society (Hewitt 1986). Language and gesture are important components of the style of the chupapegas, malandros, monos, or now jordans; they are associated with a code belonging to the streets and not always exclusively to the young. It is what the people at the Carolina describe as "lenguaje malandro." Roger Hewitt's term, "markers of identity," which he uses in his study of the relationship between language and interracial friendships in Britain (1986), is rather too strong to be applied here, but certainly young people in Caracas often do create in language, as they do in dress, cultural terms through which they wish to present and see themselves.

The television program *Radio Rochela* poked fun at and popularized the language style of the woperós and the jordans. The woperós think they sound very sophisticated when they show enthusiasm by saying, "me encanta, me encanta, me encanta" (I love it, I love it, I love it), and they give the word *chamo* (kid)—a popular way of referring to a peer or someone younger—a new intonation that is supposed to sound sophisticated—"saamo." In the *Radio Rochela* jordan sketch, the two characters moved their arms incessantly and repeated the phrase "Chamo, ¿Cuál es?" (Hey, kid! What's up?) Of course, the very presentation of these and other woperó-jordan words and gestures on a popular television program inspired youngsters who were neither woperós nor jordans to imitate these styles. Whether media exposure will lead woperós and jordans to change their styles remains to be seen, but certainly the lenguaje malandro will continue to evolve in response to cultural influences.

It was Rodilla, the fourteen-year-old hero of *Por estas calles . . .* (the soap opera discussed in Chapter 1), who has most recently captured and spread the malandro language style. Some of the young people I interviewed argued that Rodilla exaggerated the body gestures, but they continued to watch the soap opera because of him, and indeed, he owes a great deal of his success to the fact that so many young people in the barrios are such avid fans. Rodilla also appealed to wider audiences because he sympathetically portrayed the vulnerability of the young people seen around the city and categorized as street children, monos, and malandros.

It took me a long time to pick up street slang, and the youngsters constantly laughed at my attempts. It was difficult to learn because new words were always cropping up that had the most amazing origins. For example, at the Carolina, the group always referred to Lendel and others as *maquive*. The word describes someone who exaggerates all the dangerous things that have happened to him, things that never seem to harm him. When I asked the group where the term came from, one of the boys responded, "Haven't you ever seen a program on TV called *Maguiver*, where the guy does lots of things and nothing ever happens to him?" I finally realized they were speaking about the North American action program *MacGyver*.

The malandro language is not all new, and often it is not even Venezuelan in origin, but Colombian, such as the word *sicario*, which means young assassin. Much of it is a reworking of old argot often associated with delinquency. Rodríguez, who grew up at juvenile centers, wrote a record of "delinquent" argot for me, along with his own explanation for its development: "I learned that the delinquent code was a necessity because every thief has to be secretive about his intentions. That way he is free from the indiscreet ear because he has a cryptographic vocabulary. I also figured out that when somebody decides to start on the path to delinquency, he adopts the kind of language that will allow him to show that he is as cunning as everyone else" (Rodríguez 1974, 116). Studies of street talk in Colombia also provide an insight into the creativity, power, and wide use of the malandro language (see Granados Tellez 1974; Muñoz and Pachón 1980; Aptekar 1988; Salazar 1990). Some of the similarities between the vocabularies of Colombia and Venezuela are striking, and in both countries the malandro language is continually evolving not only as part of a creative process within transnational culture but also, as Rodríguez points out, for pragmatic reasons.

Many of the youngsters at the Carolina, especially the less physically strong, manipulate language and gesture to defend themselves. On the inside, language gives them power and status. Constantino, for example, was a fifteen-year-old who clearly stood out from the group because of his small physique and his "good-boy" manners. He was at the center for killing a minor with a baseball bat because the latter had come to rob Constantino's house while carrying a gun. Most everyone at the center respected and liked him, even though often he was the butt of jokes because of his buckteeth. But he grew very skilled at responding, in malandro language, to any attack with a fury that occasionally bordered on the comical. Furthermore, without being a *sapo* (whistleblower), he used the argot to manipulate information he had gathered about others in order to stop his attackers. For instance, on one occasion León and others were ridiculing Constantino for his thinness and his lack of dexterity with a basketball. Constantino said, "No vengas a hablar, llorón" (Wimp! Don't you talk. . . .), reminding León of how he had cried in fear like a baby for several days when they had shared a cell with other minors at police headquarters. León immediately stopped the harassment and convinced the others to do the same by changing the subject.

Body Style: Space, Time, and Mutilation

At various points in their lives, the young people I worked with were dispossessed and displaced. Those living on the streets of Caracas had very little material wealth, since they had few places to store their possessions and were constantly moving from one place to another, as police, angry shop owners, or culebras drove them away.[12] Those I met at the Carolina Center generally had more wealth, and though often precarious, they also had homes. However, one of the effects of living at the center was a temporary loss of their sense of body and personal space. In the context of everyday violence, the individual bodies of those living on the streets and at the Carolina, which for some is the only home they have, are continuously manipulated. Violence is exerted on young bodies by other street people, by police, by national guards, by psychologists, and by social workers. Partially in response to this outward violence, the youngsters subject their own young bodies to violence both for aesthetic purposes and as survival techniques. From body violence emerges a body style that is considered tough and masculine but that also makes them vulnerable to further abuse.

Wounds and scars are the signifiers of a terrible street violence, the publicly recognized perpetrators of which are a reified hampa or the marginal police, who sometimes come from the same neighborhood. The wounds and scars on young bodies are the ultimate metaphors for the surreal nature of daily violence in Caracas. Who is cutting the bodies of these youngsters? How can this terrible proof of violence be interpreted as representing part of a style?

Almost all the young people I studied, especially those who lived along the boulevard, had many body scars of all shape and sizes. Most of the scars were the result of fights, but some were self-induced, partly as a kind of self-protection but also as a reflection of personal style. Self-inflicted wounds are an effective tactic for escaping the authorities, since the police and national guards are reluctant to take to their headquarters a person who is bleeding; the authorities fear, especially when the person involved is a minor, that their cars or uniforms might get stained and that they will later be held accountable for the minor's wounds.

Edison has many body scars, which define him, in his own words, as a street warrior, one who has cleverly escaped the police on several occasions. Edison proudly points out a series of short cuts on his left wrist as proof of his cunning and toughness. He was robbing a store along the boulevard when the police spotted him. He left and ran hard until he entered the parking lot of a building, where some night guards looked at him suspiciously. Edison was afraid the police were getting closer, so he grabbed the half razor blade in his mouth and repeatedly cut his left arm, making a series of short, diagonal incisions, knowing that if he was bleeding when the police caught him, they would very likely let him go. "Others are like Pechundío who knocks his head against a wall when he sees police, and they think he is crazy and let him loose."

Scarification is very common in many societies. Culturally sanctioned mutilation occurs in a variety of contexts, most frequently in adolescent initiation rites. Many anthropologists (Ottenberg 1989; Turner 1969; Van Gennep 1915; Whiting, Kluckhohn, and Anthony 1958) have generally understood the purpose of these rites to be the acquisition by adolescents of new social roles and status necessary for the orderly preservation of communal life. Mutilation—often quite brutal and painful—is an integral component of these rites and seems to serve several important functions. It heightens the drama and significance of the ritual, focuses attention on the adolescents, and allows them to demonstrate their inner strength. It is also a warning about the power of the social group.

Scars among young people in Caracas signify the youngsters' personal journeys on the streets. As Edison puts it, "For street people it is important to have scars. They serve as a sign of who you are when you fall into the División de Coche (police headquarters) or somewhere else." People on the streets see each of their scars as part of a record of their life histories. Each wound and the ensuing scar has its own story; it constitutes a memory of a violent event. People living on the streets do not discuss their life histories in terms of their houses, their cars, or the courses they've taken in college like better-off young people do. Their narratives often emerge from the body. Cheo, now thirty years old and still living on the boulevard, narrates his life on the streets in relation to the scars he has. His life history is illustrated not through photographs in an album or fancy possessions, but through the degradation of his body. Every time I asked Cheo to tell me about his life on the streets he began by talking about the several scars on his face.

Cheo moved with his mother and his stepfather to Caracas from Maracaibo when he was twelve years old. "At that point," he says, "I was a healthy person. I worked and everything. I worked distributing cards and newspapers on one of those little trucks you no longer see in this city." Soon after he arrived in Caracas, he started to spend time on the streets, because, according to Cheo, his father paid no attention to him and his mother treated him like a "troublemaker." Cheo began to drink and to sniff glue with his new street friends. Later on, things got worse at the reeducation centers, though for a time he was all right: "I had a place to sleep and they gave me three meals a day. I have been in Los Chorros and in La Guaira; in the second place we did what we wanted. But later I killed a PTJ (policeman) when I was fifteen and I was sent to La Planta, where I spent seven years. I was a *pichurrito* (little one) and they called me Chino because I was *chinito* (looked Chinese)."

After being released from La Planta, Cheo returned to the boulevard. Occasionally he visited his mother and stepfather, who were "gente bien" (well-off people), though they were not crazy about seeing him. During Cheo's last visit, his parents lent him their Toyota, and he sold it to buy drugs and alcohol. He was drinking more and more as a way of coping with the injury to his face:

I drank to forget. Do you know I can't eat red meat anymore? Here, touch here, so you can see that it is broken. I still need another operation, but I got tired of them. I got tired of waiting, one week then another, and I finally left. I had a friend at the Hospital

Universitario named Dr. Carmona, and every time I went there she would say, "Fernández, how can it be you again?" She was very nice to me. I went in first with a broken arm, then with a cut on my back, and then the face. I lost several teeth but I did get that fixed, because women pay a lot of attention to that.

Cheo was very self-conscious about the deep cut on the left side of his cheek and chin, which a culebra had given him a while back. Recently several women had told him it was time to change his life: "Just look at you now, Cheo, you are all cut up." He was afraid to steal now out of fear of being punished. Recently the injury to his face had become worse and he had a new small scar on his face. Cheo had acquired this new scar when he had pinched a woman on the buttocks while he was drunk and she had kicked him several times in the face. His scars were a very real source of shame to Cheo.

Although scars can cause shame, their signifying power, as in many other societies, is partially aesthetic. Scars are a self-organized practice with social meanings. Paul Bohannon discovered that the Tiv of Nigeria, unlike some tribes that produce scars as distinctive tribal marks, scar themselves, at least on a conscious level, primarily for aesthetic reasons (Bohannon 1956). The procedure is revered not only for its beautiful results but also for its indication of a willingness to endure pain. Although most scar designs on Tiv females are traditional, unchanged for generations, for men, scarification styles tended to change from one generation to the next. Similarly, I found that some of the boys I knew were scarifying themselves with special designs, similar to tattoos.

I met Angelito at the Carolina when he was seventeen. One afternoon he came into the library and asked me if he could join the group making cards for Mother's Day. (The others in the group made fun of him, for he was a street person from the Sabana Grande boulevard who supposedly didn't have a mother.)

As he worked on his card, I couldn't help noticing the deep keloid scar in the shape of a cross on his left arm. Angelito explained that he and two other friends had made the same tattoo on their arms to assure their partnership. He said the similar scars on their arms symbolized their friendship and their power. Tattoo parlors are not common in Caracas, and skin cutting serves as an accessible, if more painful, substitute.

In his study of self-mutilation, Armando Favazza (1987) concludes that inmates of penal institutions are at a high risk for self-cutting. He argues that there is an increased incidence of self-mutilation in prisons both because of the psychopathology among institutionalized persons and because of the nature of institutional life. Feelings of desperation, demoralization, despair, and boredom among inmates may lead them to self-mutilation as a way to cope with these feelings (1987, 139). However, at police headquarters, and even at the Carolina Center, I seldom saw or heard about self-mutilation. In fact, the few times I heard about it was when the workers at the Carolina classified wounds as self-mutilation to avoid either finding out what happened or taking better care of an attacked individual. Usually skin cutting occurred in the centers when one youngster or group of youngsters did it to another. It did not appear to me that scarification within institutions was solely the result of psychopathology as Favazza implies, nor was it simply an aesthetic practice.

Inside institutions of violence scars can be very useful to the young. Scars embody potential toughness, which helps youngsters to avoid getting harassed and, in the worst of cases, raped—popularly called dancing "el baile del tubito."[13] Scars can help youngsters dominate space and the few resources available in the cell through intimidation and not just brute force. When young persons are caught by the authorities, they are first taken to police headquarters, of which the most famous and dreaded is the División de Coche. I was never allowed entrance there, because the policeman or the social worker in charge would say that I was not a family member (the police would end up eating the sandwiches I had brought for my informants), but many boys have described it to me. Recently caught young people—chupapegas, monos, malandros, or jordans—are all placed together—approximately eighteen at a time—in cells no larger than an average room and are given little food or water. In these crowded conditions, in which one has to fight for space and for food, scars are an immediate and obvious way to show what kind of *cartel* (reputation) one has outside.

There is more fighting in these overcrowded División cells than at the INAM centers. In División, the inmates, dispossessed by their families and humiliated by the police, have only their bodies and their innate creativity to help them assert themselves in the cells. Often boys who were culebras in the barrios or shantytowns are placed together, and in their struggle to control their new territory, they develop strategies aimed at their enemy's body. They make their own weapons. A common one is the *cebollita* (little onion); this consists of a bunch of matchstick heads wrapped in a plastic bag, which is then ignited on the skin of a sleeping enemy.

I readily admit that the youngsters' feelings of desperation, demoralization, despair, and boredom are exacerbated inside División, but unlike Favazza, I also believe that the struggles that occur in División have more to do with the rules of the streets—in the context of brutal institutional dynamics—than with individual pathologies. The practices of mutilation against both self and other play key roles within penal institutions. It is not just about reflections of life histories, pathologies, or aesthetics: when faced with the brutality of División, the youngsters' attitude is one of survival, of hitting before getting hit. And the body is all the youngsters have when they are thrown in there.

Monos and New Dimensions of Contemporary Torture

Although young people's testimonies of violence point out the violence they themselves are capable of, more often their stories speak of the greater violence brought upon them by authorities, police, psychologists, national guards, and doctors, stories that emerge in relation to styles, their bodies, and stigmas.

The phenomena of abuse and torture can be perceived of as diverse, comical, matter of fact, gratuitous, category based, and willful. When I talk about torture, I do not mean it only as an allocation of force. The torture young people in Caracas suffer is pervasive and often goes unrecognized by those in power.

I came to Plaza Venezuela one Saturday afternoon for an association meeting and found Edison sitting by himself. He was wearing jeans, black sneakers, and a half-open leather jacket that was too small for him. I could see a large scratch on his chest. He was testing his jaws by moving them, saying that everything hurt, and pointing to a red bump he had on his head. He then described to me how he had been mistreated by the police and the medical establishment after he stole a stroller with a friend. The abuse he endured was not perceived as such by the perpetrators, but as the only commonsensical way a mono or a malandro caught in the act of stealing should be treated.

> *Edison.* I can hardly open my mouth, everything hurts, my legs hurt.
> *Patricia.* What happened?
> *Edison.* I fell off a motorcycle.
> *Patricia.* What?
> *Edison.* I stole a police bike.
> *Patricia.* No, how?
> *Edison.* I'm just kidding—how do you think I'm going to steal a police motorcycle? I was on the boulevard and Antonio told me he had stolen a baby stroller and asked me to go in with him. I

> thought it was a good idea to have some money, because I
> needed a haircut. We were walking down the street, and the
> owner of the stroller saw us and recognized the stroller. The po-
> lice came after us and Antonio disappeared, but they got me and
> kicked me three times and threw gas at me, which irritated my
> eyes. There were shots and everything. A store owner, and I
> know who he is, started to shoot.

The three police officers took Edison to the house of the
stroller owner, who was dropping his wife and baby off at a
friend's before deciding whether to press charges. The police decided to take Edison to Cotiza (another institution where prisoners initially go). Edison was riding on the back of one of the police motorcycles, and he wanted to jump off. The officer, guess-
ing his intention, told Edison that if he jumped off, he would
make sure to run over his body with the motorcycle.

The police took Edison to a hospital to have the injuries they
had inflicted on him checked on. There the officers started what
Edison calls "a psychological war." One of the policemen asked
him, "How do you want to be killed, judicially or sexually? Do
you want a shot of adult semen?" Another one said, "I'm going
to hit you, I'm going to throw tear gas at you, I'm going to cut off
your ear." When Edison finally got to the hospital room, where
the doctor was waiting for him, he decided to act like a madman.
He walked around the room moving his head sideways and re-
peating, "I am going to kill myself" until the doctor told the
officers to watch him because "that child must have serious psychological problems—it's not normal for a sixteen-year-old to
say those things." Edison was laughing now as he was recounting how he had fooled the doctor. In the end, the stroller owner
decided not to press charges, and the police let Edison go.

Foucault has argued that power is localized and that resistance
is inherent in power relations, which, by definition, allows much
resistance to be co-opted (1978, 95–96). The boys' self-scarring or

Edison's performance may be "weapons of the weak" (Scott 1985) and the only forms of resistance available to them, but to the people running the reformatories or the policemen, they constitute evidence that the boys are crazy and dangerous, reinforcing rather than breaking down the hegemonic model of who these young people are.

Sometimes the way Edison and others are disciplined and punished, both physically and psychologically, by the keepers of the state constitutes abuse as spectacle more than as anything else. Daily shows are put on for those walking along the boulevard. Policemen, Uzis in hand, stop and harass those who appear to them as suspicious monos-malandros-jordans, especially if the youths have dark skin. There are abusive spectacles like that of Edison recoiling in pain from the kicks he received after stealing a stroller while a shop owner, desperate because of the robberies he has suffered in the past, fires his gun into the air as a form of retaliation.

The effects of punishment, abuse, and torture linger in the imagination and reverberate in the youngsters' psyches. Edison suffered from recurring nightmares about the violence in his life. He often woke up at three A.M. from a dream in which he was riding very fast on a motorcycle that was crushed by monsters coming out of the walls. He referred to this dream as "psycho-terror." While Benjamín was living on the streets, he remembers having dreams in which the Pantanero police corps were chasing him on their motorcycles along the garbage-infested banks of the Guaire River. Troy from Sabana Grande often came to the association meeting terrified that he had swallowed the razor blades he kept in his mouth for self-protection.

At the Carolina I repeatedly heard stories about the torture young people endure while at police headquarters. Ruben, who was seventeen years old, told me, "I have lived things that I never could have imagined. Taking police beatings, the torture to force you to talk and tell the truth. Even if you tell the truth you get beaten anyway. Sometimes you can't even take the torture, there are so many hard blows."[14] The youngsters told of how, when they were held captive in "la jaula de King Kong" (King Kong's cage), they were beaten with baseball bats through mattresses placed on top of them or sprayed with cold water. However the youngsters reconstruct what has happened to them in the centers or on the streets, what remains clear is that they are the target of the most pernicious physical and psychological abuse. They suffer from a violence that is directed at the marginal, the chupapegas, the monos, the malandros, the jordans, or, as the police would put it more simply, at the "carajito coño'e madres" (little bastards).

What is most horrifying about this abuse, not that torture or abuse is justifiable in any context, is that these young people in Caracas are not beaten and harassed for interrogatory purposes; there are no truths to be extracted. Rather, the violence is mostly punitive. The authorities inflict pain on these youngsters' bodies out of their frustration over their rapidly deteriorating living conditions, the political crisis, and rampant corruption.

In one of his writing assignments, Lendel told me what happened to him once when he was caught for hurting another youngster.

> On January 16 at 5 A.M., a police group came into the house where I was staying with some other minors. We were taken to police headquarters, where they tortured and mistreated us in every way possible. They used plastic bags, tear gas, and the traditional torture of the hanging eagle—putting us in a room and hanging us from a pillar with our feet in the air. After eight days we were taken to court, where they decided to send us on January 25 to a minor's detention center.[15]

At times it appears that not just the police but also the social technicians at the centers, many doctors and nurses at the hospitals, and the judges and other people with power over the minors abuse young people out of frustrations over the order of things or in a transference of the violence they themselves experience in their everyday lives. The police understand the difficulty of controlling violent conflict in the barrios, some of which is caused by the officers themselves. But because the police are categorized in the media as corrupt, violent, and inefficient, they feel compelled (to compensate for the criticism they receive) to provide solutions. And the people they can most easily harass are the chupapegas, the monos, and the malandros walking along the boulevard. Walli from the boulevard explains it clearly:

> The police used to be less violent. Now they want to kill all the minors. Now they catch you on the streets and in front of everybody they throw tear gas at your face. They also beat and kick you. They kick you as if you were a dog. They hit you, but they don't dare enter the barrios; they don't dare deal with the malandros of Pinto Salinas; they are cowards who don't dare to go to Pinto.[16]

Doctors and nurses at the hospitals are equally frustrated with the current crisis, in which there are fewer resources every day. The easiest people to reject or mistreat are the youngsters of the boulevard, since hardly anyone would find the mistreatment unfair or even cruel. In the hospitals, as elsewhere, these children are considered pests, demons, malandros, monos, barbaric, lost causes, and few of them speak up in protest. Therefore, these youngsters become the recipients of violence—from beatings to psychological abuse—that is generally accepted and even approved of.

In Venezuela people do not necessarily perceive social mobility in the same way as in the European system of mobility among the working, middle, and upper classes. In a country where transnational consumer culture came hand in hand with oil wealth, social mobility has been constructed in terms of symbolic capital. Power and status are embodied in particular styles. For the wealthy, cellular phones and expensive cars represent social status. For the youngsters from the barrios and those on the Sabana Grande boulevard, guns, motorcycles, and brand-name clothes represent status or power. The young mono may live in a rancho in the barrios, but if he has a gun and Nike shoes, he does not consider himself working class, poor, or marginal—he has a style. For young people on the streets the mono, malandro, and jordan styles are a way of living that transcends making a "fashion statement." Although they also mark youngsters as delinquents or potential delinquents, styles give them an identity and a sense of belonging in a world that offers them little else.

Conclusion

In reflecting on the central problem of representing the complex social realities and practices of poor children and adolescents in the rapidly changing and interconnected world of Caracas, I have tried to move beyond psychological and journalistic analyses. I have examined identity, selfhood, and values not just as mental categories but as expressions of the youngsters' experiences and relationships that generate choices and decisions in the current context of national economic crisis. I have not tried to emphasize the social, economic, or individual misery of young people on the streets or the violence they are capable of, and I hope that I have shown that the young people's imaginations and tactics, shaped by both local and global forces—police beatings, video-game stores, Chicago Bulls products, salsa songs, or glue sniffing—can lead us to new ways of thinking about youth in relation to consumption, the body, discipline, and punishment.

It is well known that many young people in Latin America suffer from malnutrition, disease, and abuse. More than that, it is known that lower-class children and children of particular ethnicities suffer the most from these life-damaging conditions. Nonetheless, the more powerful classes cling, however ambivalently, to distinct constructions of childhood that involve a set of universal rights. The discursive ambiguity about childhood and children serves the purpose of perpetuating social, economic, and political relations that are detrimental to many young people throughout the world. Dominant groups maintain views on childhood, which have evolved over the last three centuries, that disempower youngsters the most.

In Latin America today, the streets are more than a locus for businesses, entertainment, conversation, games, and socializing. The streets of Latin American nations also witness immense poverty, inequality, and everyday violence. In Caracas, youngsters categorized as "street children" by the media, the state, and by public and private organizations are mostly those sleeping on the streets, such as the chupapegas who live on Sabana Grande boulevard looking ragged, causing havoc, begging, playing video games and sniffing glue. In the popular imagination, these street children represent an emerging form of marginalized childhood and provoke in the public contradictory sentiments of pity and disgust (Aptekar 1988).

Discourses about these "street children" revolve around two main ideas. The first relates to the possibility of finding ways to "recover" these children from the streets and make them into "real citizens." So far, "recovering" young people from the streets has meant simply pushing them back into the shantytowns or containing them in closed institutions. The second idea involves a generalized belief that these children, already considered delinquents or potential delinquents, cannot be recovered; they are lost to society and therefore must be gotten out of the way before they "take over." Several government agents propose reducing the age for criminal responsibility from eighteen to fourteen or sixteen, which would allow them to place young transgressors in jails with adults for longer periods than they spend in centers for youths. Although not as pernicious as the Brazilian death squads, who randomly go about murdering poor children on the streets, there are extermination groups that make it their business to kill young people on the streets of Caracas.

These youngsters living on the streets, away from formal institutions such as schools, transgress by their mere presence the hegemonic social order. They are growing up on their own, hence defying the idealized model of the nuclear Western family. And these children are taking over spaces, such as the Sabana Grande boulevard, that were designed not for them, but for tourists and the middle class. In a broader sense, however, "street children" have become more than the just transgressors of order, time, and space. In the collective consciousness of those who live in Caracas, these children, increasingly a part of the urban landscape, are the most visible, tragic, vulnerable, and dangerous evidence of the imminent deterioration of the infrastructure and standards of living in one of the richest Latin American nations.

In the capital city of Caracas, with its population of four million people, the number of youngsters growing older on the streets is much larger than the few thousand categorized as "street children." The socialization process of barrio youngsters increasingly takes place on the streets rather than within the family or the school; it is on the city streets that great numbers of young people from the shantytowns are developing friendships and networks. For all those classified as street children, an equal number of young people from the barrios are fending for themselves—by finding jobs or chambas as shoe shiners, buhoneros, hot dog vendors, and books sellers, by working as artisans, or by stealing and selling drugs.

These barrio youngsters, usually older than the glue sniffers on the boulevard, are more threatening to the communities where they spend their days. They are not portrayed by the media, private and public organizations, and the state as "street children." Rather, they are called shantytown monos, malandros, and jordans and are blamed for the terrible violence in the city. Particular discourses on barrio youth allow radically different understandings of violence to emerge within social groups not sharing the same experience. The current focus is on these young people as the barbaric "other," capable of car thefts, barrio wars, or shoe-related killings; much less attention is paid to the daily violence these youth of few economic resources are subjected to.

The great majority of citizens in Caracas live in crowded spaces. They live in barrios, where often the basic services such as running water are lacking. Up in the hills surrounding the valley of Caracas, the great majority of the population endures long lines to catch the Jeeps that will take them down to their jobs; they have to walk up rickety steps to get back to their ranchos, which are so flimsy that they sometimes fall apart when it rains. In this setting, young people are finding imposed options, such as working as office boys for minimum wage, unacceptable. They take to the streets to create their own opportunities and to reproduce violence for reasons that make sense to them. This violence exists in the context of a violent city and a current sociopolitical crisis that reduces their access to basic services. Furthermore, these youngsters experience abject poverty in the vicinity of a small, but very visible, elite with great wealth.

Because of a lack of resources and a resigned acceptance of their situation, shantytown youngsters do not have access to certain places. But at the same time, the terror the young monos, malandros, and jordans can create, along with that of the authorities who try to repress them, is bringing about a reconfiguration of city space. Caracas has been fragmented into countless pockets of "red zones," some of which are in the barrios, some not. Moreover, those in wealthier neighborhoods who fear the hampa are raising their walls, closing off their streets, and adjusting to their own self-imposed curfews.

Chupapegas, malandros, monos, or jordans live on the streets partly because of poverty—that is, to find the piece of bread to tame their hunger—and some come to the streets because of intolerable family situations. Many youngsters become school dropouts early and begin the life of malandreo, hoping for fast rewards. Perhaps their lives will be awfully short, but some youngsters find a life of fast money made on the streets more appealing than a long life of hard work for only one hundred dollars a month. They come to the streets searching for what they belief is a better life—living through their imaginations. With the guns, motorcycles, the razor blades, Nikes, and Walkmans, monos, malandros, and jordans dream they are in control of their lives. Sometimes the chupapegas on the boulevard prefer to go hungry to play video games. And when they do eat, they prefer soup, McDonald's hamburgers, or Arturo's fried chicken. These youngsters can get an offer of a good place to live and they still might go back to the streets—"it's more fun." Despite the abuse young people endure on the streets, they believe they are finding freedom. In other words, the streets offer their imaginations a wider range of possibilities.

Official discourses describe the priorities and practices of young people on the streets in relation to a loss of morality. Nonetheless, the current morality of young people on the streets is the dominant morality of the last three decades of "The Great Venezuela." The youngsters' recent memory is one of generalized corruption, impunity, and consumerism, all in the name of gaining power and status. Powerful role models—presidents, politicians, bankers, and colonels—are continually involved in scandals. State authorities who have taken other people's money and government finances end up unpunished and living in comfort in Costa Rica, Europe, or the United States. Is it so surprising, then, that youngsters also seek quick success and money? Now shantytown jordans and corrupt politicians share the same set of morals.

Crying "loss of morality" and "the collapse of the family" are just two of the discursive strategies used to support a type of social control through which the state attempts to maintain its force and legitimacy. In this period of volatility, when using public spaces to protest utter desperation at the systemic collapse has become more common, the presence of young people on the streets is threatening. The state exerts social control partly through the brutal force of operativos and partly through general abuse at the hands of the police. Within this repressive context, the policy toward minors on the streets is to incarcerate and to punish.

The state, dominant classes, and various organizations are failing in their attempts to deal with these young transgressors of the social order, whom they both homogenize and objectify. They seem unable to make a connection between the behavior of young people on the streets and the complex social fabric of present-day Venezuela, where youngsters are influenced and attracted by things far beyond the geographical boundaries of the Sabana Grande boulevard. These youngsters on the streets, with their Nintendo dreams and Nike shoes, experience life in the larger context of global and transnational processes.

In *Anthropology as Cultural Critique*, George Marcus and Michael Fischer state that in a modern world of interdependence among societies, "The present is a time of reassessment of dominant ideas across the human sciences (a designation broader than and inclusive of the conventional social sciences), extending to law, art, architecture, philosophy, literature, and even the natural sciences" (1986, 7). It is also, I shall add, a present in which hungry boys can kill for a pair of shoes or be assassinated by death squads. At a time when more and more young people, who are both frightened and frightening to entire communities, live amid vast symbolic, political, and economic violence, anthropologists must not remain silent. Social scientists must further the "experimental moment" (this "reassessment of dominant ideas across the human sciences") and reassess hegemonic discourses about young people. In this study I have attempted to open up a space in which to listen to children and adolescents without trivializing them or stifling their voices. I hope that this work serves to illustrate the urgent need to develop new models for better understanding of what it means to grow up under trying circumstances.

Reference Matter

Notes

Introduction

1. I am aware that the more idiomatic way to describe the process of aging would be "to grow up," but in many instances I prefer the term "to grow older," because it places less of a value judgment on the aging process. "To grow up" implies that aging is about arriving somewhere.

2. In "Up the Anthropologist" (1972), Nader urged anthropologists to "study up" as well as down, that is, to look at an issue, problem, or group in relation to spheres of local, national, and global power. Nader 1980 expands on this idea of studying up with the notion of the "vertical slice." Examining the lives of children in the United States, she looks beyond the family as the site of child development to investigate the role of corporations and government organizations in shaping children's health, nutrition, and housing, among others.

3. I chose nine to be the lower age because I never met street children living in the Sabana Grande boulevard who were younger than that. Eighteen is the age of majority in Venezuela.

4. Many of the older street people I met became *lateros* (can collectors), who searched for soda cans throughout the city to exchange for money and drugs.

5. The word *mono* literally means monkey and has very racist connotations. In the past, monos were also called *niches*. Today monos are most often known as "jordans" for their basketball haircuts and particular style of dressing.

6. At the beginning of my fieldwork, I became friends with a fifteen-year-old girl who called herself Jinette. I met her and her one-month-old baby on the boulevard, though she was regularly in the Bellas Artes area. Soon, I was too involved with Jinette, trying to get her life history while foolishly attempting to solve her problems. Jinette's lover did not want us to hang out, and he beat her every time she saw me, so I stopped meeting her. I despaired for a long time afterward in a way I never did over the males. On top of the differences I would have encountered between the daily lives of males and females on the streets and the difficulties of handling too many things at once, I felt emotionally unprepared to deal with the abuse females endured as well as the enormity of the risks they were taking.

Chapter 1 • The Streets of Caracas

1. Official estimates declared approximately three hundred people dead; unofficial figures vary between one thousand and two thousand deaths.

2. In Caracas, motorizados constitute a large group of young working males. They are a solution for businesses attempting to carry on in the midst of chaotic traffic and inefficient communication systems. Motorizados can be very abusive on the streets: they respect hardly any traffic regulations, and some groups have snatched goods from pedestrians. Many ride stolen bikes that they have repainted or altered. For these reasons, motorizados are frequent targets of police *operativos*, which inevitably involve roughness on both sides and further disrupt traffic.

3. Briceño-León argues extensively that the effects of oil in Venezuela have been perverse in the sense that they have led to a society dominated by consumerism and passivity (1990, 87). High oil revenues led to the development of a system in which it was easier and cheaper to import than to produce.

4. Political economic processes have developed in direct proportion to the emergence, development, and diminishment of oil wealth during the dictatorship of Juan Vicente Gómez (1908–35), and continued into the military regime of Pérez Jiménez in the 1950's and the negotiated democracy of the last three decades (see Karl 1987).

5. *La Gran Venezuela* (The Great Venezuela) was the slogan for a multi-

million-dollar plan to rescue the nation from underdevelopment and transform it into an industrial power during the 1970's oil boom. Large amounts of oil revenues were used to promote government projects and modern infrastructure.

6. During Herrera Campíns's administration, Venezuela's official foreign debt increased from nearly 9 billion dollars to 24 billion dollars. The currency devaluation in February 1983 was an effort to activate the economy. However, it failed to raise productivity, because it was accompanied by subsidies for "essential" imports for protected industries (Coronil 1997, 370).

7. During the 1980's, income per capita throughout Latin America dropped an average of 9.4 percent; in Venezuela, it dropped by 20 percent. By 1988, the number of households living below the poverty line had increased tenfold since 1981 and real per capita income had sunk to 1973 levels (Naím 1993, 43).

8. This is not to say that the crisis has not been difficult for those who could be considered middle class. For the middle class, increasing interest rates, the collapse of the bank system, the devaluation of the bolivar, and other problems have significantly lowered living standards. In fact, many believe that the middle class has ceased to exist in Venezuela, that there are only the rich and the poor.

9. I was not able to discover the reasons that the students covered with hoods—called *encapuchados* (hooded ones)—protest only on Thursdays. I thought their protests were related to public transportation fare increases. However, many people I spoke with believed that encapuchado protests were caused by a wide variety of reasons, ranging from dislike for the president to opposition to government policies, which often did not affect them directly. Some people I spoke with even thought that the encapuchados were an organized group of policemen who were causing havoc to change the ruling that bans police forces from entering university grounds.

10. A disturbio is the name most often given to any student protests. Today, many marches and protests are presented by the media as ending in a disturbio.

11. The banging of pots and pans in collective protest is known as *el cacerolazo*, an increasingly used accompaniment to the manifestation of discontent. The cacerolazos (*cacerola* means saucepan) became very popular during the military coup attempts of February 4 and November 27,

1992. People from all over the city who supported the military leader Lieutenant Colonel Hugo Chávez banged their pots at specific hours.

12. In 1993, approximately 89 percent of all Venezuelan households had television sets, and ownership rates were higher in Caracas, where there were television sets in 97 percent of households. A popular soap opera might reach 50 percent of the population in a prime-time evening slot (Enright, Francés, and Saavedra 1996, 75).

13. The soap-opera industry in Venezuela is considered one of the most competitive in the nation. Venezuela's soap-opera export earnings are on par with export earnings from other domestic industries such as automobiles (fifty-three million dollars), clothing and textiles combined (forty-nine million dollars), and pulp and paper (forty-five million dollars). According to Enright, Francés, and Saavedra, Venezuela has achieved a leadership position in foreign licensing of soap operas, even though rivals Mexico and Brazil have the two largest television networks in Latin America and together account for 54 percent of Latin American television stations (1996, 70).

14. The soap opera revolved around people from a barrio named Moscú and their relation to spheres of power. Each episode tried to incorporate real events from daily life such as presidential elections, a bomb explosion at a shopping mall, the return of a corrupt politician, and so on.

15. There were several car explosions in Caracas—notably at the trendy shopping mall CCCT. The police later discovered that the explosions were the work of a group of yuppies who were trying to instigate panic among the population to influence stock prices.

16. Today, even the games children play in the barrios are influenced by violence. While visiting a barrio, I watched a group of children playing encapuchado, in which they wrapped their T-shirts around their heads to cover their faces and then mocked a disturbio, pushing one another around.

17. Grupo Lince is one of the best known of the motorcycle police corps that go into the barrios. I heard several times on the streets that the leaders of the group were two police agents known as Robocop and Terminator.

18. Tupac Amaru was the leader of an eighteenth-century peasant revolt against Spanish rule in Peru. During the second half of the twentieth century, several groups in Latin America were named after the Peruvian revolutionary, such as the National Liberation Movement Tupamaru from

Uruguay and the Revolutionary Movement Tupac Amaru (MRTA) from Peru. When the neighborhood 23 de Enero was created in the late 1950's and early 1960's, several people from the Venezuelan guerrilla movement lived there. According to my informants, their previous influence and their discourse about change inspired this new generation of vigilantes to choose the name of Tupas.

Chapter 2 • Young People on the Streets

1. *Hampa* literally means underworld. The word is said to come from Andalucía, Spain, where it was used to refer to the life of a company of rogues and vagabonds. In Venezuela, the word *hampa* is used in reference to delinquency.

2. "Vagos y maleantes" are persons whom the authorities consider "undesirables," not because they have committed any clear offense, but simply because they are thought to be transgressing the social order. They are taken off the streets and often placed in prison through the 1956 *Ley sobre vagos y maleantes*. In the 1950's, the law was regularly applied to those who opposed the military regime of Pérez Jiménez; recently it has been used against university and high school students who stage protests outside their institutions.

3. Operativos are organized police corps crackdowns, such as the entering of a particular barrio to look for arms. Other operativos are no more than systematic searches of motorcycle messengers on crowded downtown streets, during which the police demand identification papers for the messenger and the vehicle. These operativos are popularly known both for the police's arbitrary use of force and authority and for their failure.

4. Bazuko, an end product of processed cocaine, is a brownish rock that is later shredded and smoked in a cigarette. When lighted, it produces a particular sound called *chirre*, and to smoke bazuko is often called *chirrear*. Bazuko is sold on the streets in small strawlike packages.

5. The nickname Caracortada means scarface; el Feto means the fetus; Chino is a nickname given to anyone who has eyes resembling those of the Chinese; Mascota means pet.

6. The addictive narcotic in shoe glue is toluene. In some areas of the United States, glue containing toluene also contains oil of mustard (allyl isothiocyanate), which makes sniffing the glue painful.

7. A shorter version of Edison's writings on glue sniffing was later published in the Association for Street Children's newsletter, *Nosotros también
soñamos* . . . (We also dream . . .).

8. ¿Qué respuesta puede tener una lata de cerveza en el medio del
Pacífico? La respuesta es soledad, un mal que nos turba y nos enferma.
Piensen todos un poco, pónganse en el lugar de esa lata en el medio del
océano y sabrán lo que se siente ser un muchacho de la calle. Ese niño,
ese ser inocente que por hambre, por frío o por falta de cariño consume
pega. Consume para olvidar el hambre o para olvidar el dolor. Esa
criatura busca cómo olvidarse de que cada noche que se acuesta en un
piso frío con el estómago vacio. Duerme con la duda de saber si al día
siguiente habrá que comer. Así sigue la rutina para ese niño, esperando
que a alguien le de lástima y se le hablande el corazón y le brinde algo.
La lluvia: unos la prefieren y a otros les encanta. Unos la aprovechan
para dormir porque tienen un lugar seguro donde hacerlo. Pero para los
muchachos de la calle es fastidiosa porque si no corren rápido a un lugar
donde protegerse ya saben lo que les espera. Ustedes piensan que en la
calle puedan haber sitios seguros para esconderse de la lluvia. ¿Qué tan
seguros pueden ser? Aun cuando conseguimos un lugar donde no nos
mojamos tenemos que evadir el frío. Buscamos cartones para arro-
parnos. Combinen un poco el frío y el hambre que se siente y sabrán por
qué uno dice: "menos mal que existe la pega o si no cómo lo aguanto."

9. In 1963, Srivastava, in his study of juvenile vagrants in the Indian
cities of Kanpur and Lucknow, concluded that homosexuality was common among these children. Although homosexuality and drug use
among Caracas youth on the streets today make them a high-risk population for HIV infection, I never encountered any boys infected with
AIDS, or heard any references to them.

10. Hay una detrás de la funeraria San Martín a una cuadra del hotel
Orfeón, como la mayoría de las caletas ésta es un hueco. Es una superficie
más o menos larga debajo de una cloaca donde ponen los cables. Te
metes por una alcantarilla, "¿tú no has visto las tortugas Ninja?" abres tu
alcantarilla y te metes tipo topo, llegas a la vaina y tienes tu cobija o tu
colchón, es como para cuatro personas.

11. In Venezuela there is a legal obligation to care for the sick and injured. Medical services, however, are often denied to homeless people because, with the increasing collapse of the public health system, many
doctors, nurses, and hospital administrators do not consider the home-

less to be a priority. During my fieldwork, I witnessed several instances of street children being denied medical treatment. They were not turned away, but they were made to wait so much longer than other people that they finally left. In one case, Jorge from the Bellas Artes area had been badly cut while he was waiting to meet me; some artisans told me that a group of youngsters had come from another area and slashed Jorge's arm and back. Jorge and a couple of his friends had gone to the Red Cross (a relatively inexpensive hospital), four blocks away. When I arrived, Jorge was waiting outside an office. A nurse told me that I had to pay a fee before the boy could be treated. I explained to her I saw no reason to pay because I was his friend, not his guardian. I eventually had to explain the situation to the doctor, who agreed to treat Jorge if I would buy the antibiotics the child supposedly needed. Meanwhile, Jorge wanted to leave the clinic because he thought everyone was looking at him suspiciously. This, and the nurse's attitude, meant to him that, as usual, they did not want to give him the treatment he needed.

12. In Petare, a large barrio neighborhood on the easternmost side of the city, there is a group of street children who prefer to take drugs (Rupinol, a tranquilizer) mixed with liquor (especially anise). They believe that those on the boulevard are fools to prefer glue.

13. La Planta is a jail for those over age eighteen. However, it is increasingly more common for youngsters who are between fifteen and eighteen and are considered to be "de alta peligrosidad" (very dangerous) to be sent there also.

14. The expression "un calienta culo" comes from the pain caused by *peinillas*, which are flat metal instruments used by policemen to beat people in crowds. Police officers often beat people on their buttocks and legs, and calienta culo literally means "ass warmer."

15. It is interesting to note that most youngsters pronounced Nike the way they think it is said in English, "nīk."

16. A study done in Caracas about stereotypes of delinquents concluded delinquents are assumed to have little education, are unemployed and unattractive, and have "black" features. It further concluded that policies against delinquents were clearly discriminatory and supported by a general stereotype of the delinquent person (Ceballos and Malaver 1984, 146).

17. There are many reasons a person might be undocumented. These are the three most common: he or his family migrated illegally from a

nearby country (especially Colombia); his parents did not register him at birth; or he never requested his *cédula de identidad* (identification card). Usually a child's parents or legal guardian request the card when the child is about ten years old.

18. Wright found that most Venezuelans are aware that some subtle forms of racial discrimination still exist in their nation. Occasionally, they will acknowledge that blacks meet with some not-so-subtle forms of discrimination. Vestiges of the hierarchical colonial society that was based on the racial supremacy of whites linger on. Consequently, for most blacks still mired in poverty, the concept of racial democracy holds little more than a hollow promise for improved social status at some future date, dependent on their own ability to improve their lot economically. "Whitening" has become a prerequisite for social mobility, both in cultural and racial terms (1990, 130).

19. The term *woperó* comes from a popular song in English that has the repetitive phrase "pump it up." The phrase was sung by people in Caracas as "woperup."

20. In one way, Prince is different from many of the other street people I met. A childhood illness left him with short, deformed legs that made walking difficult. I assumed he had polio or was severely malnourished when he was born, but he was never able to confirm either. In fact, Prince partially believed the story that his grandmother had told him: his parents had thrown him to the floor during a fight.

21. Yo llegué a la calle a mediados del '87, y ya caminaba así. Llegué equivocadamente porque agarré una camioneta, en esa época no conocía bien a Caracas, llorando y tal. *¿Por qué estabas llorando?* Por lo de mi mamá. Bueno, llegué equivocadamente a Chacaíto y ví toda esa gente y me sentí como un inmigrante: "Todo esto será mío" y tal, osea, yo tenía esa mentalidad de los televisores, que el tipo llegaba y "toda la ciudad va a ser mía."

¿Tenías plata contigo? Si tenía plata porque ese Domingo había trabajado en el mercado de Guaicaipuro vendiendo bolsas y entonces tenía plata, trescientos bolívares. En esa época trescientos bolos era bastante real. Entonces esa semana me dí una vida a lo Boulton, pero después si me tocó, coño, dormir en el piso, en cartones.

¿Y el primer día cómo fue? Los primeros días dormí en las sillas de los restaurantes, si no, amanecía caminando. Más de una vez me metieron en el modulito que está allí, pero no en el módulo, sino donde está Pida Pizza, allí había un modulito y más de una vez dormí allí.

¿Cúal fue la primera persona que conocistes? Pechundío, eso fué porque yo empecé a martillar porque me acordé de la vaina de mi abuela, "¡Ah! así no paso hambre", y entonces llegó Pechundío: "Chamo, ¿qué haces por aquí?" y tal "ese bolso está bonito ¿Dónde vives tú?" porque el tipo ya me estaba viendo todo sucio "¿Tienes dónde vivir?", "No chamo yo me fuí de mi casa," "¡Ah! si y ¿no quieres volver?" "No chamo porque mi abuela me pega mucho," "Bueno vente" y me llevó a La Cortina. Después seguí y andaba con la misma ropa más de un mes, sendas greñas tipo Marco Polo. Y hacíamos la comuna martillando, al principio comía solo y decía, "Tengo que aprender a conocer esto." Me empecé a unir con Pechundío, con Nava, con Kilian y con un poco de carajos que ya ni están y algunos ya se me va la memoria.

¿Qué edad tenías? Como catorce años. *¿Y Pechundío?* Once o doce. *¿Era chupapega?* Yo creo que el empezó a chupar pega desde que el venía para acá a Los Caobos donde había un módulo que veníamos a dormir aquí.

¿Y qué hacían? Mira, unos preparaban cuchillos con las bromas de las latas y se enseñaban entre ellos mismos los trucos de pase y cadenetas para agarrar a uno así ¡aghhh! Nosotros mismos hacíamos combates de cangrejos nos tirábamos en el piso y con una mano nos sosteníamos y con la otra peleabamos tipo cangrejo, era para las circunstancias mayores. Te pones en el piso y el otro así acostado así como haciendo flexión y a la cuenta de cinco, este es un juego malvado, pero lo aprendí en la calle, a la cuenta de cinco tu te apoyas con una mano todo el peso de tu cuerpo y con la otra andas tipo cangrejo el que tumbe al otro haces que pague la penitencia. *¿Entonces era un juego?* Si, pero a mi me sirvió bastante en Playa Grande para defenderme así peleando. En la playa lo aplicábamos mucho, yo y Pechundío aplicabamos trampa con la arena, tácate, "¡Toma maldito!"

¿De dónde viene Pechundío? ¿Conoces a su mamá? Yo conocí a su mamá de vaina por Carmen la chama del CONAC, y bueno entonces, la mamá es gordita bien simpática. *¿Por qué se fue a la calle, nunca hablaban de sus familias?* No, el se ponía a llorar *¿Por qué ?* No sé, él se fue por problemas de comunicación aunque él siempre dice que su papá es un borracho. Siempre que él está full de pega o está tomado saca a relucir al papá, verma.

¿Qué otras cosas hacían? Después si aplicabamos la ley del grupo, tienes que ir a dormir al cementerio *¿Qué sucedía?* Que los que se iban todos cagados no ingresaban en el grupo, hubieron como seis chamos que se quedaron en la puerta y les decíamos, "Métete, métete o te vamos a echar los perros."

22. Lo que pasa es que antes habían más grupos, los grupos eran más unidos. Antes habían los Anticristos, que no creían en Cristo pero ayudaban mucho a la gente y vivían tipo gitanos, dormían una noche aquí y una noche allá. Ellos nos enseñaron a Pechundío y a mi casi todos los edificios abandonados de Caracas. *¿De dónde salió este grupo?* Era un grupo de los setenta, rockeros. Había uno que se llamaba Leroy que ahora es un pastelero arrechísimo. El nos enseñó más que todo a ser guerreros. Hay un puente en los Chaguaramos que es en el Guaire y nos ponía a hacer esas competencia de pasar el puente, tipo soldado, Pechundío, yo y otro. Pero inclusive uno de mis primeros atracos de quiosco con ellos, tuvimos que pasar por ese puente con las bolsas así, Nava y yo nos traímos los reales y las chucherías así por dentro. Tenías que robar algo para que te aceptaran. *¿Qué te pareció eso?* Terrible estaba más asustado ¡No joda! *¿Cuántas veces hicistes eso?* Como tres. Después si lo tuve que hacer por hambre porque me daba pena martillar, entonces me metí en el Cada y me robé unas galletas y frutas.

¿Y después que entraron en el grupo? Bueno, Pechundío y Leroy te enseñaban, Leroy era sendo ratero de caleta: a abrir los carros con llaves chimbas, a inyectarle agua a los carros de seguridad para robarlos. Pechundío todavía roba reproductores de esa manera, como hoy en día en los carros hay muchos sistemas eléctricos, con agua se abren los sistemas de seguridad, pero eso es en los carros caros, y los vende en los negocios o si está muy pelando te dice "vamos a hablar como caballero." A mi me gusta Pechundío, el tipo es "vamos a hablar como caballeros" y él te abraza, "mi amiguito, mi tío" cuando el carajo te abraza el quiere algo "mira tengo hambre vamos a hablar, tengo algo para ti cuánto me puedes dar," "bueno te puedo dar tanto más la comida."

Yo una vez me metí en una tienda con él y me traje tres camisas y un pantalón para mi y unos zapatos más feos que parecía el payaso Cepillín, verga que horrible. Entonces el bicho se paleó un pocote de bolsas y nos agarró la guardia "¡QUIETOS! ¿qué hacen allí?" "No," dijo Pechundío, "esto es basura porque nos pagan para trabajar aquí cargando la basura," porque estabamos al lado de un quiosco, entonces agarró una navaja y abrió una de las bolsas y dió la suerte que era de basura. Tranquilos y tal. Entonces nos fuimos a Quebrada Honda y nos metimos en un edificio. Entonces él se ponía con papel a quemarse el cuerpo para darse calor, pero después empezó con su nota chimba a hacerse tatuajes y a darse viajes con cuchillos. Pero creo que se le borraron ya. La mayoría de mis aventuras fueron con Pechundío, porque él no es traicionero sabes.

¿Cómo era la situación de la policía? Había represión. Un menor de la calle no podía estar porque te llevaban a un INAM, pero ya es un problema mundial, la niñez abandonada es tan grande. *¿Cómo te trataba la policía y la comunidad?* La policía chimbo y la comunidad como si no existiera. Ahora hay más policía, pero fíjate la mayoría de la policía han sido malandros o han vivido en la calle. Como ellos se moldean con los rateros te dicen, "mire, panita, eso no es así porque si usted come yo también como, entonces no me lo puedo llevar preso por tal y tal, vamos a hacer algo, qué te pareces si me das esto y nos vemos después," o como te dije hay policías que mira, que les gusta coño, hay policías que también saben se criaron en el barrio como uno. Ellos se meten en la policía porque saben lo que van a buscar.

Me separé de Pechundío a mediados del '89, yo siempre le decía "vamos a estudiar," porque yo siempre he querido estudiar y vivir fuera de este país lo que pasa es que estoy muy achantado. "Coye nos vamos a vivir fuera," él tiene mucho talento para imitar, hacer bromas de payaso, "Pecho nos podemos ir como circo rodante, nos va a ir bien." El decía, "no," se ponía fatalista. Pero cuando mataron a Zambrano si que nos disolvimos. El era un muchacho que vivía en la calle y por bromas de drogas lo mataron. *¿Por qué eso los separó?* Porque Pecho era muy amigo de él y se quería meter en ese mundo de lleno, pero yo no quería entonces nos separamos. Yo le dije que seguiríamos siendo amigos, pero no íbamos a andar juntos. Ahora a veces nos vemos y conversamos y compartimos la papa. El y yo a veces corregimos a los chamos porque siempre dicen "pa'segundo" y los enseñamos y Pechundío los trata como un padre: "estos muchachos no quieren aprender" y les da sendos lepes y yo si le digo "pero no, Pecho, no les pegues."

23. He is referring to a famous case in which Ramón J. Velázquez (1993), interim president after the impeachment of Carlos Andrés Pérez, apparently mistakenly signed a pardon for drug dealer Larry Tovar Acuña: ¿Por qué tenemos que soportar el acoso de la policía? Vienen a San Agustín a atacar, y decir que el plan de desarme era conjunto con las comunidades para sabotear porque no les interesa que nos organicemos porque aquí hay un negocio con la violencia. Fijense que aquí el Ministro de Justicia pide justicia porque no sabe lo que pasó con lo del narcoindulto. Lo que demuestran es que Venezuela no sirve. Yo vi unos policías

que subieron a Marín y armaron a dos menores de diecisiete años, ellos
generan violencia.

24. La verdad que es difícil hablar de paz cuando se es violento, y la
verdad es que soy un hombre violento. La pobreza genera violencia. No
somos un punto aislado dentro de tanta violencia. . . . Los culpables son
los que se han olvidado de nosotros. No existe la justicia social. Es difícil
ser un hombre de paz cuando se va a una escuela bajo de un puente, no
hay teatro que no le impidan entrar como en el Teresa Carreño, que
porque eres negro, pobre y marginado no puedes entrar allí. Donde cen-
tros de asistencia médica son horribles es difícil ser hombre de paz.

Chapter 3 · Young People and Family Life

1. In *Familia y televisión*, Leoncio Barrios asserts that Venezuelan families, and especially those from the middle and lower classes, can be considered extended by comparison with the number of people in the average European family. The average in Venezuela is about five in the upper-
class family, seven in the middle-class family, and eleven in the lower-class
family (Fundacredesa 1987, in Barrios 1992, 61).

2. In 1546, the Libro de Indias established that all the governors and
other authority figures who were married in Spain had to come to South
America with their wives (Troconis de Veracoechea 1990, 26).

3. However, Troconis de Veracoechea argues that giving their bodies to
the owner, over which they probably had no choice, sometimes increased
women's chances of gaining freedom from their owners (1990, 49).

4. José Luis Vethencourt is a well-known psychiatrist and criminolo-
gist who has written several influential articles about the family and appears frequently on television and radio programs. His writings on Venezuelan family types are quoted as unquestioned fact in most theses about
family I read at the Universidad Central de Venezuela.

5. Higher rates of marriage occurred among Indians, because they
lived under the close supervision of the Church (Lombardi 1976, 82).

6. Former president Jaime Lusinchi epitomizes the double standard.
When he became president, his wife, Gladis de Lusinchi, accompanied
him as the First Lady. However, it was well known that his private secretary, Blanca Ibañez, was his mistress. While politicians in the United
States can be severely undermined by public knowledge of their infideli-

ties, in Venezuela, the situation was accepted. It was only criticized when it became increasingly evident that Ibañez was using her position to obtain more power and material wealth for herself and her family. Gladis de Lusinchi finally divorced her husband at the end of his term. Lusinchi and Ibañez married and, at the time of this writing, live in Miami and Costa Rica. The Venezuelan government currently intends to bring them to trial on charges of corruption.

7. Venezuela experienced the fastest rate of urbanization in Latin America. Concurrently, the proportion of the workforce engaged in rural activities declined rapidly, from 71.6 percent in 1920 to 33.5 percent in 1961 (Karlsson 1975, 34).

8. This appears to be a universal assumption. In England, after the murder in February 1993 of a small boy, not quite three years old, allegedly by two ten-year-old boys from a working-class neighborhood, the media started a moral panic. One of the older boys was from a single-parent family, and even though the woman had left her husband (whom she had married at age eighteen) and was trying to raise her six legitimate children (all boys), the media focused on teenage mothers, denigrating parenting skills and the moral recklessness of having children without the emotional and financial support of a father (McRobbie 1994, 200).

9. La delincuencia no es sólo en los barrios. Hoy en día el cien por ciento de los menores son malandros así sean de la familia que sean. Porque si no son malandros que atracan esos andan por ahí fumando marihuana. Muchos malandros se visten de Paltó pero ese es diputado. Hay mucha gente como tu oliendo perico. Pa'l 23 iban comprar perico gente hasta del este. Va Joselo, coroneles, en carro fino pa' el bloque 25.

10. Cuando tenía ocho años mis padres se separaron y tuve que aprender a sobrevivir. Mi mamá es de nacionalidad colombiana y se marchó llevándose a mis dos hermanos. Me preguntó si me iba con ella pero decidí quedarme con mi papá porque vi que se sentía solo. Así pasó el tiempo y poco a poco me fui alejando de mi familia, me molestaba todo lo que me decían sabiendo que tenían razón. Me sentía mal cuando mi papá tomaba y no aguantaba ser un estorbo para él. Yo continué haciendo lo que él quería que yo hiciera, que era estudiar. Pero se me complicaban los estudios porque yo quería ir con unos zapatos caros para el liceo. Mi papá no podía cubrir esas cantidades por su presupuesto económico, entonces como no tenía zapatos caros no iba para el liceo.

11. Bueno, yo me fuí para la calle porque bueno yo estaba estudiando

y estaba cuidando una casa y mi mamá se murió y entonces mi hermana la mayor alquiló la casa y no agarró medio y después la vendió y de los reales que agarró tampoco agarré medio.

¿Cómo se murió? Osea se murió de una piedra. *¿Cómo pasó eso?* Cónchale, se cayó y se murió de una piedra, pegó la barriga de una piedra, ¿entiendes? Entonces después de que se murió mi mamá. *¿Dónde vive tu papá?* Vive en el Valle. *¿Estaba casado en ese entonces con tu mamá?* No.

¿Qué pasó después que tu mamá se murió? Mi hermana vendió la casa a otra hermana mía que vive con un hombre. Entonces yo estaba viviendo en la calle y un dia le dije a mi hermana la verdad de que yo estaba pasando dificultades porque yo estaba viviendo en la calle, todo porque mi hermana, la otra, había vendido la casa y el que compró la casa fue el hombre de mi otra hermana.

¿Qué edad tenías? Doce años, entonces ella me dijo que no, que esa casa no era de ella, que esa casa era de Raulito que es el marido de ella. Bueno entonces yo pensé "si ella es mi hermana no tiene derecho por qué tirarme." *¿Qué edad tenía tu hermana?* Dieciocho. Yo pensé y dije que no los iba a ver más nunca y dure tres años sin volver. Volví ahora a los disciseis.

12. Because of the inefficient and corrupt Venezuelan bureaucratic system, the speed with which an individual case is processed often depends on bribes and family pressure for faster movement of papers from the INAM to the judges.

13. Todos los problemas de la familia vienen por la falta del padre (pon falta paterna que es la misma mierda), lo he comprobado en estos días con la tía, ella se pone "yo lo he hecho todo por ustedes porque el coño'emadre los dejó." A ráiz de que la mujer se ha quedado sola, ha hecho un doble papel, pero la mujer necesita un hombre que le de apoyo moral, cae en el error del padrastro—el colado. Casi siempre el hijo'e puta es el detective y se priva la comunicación y todos se ponen ariscos porque el quiere imponer sus maneras. Entonces comienza por parte de la madre un chantaje subliminal con los hijos "yo que te lo he dado todo" o el método de los golpes y juegos de palabras que es brusco. De allí los muchachos vienen a la calle, no soportan la imagen del usurpador. Hay padrastros muy rígidos porque el papá con todo lo coño'emadre que fuera por lo menos lo consiente. El padrastro empieza con "en mi casa las reglas las pongo yo" y no deja que un niño de diez a dieciseis años busque su propia imagen—no lo dejan ser. Se van a la calle y buscan un

apoyo, asi consiguen un carajo que le dice "yo te voy a ayudar pero tu también me ayudas . . . " y el muchacho termina de mula hasta que tome conciencia pero solo si tiene esa pensadora bien.

14. Hay un familiazgo imaginario ya que tu familia no te da ese apoyo moral. Tu dices, "coño estos extraños, tienen diferentes éticas sociales y religiosas y aunque su cultura sea insuficiente, los carajos me están dando el apoyo moral que no encontraba, es un refugio, pero es momentáneo." Eso sí, uno tiene que imaginarse que uno es un extranjero en cualquier parte.

15. Aptekar (1988) suggests that in Cali, Colombia, street children form bands of five to fifty children known as *galladas*, which constitute a substitute family and provide them with psychological benefits.

16. Cuando uno llega por primera vez al bulevar tienes que asociarte con una pandilla para ser aceptado. Entonces cuando tu consigues alguien que te oriente y que quizás vive sumergido en su miseria moral, porque sabe que puede cambiar pero no hace nada por ello. Es una miseria moral porque él la lleva dentro de él, está reflejando toda la miseria global de su país, la falta de educación, la falta de aceptación. Cuando llega a la calle tiene que sacar su otra cara, su cara del malo porque de lo contrario fueras el hazmerreir tanto de esa supuesta sociedad como de sus compañeros, entonces el tiene que aparentar ser el malo, y como no, de repente robar, de repente prostituir su cuerpo o de repente caer en el papel de la miseria y pedir dinero.

17. Tienes que buscarte alguien que te adiestre los primeros meses y después tu eres libre, y Barrabás a pesar de que nos enseñaba a robar nos ponía a leer a Pechundío, a mi y a cuatro carajos más. Nos decía como hablaban en otros lugares y, "fíjate porque en Colombia roban de esta manera" y así, "Fíjate que no tienes que estar sucio para robar mientras más elegante estés menos vas a llamar la atención" y yo "¡verma!" y así infinidad de cosas.

18. Si y no, porque yo sabía lo que él hacía. Barrabás estaba sumergido en su miseria y quería cambiar pero estaba preso en si mismo. Lo que pasa es que yo esa figura del padre abnegado no la tengo. Barrabás fue un buen guía a nivel de vida.

19. Ustedes se preguntarán, ¿Qué se siente vivir en la calle? Es como abrir la puerta a otro mundo de seres poco queridos por la sociedad humillados, despreciados obligándonos a crecer o hacernos grande desde temprana edad. Es como todo con sus altas y sus bajas muy bajas. Otra pregunta, ¿Por qué están en la calle? ¿no tienen casa? Claro que tienen

casa pero no todos. Pero el problema no es ese si no el trato que hay entre padre, madre e hijo o también cuando hay conflictos familiares. O es
decir, la madre y el padre se dejan o divorcian y luego hay madrastra o
padrastro que pocas son las veces quieren a sus hijastros y uno como es
niño inocente paga todas las culpas. Otro caso es: la madre maltrata mucho a su hijo con o sin razón y el niño como es lo que es, le afecta y un
día decide abandonar su hogar. No sabe a donde ir, puede ser uno o dos
días. En el transcurso de esos días anda solo sin conocer a nadie, y luego
se encuentra con otro niño como él, con o más experiencia en la calle o
la vida libre, después que eso pasa y han transcurrido uno o dos meses la
madre decide buscarlo. Lo encuentra y le habla el idioma callejero "le
monta la llorona": "Vente conmigo que yo te quiero," el niño se pregunta ¿Si en verdad me quiere, por qué esperó tanto para venirme a buscar? Se le va creando un odio o no tanto eso. Son poco los casos que un
niño odia a su madre, pero si le digo que le importa poco si lo buscan o
no, o sea pierden un afecto o un sentimiento, de ya no querer volver a su
hogar. Aparte de eso cuando su madre lo abraza se siente incómodo, no
se hablan, se siente extraño. Y lo peor del caso es que cuando empienzan
a consumir drogas se les hace más difícil todavía dejar la calle, o sea, su
nuevo hogar, y ya no se sienten o sentimos (y digo así porque yo no se si
soy o no soy un muchacho de la calle. Sin preguntas por favor. Olvidán-
donos de eso seguimos.) iguales ya nos consideramos de otra especie
diferente como: Rebeldes muy capacitados para sobrevivir como unos
guerreros y parte de nosotros somos una familia aquí te hablo por los
muchachos que conozco y he conocido.

Chapter 4 · Media, Law, and the State

1. In May 10, 1994, a friend gave me a pamphlet inviting people to
participate in a protest called "luces contra el hampa" (lights against the
hampa). People were asked to turn on the lights of their vehicles and to
wear yellow during a particular day and time to show support for a project that would fight delinquency. The slogan was "mano dura contra el
hampa" (hard hand against the hampa), which proposed to (a) close
"marginal immigration" (probably meaning Colombians, Haitians, Ecua-
dorans, and Peruvians) and deport illegal residents, (b) disarm the shantytowns, (c) increase police presence, (d) increase the budget for security,

(e) enact strict laws for arms permits, and (f) set up militarized centers for "dangerous" minors.

2. In 1955, during the dictatorship of Pérez Jiménez, the government proposed a reform to the penal code to lower the age of responsibility for a crime from eighteen to twelve years old. In 1963 and again in 1964, the same proposition emerged. In the 1960's to be young was identified with being in the guerrilla or communist movements. Today being young and poor is associated with being a transgressor (Montero 1989, 117–18).

3. The mayor of Sucre county, Enrique Mendoza, also established a 9:00 P.M. curfew for minors. However, the authorities have found that they have no place to put the minors who are on the streets alone after hours.

4. The word *hampa* is being increasingly used to mean an "alien invader," especially by the upper classes, to categorize minor and adult delinquents as well as so-called marginal immigrants.

5. According to Trotman's *Crime in Trinidad*, when the public was restless over poor economic conditions in nineteenth-century Trinidad, the law enforcement agencies increased their activity. This generated higher criminal statistics, but did not always represent a real increase in criminal activity. The level of legal skill and popular attitudes toward the court also affected the rate of conviction, and the statistics on convictions were not completely reliable indicators of the rate and nature of violence (1986, 70, 136).

6. In 1935, 82 percent of the children between seven and fourteen years old did not go to school (Salcedo Bastardo 1974, 192). Can it then be said—and many do say—that today's young are out of control because of school desertion?

7. For instance, a professional psychologist who formerly worked at INAM told me that the center's statistics are continually manipulated to assure the public that INAM is controlling large numbers of young people despite the criticisms they receive. The psychologist also informed me that recidivists at an INAM center, and those who escape and return, may be counted twice or more.

8. The most organized census on street children on the Sabana Grande boulevard was done in 1992 by the Association for Street Children, which estimated that there were one hundred minors living there.

9. In 1978, official reports said that 50 percent of the total number of criminal activities were the work of minors (Montero 1989, 119).

10. Aries is vague about what was behind the "discovery" of child-hood, simply implying the significance of modernizing social processes (Johnson 1990). Recently, several anthropologists and historians have discredited Aries's argument of the progressive emergence of the figure of the child (Shahar 1990; Wilson 1984).

11. This happened under the influence of "Children's Savior," an upper-class social movement (Platt 1988, discussed in Beloff 1994).

12. I was unable to find the original source on which the newspaper article was based, though I searched in many libraries in Caracas, including the Biblioteca Nacional.

13. The code of 1863 was created partly to counter increasing crime rates. In 1854, President José Gregorio Monagas abolished slavery but offered the former slaves little opportunity to find jobs.

14. En Los Chorros duré dos semanas por mi condición física y en Caracas Uno duré tres semanas. Me fugué y me volvieron a llevar y duré tres semanas y después a Los Chorros donde me hicieron una carta especial para que me buscaran una beca especial para estudiar y me llevaron para el Francisco de Miranda de Los Teques que era peor, una casa hogar. Yo llegué y duré como dos semanas a mediados del '88. Yo notaba que la sección que me tocó eran muchachos mayores que yo y se caían a piña y le robaban a uno las pertenencias, los vigilantes no le paraban bola a uno, pensaba "si en Sabana Grande no me corrompí, aquí si me voy a corromper porque estos carajos no me van a tratar con suavidad como me trataba Pechundío."

15. Habían unos policías, Barriento y Malagón, que porque los vecinos se quejaban de que nos metíamos en los negocios y agarrabamos ropa limpia, se quejaban también de que dormíamos en los negocios y se volvieron algo así como la Mano Negra en Brazil, nos perseguían. Después de un mes de tantas entradas en el Recreo nos dijeron "a ustedes les toca zona siete" yo pregunté aterrado porque no había hecho nada, "¿qué es eso, qué es eso?" Pechundío que había estado allí dijo, "tranquilo que eso es como esto y nos van a poner en otra celda aparte con otros menores." "¿Estás seguro?" "Si, chamo tranquilo."

16. Even today, mothers with few economic resources who think they will not be able to care for some of their children take them to INAM centers. In addition, mothers who have been left by their child's father and who find a new partner often take the child to an INAM center.

17. Retén de Catia was blown up in a public spectacle in February

1997. The event was shown on all public television stations in Venezuela as a symbol of the new penal reforms that President Rafael Caldera's government was to implement. However, as of today, the terrible conditions and the lack of basic services for prisoners still exist.

18. All these names are pseudonyms.

19. Había un muchacho que se llamaba Freddy apodado el "Aldillón," cuando éramos pequeños peleamos dos veces en el barrio donde vivíamos. Luego él se mudó al barrio San José, entonces se volvió malandro, y regresó al barrio. Consumía drogas, tenía una pistola, le gustaba poner a los menorcitos a mamar guebo. Una vez me dijo a mi todo drogado que me quedara parado en una esquina donde yo estaba para ponerme a mamar guebo, entonces yo me fui corriendo, me lo dijo cuatro veces y siempre me le iba corriendo.

Un día yo venía con mi novia de una fiesta en el Llanito cuando regresamos a mi casa él venía corriendo y yo subí corriendo con mi novia, más arriba me pasó y me dijo: "¿Por qué saliste corriendo?" y yo le dije, "yo soy un hombre y tu quieres que te mame el guebo," entonces me dijo "no hombre bruja, no te pongo a mamar guebo porque andas con tu geba," y yo si le dije "chamo, quédate tranquilo y baja esa pistola que se le puede ir un tiro," la desmontó y me dio por la cabeza, me dio con el cañón por el pecho y luego empezó a faltarle los respetos a mi novia, manoseándole el cuello y yo le dije "deja el abuso" y me dijo "cállate, porque si no voy a explotar" y después me dijo "bruja, vete de aquí" y me dio una patada, le dijo a mi novia, "pendiente mamita que a vas a ser mi mujer."

Después un viernes como a las 2:00 P.M. me vio en el matiné y me dijo "quieres ver como te exploto aquí mismo" y le dijo a mi novia "si estás sexy, estás como para hacerte el amor, nosotros dos junticos" y luego se fue porque lo llamó un malandro y bajaron, tenían una moto robada con la que pasaban para allá y para acá, echando tiro al aire. Luego subieron y él empezó de nuevo a humillarme, me dio dos cachetadas, fue tanta la pena que me fui de la fiesta.

Como a las cuatro, me puse a jugar basket y luego como a las seis de la tarde, vino un muchacho y me dijo que estaban vendiendo una pistola y yo le pregunté de quien era. El me dijo que no sabía y yo le dije si es de un policía de todos modos voy a todo riesgo porque era para asustar a Freddy que me tenía hastiado con tanta humillación.

En la noche como a las 8:30 P.M. venía yo de la casa de mi novia, cuando iba por la escuela Cecilio Acosta, estaba parado porque esta vez si tenía que mamarle el guebo, que si me iba me iba a matar, yo le dije, "está bien me voy a quedar aquí parado," venía comiéndose la mitad de una hamburguesa y me dijo "sígueme." Me llevaba para el sitio donde ponía a los amorcitos a mamarle el guebo, cuando llegó al sitio se terminó de comer la hamburguesa y luego se iba a sacar la pistola de la cintura, cuando yo vi la cacha me asusté y saqué la pistola y le di un tiro en el pecho. Luego salió corriendo y yo pensé que iba a venir la familia de él que son malandros y me iban a matar. Yo le zumbé dos tiros mas—casualidad que los pegué—salí corriendo y voté la pistola para el Guaire.

20. Proyecta un tipo emocional coartado indicativo que responde con dificultad ante los estímulos del mundo externo como interno. En él se encontró: bloque psicológico, abulio, afectividad reducida, inestabilidad, culpa masturbartoria, infantilismo, inmadurez, falta de orientación y metas claras en la vida, deseos de compensar insuficiencia corporal.

21. Anton Makarenko (1888–1939) was a Soviet teacher and social worker. In the 1920's he successfully organized a rehabilitation settlement for children made homeless by the revolution, who had been roaming throughout the countryside in gangs. Makarenko rejected slogan-based education, maintaining that lectures and exhortation were the least effective means of exerting influence. He regarded work as basic to intellectual and moral development.

22. Ayuda Juvenil (Children's Aid) is one of INAM's prevention programs.

Chapter 5 · The Institutionalization of Violence

1. While I was doing research at the Carolina Center, one of the counselors was stabbed outside the center. I asked several staff members what had happened, but their answers were vague. When the injured counselor returned after several weeks, he told me that he had been assaulted and implied that it had been by someone he had met at the center.

2. The chupapegas from Sabana Grande seldom spent more than a week at Los Chorros. Most of them escaped through the main door, which at that time was left unguarded. However, over time, the youngsters found other ways to get out. At one point, the children were denied almost all clothing to keep them from leaving. They nonetheless man-

aged to escape, and the neighbors complained about half-naked children running around their fancy neighborhood.

3. I quit when I was told by the director that I would have to be at the center every day from one P.M. until nine P.M.

4. By the end of 1994, the Los Chorros center was transferred for a five-year period to the NGO Fundación Atenea. Four years later, Fundación Atenea has achieved a great many improvements in what I here call the Los Chorros complex. The boys are no longer mistreated and have a wide variety of educational activities. Fundación Atenea has been very successful in completely reorganizing administrative practices and evaluation procedures, increasing its funding, and attracting many new volunteers.

5. One building houses girls, another boys who are "at risk." The third building, the Centro de Atención Inmediata (Center for Immediate Attention), is where boys are evaluated and observed.

6. To save costs and to prevent them from escaping (or so the staff thought), the youngsters are not given underwear.

7. On one occasion, I went to the barrio Carapita to visit a child's mother. The boy had asked my friend Gustavo to find her. When we arrived at the barrio, we stopped at a *bodega* (small grocery shop) and asked for directions to the mother's house. The shop owner explained that he was willing to pay the child's expenses to keep him in Los Chorros. He did not want the boy to return to the barrio, because his mother was a drug addict who did not take care of any of her children, and the boy himself was a young malandro of whom many people in the barrio were afraid.

8. Mira carajito, tu eres nuevo aquí. No estás en tu casa. Y para que lo sepas y no lo olvides tienes que andar con pies de plomo! Y si te resbalas coges plan por ese culo! (Rodríguez 1974, 22)

9. The center is popularly known as the Carolina, after the upper-class woman who donated it. Huggings (1987) wrote a detailed study of the center's dynamics before 1986, when it housed young females.

10. For example, at the CAI in Los Chorros, all the cases were delayed for a few months because the typist had left and the INAM main office had not sent another. Even though there were several psychologists, social workers, and teachers at the center, it appeared that none of them considered typing their own cases to speed up procedures.

11. Corazoncito got his nickname because when he arrived, he was

taken to the infirmary, where the doctor asked him if he suffered from any diseases. He said that he occasionally got a pain in his heart; another youngster overheard this, and the group mockingly called him Corazoncito ("little heart") thereafter.

12. Esa misma tarde conocí a una joven muchacha llamada Patricia que venía siempre a enseñarnos cosas como el ambiente, la fauna, animales, montañas, etc. Lo cierto es que ella está escribiendo un libro y me pidió que escribiera algo de mi vida y yo se lo escribí. Ella es muy intelectual, es la única distracción que tienen los menores aquí.

13. Martes, 4 de Mayo: 2:00 P.M.

Me subieron para fase inicial, allí fue el peor día de mi vida, estaba realmente asustado y en el cuarto donde a mi me pusieron estaba Oveiwin, un chamo muy alzado y también metieron al muchado que yo conocí en División y a otro menor. Comí y no hubo pelea, pero sabía que pronto me iba a tocar la hora de pelear. Lo peor ocurrió en la noche cuando el maestro de la guardia de la noche dió las galletas y se fue. Oveiwin se me lanzó encima y me pegó unos golpes. Yo le dije para pelear. Enseguida se metió León que era el otro muchacho que yo conocía y me empezaron a golpear los dos. Yo les dije otra vez que si querían pelear, OK, pero uno primero y después el otro. Y asi ocurrió, pero cuando estaba peleando con León Oveiwin se me lanzó encima porque le estaba ganando. Esa noche y cuatro noches mas fueron de amargura y sosobra. Después me cambiaron para el cuarto A de fase inicial. Allí conocí muchos menores como Lendel, Gonzalo y otros más.

14. Oveiwin is the same person I sympathetically portrayed in Chapter 4. His aggressive behavior toward Corazoncito reveals the attitude often found in the initial phase in which you establish alliances with some youngsters and attack others before they can hurt you.

15. Martes, 11 de Mayo: 11:00 A.M.

Subimos y nos encierran, cuando llegue al cuarto vi a un chamo acostado en los colchones. Le pregunte de dónde era.

—De Propatria.

—¿Por qué caistes?

—Porque maté a dos chamos que me tenían obstinado.

—¿Cúal es tu nombre?

—Orlando y me llaman el Chivo.

En ese momento Eric un chamo de grupo dos entró para fase y le dijo al Chivo que diera sus zapatos pero él no los quería dar. Yo le dije que los diera porque así como le dieron la llave de la puerta de la entrada para fase le podían dar la llave de los cuartos. El Chivo dió sus zapatos, ahora supuestamente los zapatos que le quitaron al Chivo los tiene el maestro del turno de la mañana del grupo dos, el maestro Guariguata. El Chivo era un chamo bien pero yo no confiaba ni confío en nadie.

16. Al llegar me subieron a un cuarto donde se duraba ocho días para salir al patio. En esos ocho días tuve un problema con un menor llamado Felipe que quería puñaliarme [Lendel's word for stabbing] y yo pensé "adelante, defenderme y darme a respetar." Pasó una noche y estaba arrepentido, solo y triste, no pude dormir pensando todo tipo de cosa: si me fugaba o me quedaba. Amaneció y el menor Felipe me llamó y me dijo que yo tenía problemas con un primo de él, y él intentó puñaliarme y luchamos hasta que se dió cuenta de que no iba a ser fácil puñaliarme. Yo no me preocupaba de Felipe, sino de los problemas que me esperaban afuera cuando saliera al patio, y las ganas de fugarme no dejaron de pasarme por la mente. El día 28 de Abril llegó mi madre a visitarme y vi el sufrimiento que sentía mi madre al ver el problema en que me encontraba yo, decidí quedarme a afrontar mi problema pasara lo que pasara. Después de los ocho días salí al patio y me encontré con menores que estaban por distintos problemas, algunos se hicieron amistades por mi ropa, uno de ellos más grande que yo me invitó a pelear mis zapatos y yo tuve que pelear aunque sentía mucho miedo, perdí y me los quitó, de repente apareció un menor que yo conocía del barrio habló con él y le dijo que me conocía y llegaron a un acuerdo y me devolvieron mis zapatos. Ese día me la pasé conversando, haciendo amistades.

17. Después de encontrarme en el centro me encerraron en un cubículo donde iba a durar cinco días, fue otra experiencia, para mi otra vez las ganas de fugarme no me faltaron, pero al saber que con fugarme no solucionaba mi problema decidí quedarme, no tuve ningún tipo de problema, porque allí se encontraban varias amistades mias, ahora tengo nuevezmeses, casi estoy cumpliendo mayoría y esperando mi libertad.

18. Luisa Cáceres de Arismendi was the wife of a well-known nineteenth-century independence fighter. She became a heroine when she was incarcerated by the Spaniards in a small isolation cell at the Santa Rosa castle; she was pregnant and miscarried while in captivity.

19. Martes, 18 de Mayo: 3:00 P.M.

A todo joven que pasan para un grupo lo enseñan desde fase que tiene que cumplir con sus comisiones, es decir limpiar el lugar que le sea asignado por el maestro y levantarse a las 7:00 de la mañana para cantar el himno nacional y a las 7:30 ir al comedor con un uniforme de pantalón azul, franela blanca y zapatos normales preferiblemente que no sean de marca para no traer discordia entre los mismos menores. Mi primera comisión fueron las escaleras y mi primera puntuación fue de 450 puntos. Lo de los puntos los hace el maestro. Mi segunda y tercera comision siguieron siendo las escaleras con los puntos de 570 y 578. Despúes en la cuarta y quinta tuve un puntaje de 597 y 585.

20. The director at one of the INAM centers told me that often the staff at the centers would have something like chicken breast on the menu, but the personnel in charge of food charged for breasts, gave the minors wings, and pocketed the difference.

21. Aquí en el Centro estoy viviendo momentos inolvidables como motines, peleas. Todo sin fechas exactas con la excepción de un motín. Estábamos los jóvenes del Centro A en la piscina y unos jóvenes del Centro B estaban afuera cerca de la piscina. Le dijeron al maestro William que les dieran una "cancha" conmigo. Pasó un rato hasta que llegó la noche y el maestro sacó para el pasillo de afuera a Asdrúbal y a Yoris y se pusieron a pelear con los del B. Como Asdrúbal le estaba ganando a uno de los chamos del Centro B, los mismos sacaron un chuso. Nosotros estabamos en la parte de adentro pero cuando vimos que esos chamos sacaron unos chusos nosotros empezamos a empujar la puerta y sacamos unos bates. Perseguimos a los chamos hasta la avenida. Hubieron varios heridos y al día siguiente hubo una asamblea con los directores y maestro. Pero este problema no llegó a tribunales pues a ninguno de los dos directores les convenía que esto llegara a los tribunales. Y así pasaron muchos días y muchas cosas, se fueron de libertad pocos y se fugaron muchos por motivos de traslados. Mi cuñado venía y me traía comida. Una vez mi novia me mandó drogas, pero no porque ella quiso sino porque yo se lo pedí y le dije que si no la traía me iban a golpear los chamos que estaban aquí, pero puro para porque si le digo que era para mi no me la traía. Así fumé droga, pastillas y tomamos anís todos los días.

22. Hoy, lunes, 2 de Agosto, estoy todavía aquí y me siento otra persona. He aprendido muchas cosas buenas y malas. Dentro de dos días cumplo tres meses y aparte de eso cumplo mis dieciocho años y me da mucha tristeza el tener que pasarlos aquí. Los tribunales siguen en huelga y no sé hasta cuando esté aquí. Yo quisiera salir de aquí como un muchacho normal, trabajando y estudiando, yo lo pienso hacer pero también

quiero que el Bladimir que era yo vuelva a vivir porque lo considero muerto. No soy el mismo, mis pensamientos se basan en tomar venganza por nada y sé que estoy mal, por eso le pido ayuda a Dios para conseguir a aquel muchacho alegre y no a este que sólo piensa en matar a X persona, yo tengo fé de que sí va a volver a existir aquel Bladimir. Es más, tengo fé que ese Bladimir va a nacer de nuevo pero acomodado con ganas de ser alguien en esta vida. Por eso digo que tengan mucha fé en Dios ya que él todo lo sabe y todo lo ve, porque para Dios nada es imposible. Me despido diciendo que no es nada fácil vivir con una tormenta de que matastes a alguien y sin querer hacerlo. Esta historia la hago en memoria de ella.

23. Carmen Gregoria was a friend of his whom he killed accidentally while playing with a gun.

Chapter 6 · Consumption, Language, and Violence

1. Mi vida en la perdición del malandro comenzó hace aproximadamente dos años cuando yo le decía a mi papá que quería un par de zapatos de ocho mil boívares y él no me los daba. Mi papá se gastaba todo en los caballos y en el alcohol. Yo andaba molesto cuando un pana me preguntó si quería tener real. Le contesté "si chamo, me quiero comprar un par de zapatos y mi papá no me quiere dar para comprarme los que quiero." Entonces el chamo me daba droga para que la guardara y me daba dos mil bolívares por semana. A penas vi que todo estaba funcionando bien me compré los zapatos que quería y siempre tenía real en los bolsillos. Después me asocié con otro chamo y los dos empezamos a guardar drogas hasta que un día le tumbaron la droga al otro chamo y se fue del barrio. Me quedé yo solo para afrontar el problema. Me le escondí al chamo al que yo le guardaba la droga porque me quería matar. Un día inesperado el chamo me sostuvo de espalda y me dio unos coñazos mientras me decía: "no te mato porque tu eres un menor que está empezando en el malandreo." Decidí desde ese momento no seguir guardando drogas sino venderla. Me la fiaban y después la pagaba, así poco a poco me fui montando en el negocio hasta que tenía unos buenos reales y me compré ropa.

2. Chamita, recuerdas esta canción "¿Por qué la vida es así?" Me supongo que si, esto quiere decir que como tu y yo hemos cometido var-

ios errores deberíamos de darnos perdón los dos. Mamita, te acuerdas de la carta que me escribistes donde decías que el corazón del ser querido buscaba de sentir con el corazón del otro, a eso es a donde pretendo llegar a esa herida tan profunda que te hice para limpiarla con cada gota de lágrima que corra por mis mejillas y que me las cobre por cada una de tus lágrimas que hice que brotaran de tus ojos. Joselyn, perdóname porque nunca quise causarte semejante dolor, me siento como el tipo más despreciable del mundo. Tu dirás que soy un exagerado pero es la verdad: yo también me causé un gran dolor. Si tu no me crees la próxima vez que nos veamos te lo voy a demonstrar. Espero que haya una próxima vez porque yo te quiero y tu me quieres a mi. Además tenemos un amor mutuo y una responsabilidad en "nuestro hermoso hijo." Dirás que soy un desconfiado pero es que realmente yo te quiero y te celo de todas las personas que son cercanas a ti. Por favor, compréndeme como un niño que sólo sueña con que seas para mi nada más.

3. *Rochela* comes from *rochelear*, "to jest."

4. Matute was the name of a cop in a very popular Hanna-Barbera television cartoon, "Don Gato y su pandilla," which was shown every afternoon during the 1970's.

5. Igual que los woperó, como se visten así le dicen a uno que somos unos monos porque andamos vestidos de marca, un policía te ve vestido de marca y te para "Ah no, este es un malandro." Muchos malandros se visten de paltó, pero ese es diputado.

6. The situation in Colombia appears to be even more desperate than that in Venezuela. There, young paid assassins known as "sicarios" take consumer culture to extremes. Their own lives and those of their victims become the object of economic negotiations. Therefore, death becomes an everyday event and lives are reified as disposable objects (Salazar 1990, 200).

7. Elvis is his real name. I asked him why his family had given him that particular name and he looked at me as if to say, "How can you ask that?" His mother had heard of the North American singer Elvis Presley and had always liked his name.

8. The name of his friend was in fact Jhon, not John.

9. Fue un 16 de Abril de este mismo año cuando por unas discusiones con unos muchachos de mi barrio tuve que cometer el error más grande de mi vida. Ese error fue matar a uno de los muchachos que se metían conmigo y mi compa(dre), un amigo que se llama Jhon. Bueno, todo

comenzó cuando cada vez que ellos me veían me buscaban de robar y humillarme delante de cualquier persona que estuviese presente. Entonces fue cuando quise vengarme de ellos y me puse a ahorrar dinero para poder comprar un arma para defenderme. No pasaron muchos días cuando ellos me encontraron con mi compa y un hermano de él y me dijeron:

—Quítate los zapatos y la chaqueta de cuero.

Ymi compadre le dijo.

—Chamo ese es el compadre mío por qué lo van a robar.

Yellos le dijeron:

—No te metas Jhon que contigo no es el problema y vete de aquí.

Yo les dije, "miren yo no les voy a dar nada porque a mi no me gusta que ninguno me venga a robar" y uno de los muchachos me puso un .38 en el estómago y me dijo:

—Quítate los zapatos porque te voy a dar un tiro.

En eso mi compa le dijo:

—Dame el tiro a mi.

Yél dijo:

—No a ti no porque yo te conozco desde que éramos unos chamitos.

Ya mi me dio mucha rabia y les dije:

—Bueno, si me van a dar háganlo de una vez porque yo no les voy a dar mis cosas.

En eso el muchacho me puso el .38 más cerca y me dijo:

—¿Quieres ver como te lo doy?

—Bueno, dámelo de una vez.

El se quedó un momento pensativo y luego disparó y yo me empecé a echar para atrás y él también diciendo.

—Chamo, vámonos, que este chamo está cruzado.

Yo al ver que el revolver no detonó me metí detrás de un carro y él empezó a disparar. Luego salí corriendo para el Plan. Después llegó mi compa asustado y me preguntó si me habían dado un tiro y yo le dije: que no y desde ese momento me dieron más ganas de comprar el arma.

10. La rescordia, le tienen rescordia a uno. El lugar donde vivíamos era un lugar sano, entonces salimos nosotros, empezamos a sacar y toditos teníamos pistola y la gente nos tenían envidia, habíamos comprado carro, teníamos motos, mujeres, y siempre ahí está el más malo a caernos a tiro. Si yo quiero estar tranquilo, ahí van otros que dicen: "Mira, ese anda en una moto, trae unos reales vamos a quebrarlo."

11. The group at the Carolina always told me that I should carry a .22

because things were dangerous now. One of them even offered to get me a gun when he had the chance.

12. When the chupapegas had material possessions such as Walkmans, new shoes, or notebooks, they lost them, sold them, or they got stolen very quickly. Because they have no one place to leave their things, they hide them wherever they find a hole. Later, they may forget where the hole is, or return to find their possessions have been taken.

13. This expression came from a merengue song, popular at the time, called "El baile del perrito" (Doggy dance).

14. He vivido cosas que nunca me había imaginado que fuesen así. Llevar los golpes de los policías, las torturas para que uno hable y diga la verdad. Aun si uno dice la verdad le dan golpe igual, torturas que algunas veces unos no las aguantan, son demasiados golpes fuerte.

15. El 16 de Enero a las 5 de la mañana una comisión de la PTJ allanó la casa donde me encontraba con los demás menores fuimos llevados a un centro de la PTJ donde nos aplicaron todo tipo de tortura y maltrato, cuales como la bolsa, el gas y la tradicional tortura de la guindada del ave: en un cuarto guindando en una columna con los pies en el aire. Después de ocho días fuimos pasados a la orden de los tribunales cual decidió mandarnos el día 25 de Enero del mismo año a un centro de rehabilitación inmediata.

16. La policía antes era menos violenta, ahora quieren matar a todos los menores. Ahora lo agarran a uno en la calle y delante de la gente le echan gas en la cara a uno, le caen a golpe y a patada, le dan patada a uno como si uno fuera un perro. Le dan palo a uno, pero no se meten en los barrios, con los malandros de Pinto Salinas, son unos cagones, no se meten en Pinto.

Glossary

ajuste de cuentas	to set things straight. Used in connection with drug-related transactions and violence
arrecho	tough; to be angry
artesano (artisan)	craftsperson and merchant on the Sabana Grande boulevard
artista (artist)	arrogant
argoya	homosexual
bajé el cierre	to finish a cigarette
bandera (flag)	something good
barrio	shantytown
bástese	time to end the conversation
batanear	to steal from a friend while he is occupied with something else
bazuko	poisonous residue left after processing cocaine
becerro (calf)	cocksucker
bruja (witch)	snitch
buhonero	street merchant
caleta	*ser caleta*: to be stingy; *una caleta*: a place where street people sleep
campanear	to stand watch while your group commits a robbery
carajo(s)	guy(s)
cartel	reputation
cerro (hill)	hill full of shantytowns
chalero	charlatan

chamba	odd job, often in the informal economy
chamo	popular term for a young person or friend
changa	type of pop music
chiguire (capybara)	person who has been forced by cell mates into certain services, such as washing clothes
chiguiriar	to do services for other people
chirre	*bazuko* joint; from the sound that is produced when the *bazuko* is burning
choro	thief
chuso	homemade weapon
cocoseco (dry coconut)	weak of mind, dumb
coronar	to commit a successful assault
culebra (snake)	enemy
diablo (devil)	loser
echaíto pa'tras	cocaine
El Guaire	polluted river that runs through Caracas from west to east
encapuchado	transgressor who wears a hood
equivocado (mistaken)	person who robs another in a similar condition
falso (false)	double-faced
fanfarrón	arrogant liar
frito (fried)	poor person, without brand-name clothes
guerrero	warrior
gorila (gorilla)	addicted to drugs
hierro (iron)	gun
ignorante	dumb
jeva	woman; *mi jeva*, "my girlfriend"
jíbaro	drug dealer
jordan	new word for *mono* (q.v.), derived from Michael Jordan's name
joya (jewel)	homosexual
lacreo	cool
latero	can collector
le ronca (to snort)	very tough
librero	street bookseller
malandro	thug

mamahuevo	cocksucker
mamerto	cocksucker
mano peluda / mano negra (hairy hand / black hand)	according to some, hooded police agents who kill youngsters on the street
maquive	liar
martillar	to ask for money
mono (monkey)	person from the barrios, also known as *jordan* (q.v.)
motorizado	motorcycle messenger
niche	person from the barrio
no joda	"no shit"
pagando cana	to be in jail
pana	buddy
pantanero	special police group
pavo/pavito	rich youngster
pepo	drugged with pills
perversa	whore
pichar un conejo (to catch a rabbit)	to deal with a potential drug buyer
pinta	outfit
pistolita (small gun)	a cigarette made of *bazuko* (q.v.) and marijuana
prensado	cocaine addict
preparar un yodo	to roll a joint
psicópata	hired killer
rancho	shantyhouse
rayado	*estar rayado*: to have a bad reputation
rebuscarse	to find ways to make extra money
recogelata	can collector
rescordia	envy
ropa de marca	brand-name clothes
ruso (Russian)	mix of marijuana, cocaine, and *bazuko* (q.v.)
sapo (frog)	snitch
seria (serious)	"things are smooth"; elegant
sicario	hired killer

soldando	smoking *bazuko* (q.v.)
tumbado	to get mugged
vikingo	poor
volado	to be high
woperó	middle-class adolescents who hang out on the streets of Caracas
yunque	stingy

Works Cited

Albano, Deanna. 1992. "La solución para los menores infractores no está en mayores recursos." *La Red*, no. 7: 4–5.

Allsebrook, Annie, and Anthony Swift. 1989. *Broken Promise: The World of Endangered Children*. Kent, Eng.: Headway.

Appadurai, Arjun. 1990. "Disjuncture and Difference in the Global Cultural Economy." *Public Culture* 2, no. 2: 1–24.

———. 1991. "Global Ethnoscapes: Notes and Queries for a Transnational Anthropology." In Richard G. Fox, ed., *Recapturing Anthropology*. Santa Fe, N. Mex.: School of American Research Press.

Aptekar, Lewis. 1988. *Street-Children of Cali*. Durham, N.C.: Duke University Press.

———. 1989. "Characteristics of the Street Children of Colombia." *Child Abuse and Neglect* 13: 427–37.

———. 1991. "Are Colombian Street Children Neglected? The Contributions of Ethnographic and Ethnohistorical Approaches to the Study of Street Children." *Anthropology and Education* 22, no. 4: 326–50.

Arellano, A. 1967. *Caracas, su evolución y su régimen legal*. Caracas: Ediciones del Cuatricentenario de Caracas.

Aries, Philippe. 1962. *Centuries of Childhood*. New York: Vintage.

Baiz, Abraham. 1944. *Los menores delincuentes*. Caracas: La Nación.

Barrios, Andrea, Livia Cárquez, and Magdalena Frigo. 1989. "Niños de la calle: Una aproximación a sus historias de vida." Diss., Universidad Central de Venezuela.

Barrios, Leoncio. 1992. *Familia y televisión*. Caracas: Monte Avila Editores.

Basaglia, Franco. 1987. "Institutions of Violence." In Nancy Scheper-Hughes and Anne Lovell, eds., *Psychiatry Inside Out: Selected Writings of Franco Basaglia*. New York: Columbia University Press.

Beloff, Mary Ana. 1994. "De los delitos y de la infancia." *Nueva sociedad* 129: 104–13.

Beroes, Juan Bautista. 1938. *Etiología de la delincuencia juvenil*. Caracas: Empresa El Cojo.

Blos, Peter. 1979. *The Adolescent Passage*. New York: International University Press.

Bohannon, Paul. 1956. "Beauty and Scarification Among the Tiv." *Man* 51: 117–21.

Bolívar, Teolinda. 1993. "Densificación y metrópoli." *Urbana* 13: 31–46.

Bourdieu, Pierre. 1977. *Outline of a Theory of Practice*. Cambridge: Cambridge University Press.

Bourgois, Philippe. 1995. *In Search of Respect: Selling Crack in El Barrio*. New York: Cambridge University Press.

Briceño-León, Roberto. 1990. *Los efectos perversos del petróleo*. Caracas: Fondo de Ediciones Capriles.

Brizuela, Ramón Antonio. [1974] 1991. *Soy un delincuente*. Reprint, Caracas: Pomaire-Fuentes Ediciones.

Campos, Mercedes, and M. T. Colmenares. 1991. "Aproximación al estudio de la violencia estructural, su incidencia en el homicidio: El caso de los menores de edad." Diss., Universidad Central de Venezuela.

Camuñas, Matías. 1993. "Vida en los barrios: La sobrevivencia de los más débiles." In Tulio Hernández, ed., "Composición y recomposición de identidades en los territorios populares contemporáneos." Unpublished manuscript.

Carvallo, Gastón. 1994. *Próceres, caudillos y rebeldes: Crisis del sistema de dominación 1830–1908*. Caracas: Grijalbo.

Cashmore, E. Ellis. 1984. *No Future: Youth and Society*. London: Heinemann Educational Books.

Castillo, Anabel, and Coromoto Castillo. 1994. *La política del estado venezolano hacia el menor transgresor (1980–1990)*. Cuadernos de Investigación no. 10. Caracas: FEGS.

Castro, Ina Elias, and Geraldo Samenzato. 1978. *A crianca o meio urbano do Brasil*. Rio de Janeiro: Fundo das Nacoes Unidas Para a Infancia.

Ceballos, Luis R., and Jesús R. Malaver. 1984. "Estereotipos del delincuente en el area metropolitana de Caracas." Diss., Universidad Central de Venezuela.

Ceballos, Nidia. 1983. "La familia actual y los cambios operados por la mujer." Diss., Universidad Central de Venezuela.

Cloward, R. A., and L. E. Ohlin. 1960. *Delinquency and Opportunities.* Glencoe, Ill.: Free Press.

Cohen, Albert. 1955. *Delinquent Boys: The Culture of the Gang.* New York: Free Press.

Cohen, Stan. [1972] 1980. *Folk Devils and Moral Panics: The Creation of the Mods and Rockers.* Reprint, Cambridge, Mass.: Blackwell.

Coles, Robert. 1986a. *The Political Life of Children.* Boston: Atlantic Monthly Press.

———. 1986b. *The Moral Life of Children.* Boston: Atlantic Monthly Press.

Colomine Solarte, Feijoo. 1974. *El Menor en situación irregular en Venezuela.* Caracas: Universidad Central de Venezuela.

Consejo Venezolano del Niño. 1973. *Familia y abandono de menores.* Caracas: Consejo Venezolano del Niño.

Coppedge, Michael. 1994. *Strong Parties and Lame Ducks: Presidential Partyarchy and Factionalism in Venezuela.* Stanford, Calif.: Stanford University Press.

Coronil, Fernando. 1988. *The Magical State: History and Illusion in the Appearance of Venezuelan Democracy.* Working paper. Helen Kellog Institute for International Studies.

———. 1997. *The Magical State: Nature, Money, and Modernity in Venezuela.* Chicago: University of Chicago Press.

Coronil, Fernando, and Julie Skurski. 1992. "Dismembering and Remembering the Nation: The Semantics of Political Violence in Venezuela." *Comparative Studies in Society and History* 33, no. 2: 288–337.

Coronil, María Elena. 1977. *Islas dentro del tiempo.* Caracas: Miguel García e Hijos.

De Certeau, Michel. 1984. *The Practice of Everyday Life.* Berkeley: University of California Press.

De Freitas, Julio. 1993. "Bárbaros, armados y peligrosos: La eficacia del discurso sobre violencia popular urbana." Unpub. ms.

De la Cruz, Rafael, and Patricia Márquez. 1996. "Fundación Atenea: Responsabilidades públicas del sector privado." IESA: Unpub. ms.

Dimenstein, Gilberto. 1991. *Brazil: War on Children.* London: Latin American Bureau.

Elwin, Verrier. 1968. *The Kingdom of the Young*. Bombay: Oxford University Press.

Enright, Michael, Antonio Francés, and Edith S. Saavedra. 1996. *Venezuela: The Challenge of Competitiveness*. New York: St. Martin's Press.

Erikson, Erik. 1950. *Childhood and Society*. New York: W. W. Norton.

Ewell, Judith. 1984. *Venezuela: A Century of Change*. Stanford, Calif.: Stanford University Press.

Favazza, Armando. 1987. *Bodies Under Siege: Self-Mutilation in Culture and Psychiatry*. Baltimore, Md.: Johns Hopkins University Press.

Feldman, Allen. 1991. *Formations of Violence: The Narrative of the Body and Political Terror in Northern Ireland*. Chicago: University of Chicago Press.

Foucault, Michel. 1978. *The History of Sexuality*. Vol. 1, *An Introduction*. New York: Random House.

———. 1979. *Discipline and Punish*. New York: Vintage.

Freud, Anna. 1958. "Adolescence." *Psychoanalytic Study of the Child* 13: 255–78.

García Canclini, Néstor. 1988. "Culture and Power: The State of Research." *Media, Culture, and Society* 10: 467–97.

———. 1993. *Transforming Modernity: Popular Culture in Mexico*. Austin: University of Texas Press.

Gibson, Charles. 1966. *Spain in America*. New York: Harper & Row.

Gillis, John R. 1974. *Youth and History: Tradition and Change in European Age Relations, 1770–Present*. New York: Academic Press.

Gingold, Laura. 1992. "Feos, sucios y malos. El poder de sentencia de las etiquetas sociales." *Nueva Sociedad* 117: 104–19.

Glasser, Irene. 1994. *Homelessness in Global Perspective*. New York: G. K. Hall.

Goffman, Erving. 1961. *Asylums: Essays on the Social Situation of Mental Patients and Other Inmates*. Garden City, N.J.: Anchor.

Granados Téllez, Marcos F. 1974. *Gamínes*. Bogotá: Ediciones Tercer Mundo.

Hall, Stuart, and Tony Jefferson, eds. 1976. *Resistance Through Rituals: Youth Subcultures in Post-War Britain*. London: Unwin Hyman.

Hall, Stuart, Chas Critcher, Tony Jefferson, John Clark, and Brian Roberts, eds. 1978. *Policing the Crisis: Mugging, the State, and Law and Order*. New York: Holmes and Meier.

Hardoy, Jorge, and Marta Savigliano. 1984. "La Ciudad y los niños." *Revista Paraguaya de sociología* 21: 159–81.

Harvey, David. 1985. *The Urban Experience*. Baltimore, Md.: Johns Hopkins University Press.

———. 1989. *The Condition of Postmodernity*. Cambridge, Mass.: Blackwell.

Hebdige, Dick. 1979. *Subculture: The Meaning of Style*. New York: Methuen.

Hewitt, Roger. 1986. *White Talk Black Talk: Inter-Racial Friendship and Communication Among Adolescents*. New York: Cambridge University Press.

Huggings, Magally. 1987. *Las menores internas: Un caso de sanción moral*. Caracas: Universidad Central de Venezuela.

Johnson, David. 1990. "A Multidimensional Theory of Early Modern Western Childhood." *Journal of Comparative Family Studies* 21, no. 1: 1–11.

Karl, Terry Lynn. 1987. "Petroleum and Political Pacts: The Transition to Democracy in Venezuela." *Latin American Research Review* 22, no. 1: 63–91.

Karlsson, Weine. 1975. *Manufacturing in Venezuela: Studies on Development and Location*. Stockholm: Almquist & Wiksell.

Lerner, Elisa. [1984] 1995. "Nuestra igualitaria ilusión." In Moisés Naím and R. Piñango, eds., *Caso Venezuela: Una ilusión de armonía*. Reprint, Caracas: Ediciones IESA.

Lombardi, John. 1976. *People and Places in Colonial Venezuela*. Bloomington: Indiana University Press.

López-Sanz, Rafael. 1993. *Parentesco, etnia y clase social en la sociedad Venezolana*. Caracas: Universidad Central de Venezuela.

Marcus, George, and Michael Fischer. 1986. *Anthropology as Cultural Critique: An Experimental Moment in the Human Sciences*. Chicago: University of Chicago Press.

Marrero, Carmen. 1988. "Aproximación al estudio de la familia venezolana." Diss., Universidad Central de Venezuela.

Maturi, Anibal. 1987. *Los chicos de la calle*. Buenos Aires: Editorial Galerna.

McRobbie, Angela. 1994. *Postmodernism and Popular Culture*. London: Routledge.

Mead, Margaret. 1928. *Coming of Age in Samoa*. Ann Arbor, Mich.: Morrow.

Meyer, Philippe. 1977. *The Child and the State: The Intervention of the State in Family Life*. England: Cambridge University Press.

Minge-Kalman, Wanda. 1978. "The Industrial Revolution and the European Family: The Institutionalization of 'Childhood' as a Market for Family History." *Comparative Studies in Society and History* 20: 454–68.

Ministerio de la Familia. 1993. *Encuesta nacional de la juventud venezolana (ENJUVE)*. Caracas: Ministerio de la Familia.

Montero, Nancy. 1989. "La imagen del niño en los medios de comunicación ¿Modelaje positivo o negativo?" *Niños* 24, no. 69: 109–20.

———. 1992. "Estudio sobre la programación institucional para menores con necesidad de tratamiento del INAM, 1936–86." Caracas: Ministerio de la Familia.

Morner, Magnus. 1973. "The Spanish American Hacienda: A Survey of Recent Research and Debate." *American Historical Review* 53, no. 2: 183–216.

Muñoz, Cecilia, and Ximena Pachón. 1980. *Gamínes: Testimonios*. Bogotá: Carlos Valencia Editores.

———. 1991. *La Niñez en el siglo XX: Salud, educación, familia, recreación, maltrato, asistencia y protección*. Bogotá: Editorial Planeta.

Muñoz, Cecilia, and M. Palacios. 1980. *El niño trabajador: Testimonios*. Bogotá: Carlos Valencia Editores.

Nader, Laura. 1972 . "Up the Anthropologist: Perspectives Gained from Studying Up." In Dell Hymes, ed., *Reinventing Anthropology*. New York: Pantheon.

———. 1980. "The Vertical Slice: Hierarchies and Children." In G. Britain and R. Cohen, eds., *Hierarchy and Society*. Philadelphia: Institute for the Study of Human Issues.

Naím, Moisés. 1993. *Paper Tigers and Minotaurs: The Politics of Venezuela's Economic Reform*. Washington, D.C.: Carnegie Endowment for International Peace.

Nordstrom, Carolyn, and Jo Ann Martin, eds. 1992. *The Paths to Domination, Resistance, and Terror*. Berkeley: University of California Press.

Oficina Central de Estadistica e Información. 1992. *El censo 90 en Venezuela: Resultados básicos*. Caracas: Oficina Central de Información.

Ontiveros, Teresa. 1989. "La casa de los barrios: Aproximación socio-antropólogica a la memoria espacial urbana." Universidad Central de Venezuela.

Ottenberg, Simon. 1989. *Boyhood Rituals in an African Society*. Seattle: University of Washington Press.

Pedrazzini, Yves, and Magaly Sánchez. 1990. "Nuevas legitimidades sociales y violencia urbana en Caracas." *Nueva sociedad* 109: 23–34.

———. 1992. *Malandros, bandas y niños de la calle: cultura de urgencia en la metrópoli Latinoamericana*. Caracas: Vadell Hermanos.

Pinto Castro, Ingrid, and Milagro Quijada. 1980. "Identidad y familia: Concepción de familia en un barrio marginal." Diss., Universidad Central de Venezuela.

Piven, Frances Fox, and Richard A. Cloward. 1971. *Regulating the Poor: The Foundations of Public Welfare.* New York: Vintage.

República de Venezuela. 1936. *Código de menores.* Gaceta Oficial no. 19027.

———. 1946. *Estatuto de menores.* Caracas: Editorial La Torre.

———. 1986. *Ley tutelar del menor y sus reglamentos.* Caracas: Ediciones Orley.

Rodríguez, R. A. 1974. *Internado del consejo Venezolano del niño: Antesala del delito.* Caracas: La Estrella.

Romero Salazar, Alexis. 1993. *Los Rigores de la urgencia: El Trabajo de los menores en la calle.* Maracaibo, Venezuela: Ediciones Contextos.

Rondón, Cesar Miguel. 1980. *El libro de la salsa: Crónica de la música del Caribe urbano.* Caracas: Editorial Arte.

Ruiz De Mateo, Lila. 1984. *Dinámica de los grupos familiares dentro de la estructura social Venezolana.* Caracas: Universidad Central de Venezuela.

Salazar, Alonzo. 1990. *No nacimos pa' semilla.* Bogotá: Centro de Investigacion y de Educación Popular.

Salcedo Bastardo, J. L. 1974. *Historia fundamental de Venezuela.* Caracas: Universidad Central de Venezuela.

Salgado, María Abigail, ed. 1985. *Rafael Vegas y la infancia abandonada en Venezuela. 1938–1950.* Caracas: Editorial Arte.

Scheper-Hughes, Nancy. 1992. *Death Without Weeping: The Violence of Everyday Life in Brazil.* Berkeley: University of California Press.

Scheper-Hughes, Nancy, and Daniel Hoffman. 1994. "Kids out of Place." *nacla* 27, no. 6: 16–23.

Scheper-Hughes, Nancy, and Margaret Lock. 1987. "The Mindful Body: A Prolegomenon to Future Work in Medical Anthropology." *Medical Anthropology Quarterly* 1, no. 1: 6–41.

Schlegel, Alice, and Herbert Barry. 1979. "Adolescent Initiation Ceremonies." *Ethnology* 18, no. 2: 199–210.

Scott, James. 1985. *Weapons of the Weak: Everyday Forms of Peasant Resistance.* New Haven, Conn.: Yale University Press.

Shahar, Shulamith. 1990. *Childhood in the Middle Ages.* London: Routledge.

Sosa, Arturo. 1993. "El Malandro: Ni héroe ni villano." *sic* 557: 307–9.

Srivastava, Shankar Sahai. 1963. *Juvenile Vagrancy.* New York: Asia Publishing House.

Tacon, Peter. 1981. *My Child Now: An Action on Behalf of Children Without Families*. New York: UNICEF.

———. 1983. *Regional Program for Latin America and the Caribbean*. New York: UNICEF.

Taussig, Michael. 1987. *Shamanism, Colonialism, and the Wild Man*. Chicago: University of Chicago Press.

Timerman, Jacobo. 1981. *Prisoner Without a Name, Cell Without a Number*. London: Weidenfeld and Nicolson.

Troconis de Veracoechea, Emilia. 1990. *Indias, esclavas, mantuanas y primeras damas*. Caracas: Alfadil Ediciones.

———. 1993. *Caracas*. Caracas: Grijalbo.

Trotman, David. 1986. *Crime in Trinidad: Conflict and Control in a Plantation Society 1838–1900*. Knoxville: University of Tennessee Press.

Tudares de González, Trina. 1989. *Familia, derecho y cambio social*. Zulia: Universidad del Zulia.

Turner, Victor. 1969. *The Ritual Process*. Ithaca, N.Y.: Cornell University Press.

Van Gennep, Arnold. [1915] 1960. *The Rites of Passage*. Reprint, Chicago: University of Chicago Press.

Vethencourt, José Luis. 1974. "La Estructura Familiar Atípica y el Fracaso Histórico Cultural de Venezuela." *sic* 362: 67–69.

———. 1988. "Cambios en la familia Venezolana." *sic* 502: 62–65.

Violante, M. L. 1985. *O dilema do decente malandro: A questao de identidade do menor*. Sao Paulo: Cortez Editora.

Walton, John. 1989. "Debt, Protest, and the State in Latin America." In Susan Eckstein, ed., *Power and Popular Protest in Latin America*. Berkeley: University of California Press.

Walvin, James. 1982. *A Child's World: A Social History of English Childhood, 1800–1914*. Harmondsworth: Penguin Books.

Watts, Michael. 1992. "The Shock of Modernity: Petroleum, Protest, and Fast Capitalism in an Industrializing Society." In A. Pred and M. Watts, eds., *Reworking Modernity: Capitalism and Symbolic Discontent*. New Brunswick, N.J.: Rutgers University Press.

Whiting, Beatrice B., and John W. Whiting. 1987. Foreword to *Inuit Youth: Growth and Change in the Canadian Arctic*, by Richard Condon. New Brunswick, N.J.: Rutgers University Press.

Whiting, John W., Richard Kluckhohn, and Albert S. Anthony. 1958. "The Function of Male Initiation Ceremonies at Puberty." In Eleanor E.

Maccoby, Thoedore M. Newcomb, and Eugene L. Hartley, eds., *Readings in Social Psychology*. New York: Holt, Rinehart and Winston.

Whyte, William F. [1943] 1955. *Street Corner Society: The Social Structure of an Italian Slum*. Chicago: Reprint, University of Chicago Press.

Willis, Paul. 1977. *Learning to Labour: How Working Class Kids Get Working Class Jobs*. Farmborough, Eng.: Saxon House.

———. 1990. *Common Culture: Symbolic Work at Play in the Everyday Cultures of the Young*. Boulder, Colo.: Westview Press.

Wilson, S. 1984. "The Myth of Motherhood: The Historical View of European Child-Rearing." *Social History* 9 no. 2: 181–98.

World Bank. 1994. *World Development Report*. New York: Oxford University Press.

Wright, Winthrop. 1990. *Café con Leche: Race, Class, and National Image in Venezuela*. Austin: University of Texas Press.

Young, Frank. 1965. *Initiation Ceremonies: A Cross-Cultural Study of Status Dramatization*. Indianapolis: Bobbs-Merrill.

Index

In this index an "f" after a number indicates a separate reference on the next page, and an "ff" indicates separate references on the next two pages. A continuous discussion over two or more pages is indicated by a span of page numbers, e.g., "57–59." *Passim* is used for a cluster of references in close but not consecutive sequence.

Library of Congress Cataloging-in-Publication Data

Márquez, Patricia C.
    The street is my home : youth and violence in Caracas / Patricia C. Márquez.
        p.   cm.
    Includes bibliographical references and index.
ISBN 0-8047-3453-4 (cloth) : ISBN 0-8047-4552-8 (pbk.)
    1. Street children—Venezuela—Caracas. 2. Youth—Venezuela—Caracas—
Social conditions. 3. Social control—Venezuela—Caracas. 4. Violence—
Venezuela—Caracas. I. Title.
HV887.V452C376   1999
305.23'0987'7—dc21   98-43805

∞   This book is printed on acid-free, recycled paper.

Original printing 1999

Last figure below indicates year of this printing:
08   07   06   05   04   03   02   01